WHAT'S YOUR DOG TYPE?

A New System for Understanding Yourself and Others, Improving Your Relationships, and Getting What You Want in Life

by Jana Collins, CEO Jones & O'Malley

and Gini Graham Scott, Ph.D.
Author of *Do You Look Like Your Dog?*

WHAT'S YOUR DOG TYPE?

Copyright © 2017 by Gini Graham Scott

All rights reserved. No part of this book may be used or reproduced by any means, graphic, electronic, or mechanical, including photocopying, recording, taping or by any information storage retrieval system without the written permission of the author except in the case of brief quotations embodied in critical articles and reviews.

TABLE OF CONTENTS

PREFACE 9
   The Dog Type System 12
   A Typical Workshop 12
   Making Choices... 14
   Understanding One's Choice 16
   Putting It Together... 18
INTRODUCTION 20
PART I: INTRODUCING THE DOG TYPE SYSTEM 23
CHAPTER 1: USING THE DOG TYPE SYSTEM 25
   How the Dog Type System Works 27
   Using the Dog Type System 27
   Learning More about Yourself for Personal and Professional
   Development 28
   Learning More about Others for Better Relationships 30
   To Gain Assistance in Everyday Life... 31
   To Just Have Fun 32
   Giving Others Insights about Themselves................................... 32
   Get Ready, Set, Go 33
PART II: DISCOVERING YOUR DOG TYPE 35
CHAPTER 2: THE DOG PROFILES 37
DISCOVERING YOUR DOG STAR.. 39
THE WORKING DOGS 41
   Are You a Siberian Husky, Alaskan Malamute, Samoyed, or Akita? 43
   Are You a Boxer, Bullmastiff, or Mastiff?................................... 45
   Are You a Doberman Pinscher or Rottweiler? 47
   Are You a St. Bernard, Bernese Mountain Dog, or Newfoundland? . 49
   Are You a Great Dane? 51
   Are You a Giant Schnauzer? 53
   Are You a Portuguese Water Dog?... 55
THE HERDING DOGS 57
   Are You a Collie, Border Collie, or Shetland Sheepdog (Sheltie)? ... 59
   Are You an Old English Sheepdog, Bearded Collie, or Bouvier des
   Flandres? 61
   Are You a Pembroke Welsh Corgi? 63
   Are You a German Shepherd or Belgian Malinois?..................... 65
   Are You an Australian Cattle Dog?.. 67

THE HOUNDS 69
   Are You a Beagle or a Basset Hound? 71
   Are You a Dachshund? 73
   Are You a Greyhound or Whippet? 75
   Are You an Afghan Hound, Borzoi, or Saluki? 77
   Are You a Bloodhound or Coon Hound? 79
   Are You an Irish Wolfhound or Otterhound? 81
THE SPORTING DOGS 83
   Are You a Labrador or Chesapeake Bay Retriever? 85
   Are You a Cocker Spaniel or a Golden Retriever? 87
   Are You an English Springer Spaniel or a Brittany? 89
   Are You a Weimeraner or Vizsla? 91
   Are You an English or Irish Setter? 93
   Are You a Pointer? 95
THE TERRIERS 97
   Are You a Bull Terrier, American Pit Bull, or Staffordshire Bull
   Terrier? 99
   Are You a Cairn, Norfolk, or Scottish Terrier? 101
   Are You an Airedale Terrier? 103
   Are You a Bedlington Terrier, West Highland White Terrier, or Soft
   Coated Wheaten Terrier? 105
   Are You a Jack Russell Terrier or Fox Terrier? 107
   Are You an Irish Terrier, Kerry Blue Terrier, or Schnauzer? 109
TOY DOGS 111
   Are You a Pomeranian, Kings Charles Spaniel, Papillion, Yorkie, or
   Silky Terrier? 113
   Are You a Chihuahua, Chinese Crested, or Pug? 115
   Are You a Miniature Pinscher, Italian Greyhound, or Toy Terrier? 117
   Are You a Pekingese, Maltese, LlasaApso, Havanese or Shih Tzu? 119
NON-SPORTING DOGS 121
   Are You a Chow Chow or Chinese Shar-Pei? 123
   Are You a Bichon Frisé? 125
   Are You a Dalmatian? 127
   Are You a Poodle? 129
   Are You a Boston Terrier? 131
   Are You a Bulldog? 133
CHAPTER 3: GAINING INSIGHTS INTO OTHERS 135
   How the Dog Profiling System Can Up Your Inner Radar 136
   Using Dog Types to Make Good Decisions about People 139

The Type of Information Gained Through Dog Type Techniques ... 140
Recognizing Different Personality Types and Behavioral Styles 143
Summing Up 149
PART III: GETTING HELP FROM YOUR DOGS 151
INTRODUCTION TO PART III 153
The Main Categories of Helpers 154
The Development of this System 154
CHAPTER 4: WHAT'S YOUR DOG? 157
Determining Your Top Dog, Watch Dog, and Underdog 157
Discovering Your Top Dog and Watch Dog 158
Using Guided Meditation or Visualization to Discover Your Top Dog or Watch Dog 160
Discovering Your Underdog 165
Working with Your Top Dog, Watch Dog, and Underdog 168
CHAPTER 5: A WORKSHOP ON FINDING YOUR TOP DOG, WATCH DOG, AND UNDERDOG 169
The Workshop Setting 169
CHAPTER 6: WORKING WITH YOUR DOG 185
Learning More about Your Dog Family – and You! 185
Celebrating Your Strengths 194
Making Your Top Dog and Watch Dog Part of Your Everyday Life 196
How the Process Works 197
Getting to Know Your Underdog 200
CHAPTER 7: FIND YOUR INNER GUIDE DOG – OR DOGS 207
Which Guide Dog Is for You? 207
Using Your Inner Guide Dog for Different Purposes 208
Some Exercises to Connect and Communicate with Your Inner Guide Dog 209
Digging Deep to Find Your Guide Dogs 213
A Chart to Keep Track of Your Guide Dogs and How They Can Help 216
Getting the Help You Need 218
Putting the Advice You Get Into Action 221
Using the Qualities of Your Guide Dog to Help 222
Some Examples of Working with Guide Dogs for Help 223
CHAPTER 8: PUTTING ON THE POWER DOG 229
Why These Exercises Work 229
Powering Up with Power Animals 230

A Collection of Power Exercises 232
To Unleash Your Creativity 235
Express Yourself More Fully 237
Increasing Your Energy.. 239
Summing Up... 240
PART IV: GETTING EVEN MORE HELP FROM YOUR DOGS.... 241
INTRODUCTION TO PART IV 243
CHAPTER 9: MAKING CHANGES: "TEACHING AN OLD DOG NEW TRICKS"... 245
The Need to Be Flexible.. 245
An Example of One Man's Self-Transformation 247
How You Can Change Your Basic Personality Traits................... 248
Creating a Better Balance in Your Personality Traits or Expressing Them.. 250
Here's How It Works.. 252
The Four Steps to Change 256
Determining How You Want to Change 257
Recognizing What or Who You Want to Become........................ 260
Changing Your Overall Personality Orientation and Specific Traits 264
Using Mental Scripting to See Yourself As You Want to Be 264
CHAPTER 10: TECHNIQUES TO UNDERSTAND AND IMPROVE YOUR RELATIONSHIPS... 269
Getting a Quick First Impression About the People You Meet........ 269
Getting First Impressions 272
Getting Advance Impressions of Someone Before You Meet.......... 273
Gaining In-Depth Insight into Others.. 274
Using Visualization and Dog Profiling Techniques to Improve Your Relationships 287
Increasing Your Power in a Relationship 292
Influencing Your Relationships in Other Ways 293
CHAPTER 11: A WORKSHOP ON WORKING WITH YOUR GUIDE DOG 297
The Workshop Setting... 297
Meeting One's Guide Dog (or Dogs) 298
Getting Help from One's Guide Dogs... 300
Gaining Insights about Another Person.. 302
Getting First Impressions 305
An Exercise on Getting First Impressions.................................... 307
A Day of Seeing Dogs... 309

    Learning from the Dog Associations 312
    Making Changes in a Relationship 314
    Setting Up Your Own Workshop 318
PART V: APPLYING THE DOG TYPE SYSTEM IN EVERYDAY LIFE 319
CHAPTER 12: GETTING SOME EXTRA HELP FOR MORE ENERGY AND POWER 321
    Getting Some Extra Help from a Rescue Dog 321
    To Overcome Stress and Tension 323
    To Increase Your Energy and Feel Less Tired 325
    To Increase Your Feelings of Confidence and Self-Esteem 328
    To Set and Achieve Goals 333
    An Example of How to Use the System 340
CHAPTER 13: OTHER WAYS OF USING THE DOG TYPE SYSTEM 345
    Increasing Your Skills 345
    Increasing Your Creativity 348
    Solving Problems and Making Decisions 356
    Using Your Intuition to Make Better Decisions 359
    New Ways to Just Have Fun 367
    Still Other Ways of Working with the Dog Type System 368
CHAPTER 14: SUMMING UP AND EVEN MORE POSSIBILITIES 371
    For Self-Understanding and Personal Development 371
    For Understanding and Improving Relationships 373
    For a Variety of Everyday Purposes 374
    Mostly Just for Fun 374
    Still Other Ways to Use this System for Getting to Know Others and Having Fun 375
ABOUT THE AUTHORS 379
    Jana Collins 379
    Gini Graham Scott 379

PREFACE

WHAT'S YOUR DOG TYPE? features a unique system for understanding yourself and others, thinking about and improving relationships, and having fun in creative, new ways. It's based on learning about yourself and others by knowing what type of dog you each like most or are most like – and calling on different types of dogs for different types of help – such as Guide Dogs for advice, Power Dogs to gain power, and Rescue Dogs for extra help. While this system can be an amusing and whimsical way to think about yourself and others, it offers psychological insights and practical advice on interpersonal relationships. Plus it provides creative ways to solve problems, make decisions, and deal with everyday situations.

I teamed up with Gini Graham Scott, who wrote the initial draft of the book, because I could see the potential for a worldwide system, akin to the Myers-Briggs system of personality types, because of the exploding popularity of dogs. A second companion book for cat lovers is *WHAT'S YOUR CAT TYPE?* I thought these books would be a natural, because there are over 78 million dogs in 44% of US households, and 85 million cats in 35% of these households, because cat owners more frequently own multiple cats, whereas dog owners tend to have a single dog. And there are even more dog owners around the world. Significantly, almost all dog or cat owners consider their pets members of the family, buy clothes and gifts for them, and otherwise closely bond with them. Thus, the dogs and cats they choose commonly reflect their own personality traits, and can help people better understand themselves and others.

Since I own several dogs and cats and I have many family members, friends, and business associates who do, I found this system especially appealing. I hope to bring my expertise as the owner of a PR company for over two decades to turning this system into an international success. I have had many dozens of clients in the entertainment, corporate, small business, and sports fields, and I hope to do for this sy7stem what I have done for my clients in turning them into household names.

This system was inspired by the *Do You Look Like Your Dog?* website, which co-author Gini Graham Scott turned into a book, game, fashion show, short documentary, and TV reality show proposal. As she gathered submissions by dog owners, she noticed that many people not only looked like their dogs, but shared many personality traits. Many people she met also commented on how they shared traits with their dog or chose their dog because of these similarities. At the same time, she was teaching psychological profiling classes for an investigative careers program, and she compared Pomeranian and Siberian Husky owners for a Cal State, East Bay Anthropology graduate seminar and found dramatic personality differences. While the Pomeranian owners were highly social, warm, and friendly, much like their highly social, affectionate dogs, the Siberian Husky owners were an independent, sometimes feisty, group, just like their spirited dogs.

As she continued going to dog shows to collect more photos for the *Do You Look Like Your Dog?* book, she noticed differences between the owners of other breeds. Soon a growing number of people shared their stories about why they preferred certain dogs whether they owned a dog or not. Many spoke of their close identification and kinship with their dog, too. They characterized their dog as a close companion and friend, and described the fun they had together as best buddies. Eventually she did a short documentary featuring owners and their dogs called *What Kind of Dog Are You?*

These comments reminded her of a variety of workshops she had participated in over the years involving encounters, hypnosis, shamanism, fantasy, theater games, dance, and play. In some workshops people picked an animal guide to help them go on a journey to gain personal insights or chose and "danced" as an animal to feel closer to it and ask for guidance. In still other programs for singles, people described their favorite animal or said what animal other group members reminded them of to better get to know each other. In some workshops, more like a party, people pretended to be different animals to release their spirit of play and just have fun.

The final piece of the *What's Your Dog Type?* workshop came together when Gini began to think about the different personality systems she taught in her classes and about the many systems popularized on the Internet. There are dozens of such systems, from Myers-Briggs Personality Typing and the Stanford Research Vals System to many quick to answer tests for self-understanding through associations, such as "What Flavor Fits You?" and "What's Your Pop Star Style?"

Eventually, all of these ideas led to the *Dog Type?* system. Then, these led to a series of workshops on using dog preferences and dislikes to better understand oneself and others and improve relationships, both in one's work and personal life. It was a way to help singles mix and mingle. Later, this same approach was used to create a system for cat enthusiasts: *What's Your Cat Type?*

As an example, at one singles mixer workshop for about two dozen women and men, everyone eagerly spoke about their experiences with different types of dogs. For example, Betty[1] identified herself as a "Poodle" person, though she had previously owned a Cocker Spaniel, explaining that: "When I was younger, I liked Cocker Spaniels because they are so friendly and outgoing, and I was much more active. But after my last Cocker died and a friend gave me a Poodle, I felt that was perfect for me. It was quieter, more self-sufficient, and more of a loner, very much like me."

When another group compared the owners and their dogs, Barbara said Mark, a company manager, seemed like a German Shepherd, since he was strong and controlled, but could explode if threatened, like this dog. "His dog is normally a sweet, lovable, great protector, like Mark. The kids tug on his hair, grab his paws, rub his stomach, and he loves it. But when a stranger approaches,

---

[1] I have used pseudonyms for the participants at the party.

he stiffens up and starts growling, till he's sure everything's okay, which is very like Mark, too."

I found it fascinating to hear Gini describe how this system emerged, and I think these stories will help to popularize the system.

The Dog Type System

Gradually, as she heard hundreds of people explain their reasons for choosing a breed and describe the traits of themselves and their dogs, the "Dog Star" system emerged, based on describing a dog's personality traits along 12 dimensions, much like the 12 houses in astrology, described in more detail in Chapter 2. In brief, these dimensions include characteristics like: size, leadership, dominance, aggression, speed, location, affection, strength, obedience, intelligence, appearance, and demeanor. As she found in the workshops, while some people make choices consciously, because they like a dog's looks or feel it has similar traits to themselves, others feel drawn to a dog, but don't know why. In either case, when told the traits usually associated with that dog, most people feel the description accurately portrays themselves or others they know.

A Typical Workshop

Here's an example of the workshops Gini used to develop the system. Each workshop had a similar format. It began with informal introductions followed by a discussion of the dogs people are drawn to and the characteristics of other people they know with these dogs. Then people shared their insights.

At one program, Andrea,[2] who lived in a small apartment complex, described some neighbors who owned a pit bull, which terrified her and several other tenants. Though she didn't know the dog's owners well and was relieved when they left after several complaints, she noticed that they had the same pugnacious, aloof, unfriendly nature as their dog. As she told her story:

"My upstairs neighbors had this female pit bull, and they called her Igor, which is a male Russian name. This dog gave me the creeps. I would come home and see her darting around and growling, though she would pull back and let me pass.

One day, she was very ferocious when I came home from the grocery store. She was baring her teeth and snarling, and she looked like she was about to jump on me...Eventually I waited it out, and after about 15 minutes, she finally turned away, ran toward a four foot fence around the house, and sailed over it. It was really freaky.

Thinking back now, I feel like these people were exactly like their dog. They kept to themselves. They were not friendly and very aloof. In fact, their dog helped them keep that wall of distance between themselves and the others in the building. "

Jim, a student and sometimes bartender, pointed out that sometimes dogs choose people, because they share certain similarities, which is how a friend got his dog. As Jim explained:

"Jerry was walking down the street when this dog appeared. It followed him home, and he fed it and adopted it. It was a tough little mutt, and Jerry is, too. I'm not sure what it was, maybe a mix of Rottweiler, Lab, and Spaniel. But whatever it was,

---

[2] I've changed the names of workshop participants to protect their identities.

Jerry really took to it, and they had a lot of similarities. Jerry would spend hours at home working at his computer, and he had a pretty solitary job in IT. But he loved to party, like he was two different people. And the dog was like that. It would go off and you might not see it for days…Then, suddenly, it would be back and ready to follow Jerry around, when Jerry began to go out and be more social."

Making Choices

In the next phase of the program, people chose the dog they most preferred or identified with, their second favorite, and least favorite. To help people choose, Gini used photos of different dogs, along with a brief description of their major characteristics, personality, and temperament. Participants chose among the most common breeds in the seven major groups of dogs, according to the American Kennel Club – working, herding, sporting, and non-sporting dogs, terriers, hounds, and toys.

After people wrote down their top two favorites and least favorite dog, and their reasons for selecting them, they shared their choices and reasons with the group. Their explanations help to show that they were drawn to qualities they saw in themselves and rejected those qualities they didn't have or didn't want. For example:

Sarah on choosing a Siberian Husky:
"A friend gave me this Siberian puppy, and I fell in love with her. She was so cute, and I liked her high energy. As she got older, I loved her free spirit and independence. She really had a will of her own, so it was a challenge to raise her. My mother wondered why I would want a dog that didn't listen to me and would run away if I left the door open, so I had to go looking for her. But I felt this close

connection, and now, that's what I would choose first – a Siberian Husky. Plus, I feel the Husky is a lot like me. I feel like I have that same kind of free spirit and independence."

Alison on choosing a Pomeranian:
"I own a Pomeranian and that's the dog I would choose first, because they're such affectionate and friendly dogs. They love to be around people, and it's such a great companion. I know some people might get annoyed because they're often underfoot. But that doesn't bother me. Sandy, my Pom, is so lovable, and she's gorgeous, too, with her long reddish brown coat."

Dan on picking a Pug:
"I got a pug, because they are such great companion dogs. They have a very gentle, friendly disposition, and I like that. They may look very pugnacious, but they aren't at all. They like to curl up on your lap, and when I'm working on my computer, my pug Tipi is right there. Tipi is very loyal and good at following orders, too."

Jack on choosing a Golden Retriever.
"For me, a Golden Retriever's a great dog, because I like to go hiking and camping, and this is a sporting dog that likes the outdoors. Plus, he's a great family dog, since he's good with the kids. He's so good natured. That's why I got this dog in the first place, and I would get it again."

As for what people didn't like, these were often the very qualities that others found endearing. But they didn't like those traits, for the same reasons that others liked them, such as illustrated by these comments:

Frank on why he liked Siberian Huskies the least:
"I know a couple of people who have Siberian Huskies, but they are so hard to control. They're like teenagers in that rebellious age. So why would I like a dog like that? They may be cute, but they are constantly getting into trouble. That's not the kind of dog I like, and that's why my favorite dog would be a Collie. They are very helpful, gentle, and eager to please."

Betty on why she liked Afghan Hounds the least:
"To me, Afghans are just plain snooty and arrogant. I know a couple who own them, and they are like that. They act like they're better than anyone and hardly give you the time of day, unless they think they can get something from you. So I don't trust them. The people are all superficial veneer, and that's what I think of Afghans, too."

Understanding One's Choice

At the end of the workshop, everyone discussed two key questions: "What are the main characteristics of the dogs you most like or most identify with?" and "How well do you think the characteristics you have listed fit you?" After listing these traits, the participants gave examples of how they expressed these characteristics, such as.

Sarah, who chose a Siberian Husky, stressed how much she valued independence:
"I've always prided myself on being independent and a free thinker. That's why I decided to go into business for myself when I was younger. I wanted only me as my boss, so I found a way to be an

educational consultant. I didn't like teaching, because I felt there was too much supervision. But as a consultant, I could set my own schedule, because I was the one making the rules."

Alison, who chose a Pomeranian, emphasized her warm and friendly qualities:

"I've always been a very warm, friendly person. My husband is the strong silent type, and I think that's what drew us together. When we go to cocktail parties and receptions, I'm usually the one who's going around meeting people, talking to them, and bringing them over to talk to my husband. He's a great creative artist, but still shy, and he likes it when I'm outgoing and help to make the connections for him."

The participants also talked about how they expressed the characteristics they associated with their dog in different situations. For example:

Frank, who chose a Bull Terrier, which he considered tenacious and feisty like himself, recalled an incident in which he stood up to his boss.

"I was feeling like I was being ignored, when it came time for promotions. I didn't think my boss fully recognized what I had done, since he was a hands-off kind of guy who liked to delegate. So I decided to stand up to him and tell what I did. I started out by being very diplomatic, telling him how I appreciated working in the group and how much our group had accomplished. Then, I pointed out that he might not have been aware of some of the things I had done, and I explained how they might help the company. And the strategy worked. I got a raise out of that meeting and an additional assignment, though it's possible I could have gotten canned."

June, who chose a Lhasa Apso, a glamour dog known for its long silky coat, recalled when she participated in a beauty pageant.

"It was one of my college highpoints, when I won a beauty contest. It was only a local event, but it made me feel really good and my boyfriend at the time was really impressed. Though I didn't enter any more beauty pageants after that, the experience made me even more conscious of fashion and style. And that's been important to me ever since."

Putting It Together

Finally, each workshop ended with a discussion about how the participants might apply what they learned in daily life. Here are a few comments to illustrate:

Jon, who chose a Greyhound:
"I realize that I've always liked to do things fast. I like quick results, and I make snap judgments in entering relationships or breaking up. But sometimes I've regretted my fast decisions, and sometimes the quick results have been wrong. So I sometimes need to take more time to do things or get more information to decide."

Barbara, who chose a Bullmastiff:
"I realize it's really important for me to be a presence, and I like the feeling of power that comes from people paying attention and listening to me. What would I change? Well, maybe there are times I come on too strongly, and I need to temper myself down a little."

Susan, who chose a Hairless Chinese Crested:
"I've always liked being unique and different. I like trying new things, as well as shaking things up – like stating a controversial opinion to see how people react. I think that's amusing and interesting, very much like the dog I like the most. I realize maybe I need to be a little more diplomatic and tactful. But otherwise, I don't want to change. I like the way I am."

These descriptions and comments illustrate how people do see themselves reflected in the dogs they choose and how they get insights they can apply in their daily life.

The following chapters reflect the *Dog Type* system that developed from these workshops and how to use the system to better understand yourself and others, improve personal and work relationships, and apply these techniques in everyday life. I found it very helpful to use the system myself and try it out on many family members and friends.

INTRODUCTION

WHAT'S YOUR DOG TYPE? is a new, fun way to understand yourself and others, improve your relationships, deal with everyday situations, meet others, and have fun in creative new ways. It draws on insights from a variety of areas – everything from psychology, lifestyles and learning to systems for personality typing from Myers-Briggs to astrology.

You'll learn about yourself and others by knowing what type of dog you each like the most or are most like – and conversely, what dogs you like least. Additionally, you can call on different types of dogs like guides, friends, or teachers for different types of help. For instance, pick a Guide Dog for advice or a Power Dog to gain power. And for more help, seek out some Rescue Dogs.

Why use dogs? One reason is that dogs have developed a very close affinity with humans due to their long history as human's closest companion. It's a relationship that goes back to the Neolithic Revolution 12,000 years ago, when humans first began to domesticate animals, and may even go back to Paleolithic times, when hunters sometimes used dogs to help with the hunt. Researchers believe the dog in Neolithic times was probably first used to herd other newly domesticated animals and as a guardian and companion. Then, over the millennia, dogs were developed for multiple purposes in different cultures around the world, resulting in more than 400 recognized breeds – plus hundreds more unrecognized ones, as well as thousands of mixed breeds. Such recent mixes include the trendy Puggle – a mixture of Pug and Beagle, and the Cockapoo, a Cocker Spaniel and Poodle mix. Over the years, some dogs were developed to work hard at a variety of tasks, such as herding sheep and pulling sleds (the herding and working dogs), finding and retrieving game (the sporting dogs), killing vermin (the terriers), and being a close companion or lap dog (the toy dogs).

It's no wonder that the different types of dogs, with their wide range of personality types and temperaments, can tell us much about ourselves. Plus, as long-time close companions, dogs can be a source of emotional support, advice, and increased feelings of personal power. In fact, people have long used connections with all sorts of personal helpers, from inner guides and teachers to the Teddy Bear a child talks to as a receptive companion. Even doctors use personal guides, whether imagined, real, or a fluffy toy animal, to help patients feel better.

To gain insights and help from different types of dogs for various purposes the book is divided into four sections:
- Part I: Introducing the Dog Type System
- Part II: Discovering Your Dog Type
- Part II: Getting Help From Your Dogs
- Part III. Getting Even More Help from Your Dogs
- Part IV: Using the Dog Type System for Success in Business or the Workplace

Read Part I first to understand the basics of the Dog Type system. Then, feel free to skip around in other sections based on your interests in applying the system. Feel free to choose among the techniques described, since different people will prefer different approaches. For example, instead of using visualization to meet your favorite dog, get advice, or make decisions, use your first impression or "top of mind" response and respond based on whatever dog first comes to mind.

So now, get started. What your Dog Type: what type of dog are you? What type of dog is your boss, cousin, best friend, or neighbor? Start by learning about the Dog Profile System in the next chapter. Then, apply it for self-development, improving relationships, and in other ways.

PART I: INTRODUCING THE DOG TYPE SYSTEM

CHAPTER 1: USING THE DOG TYPE SYSTEM

To learn about yourself and others using the Dog Type system, think about your favorite and least favorite dogs or choose the breeds you most and least identify with. Also, think about others you know in the same way. What are – or do you think are – their favorite and least favorite dogs?

Thinking about these preferences gives you insight into yourself or others, because people are drawn to dogs with corresponding qualities or with qualities they would like to have. Conversely, they are pulled away from dogs with qualities they don't have or don't like.

This identification process is much like learning about yourself by knowing your favorite and least favorite colors, cars, house styles, or other choices. This system uses dogs because there are so many different breeds with different personalities and temperaments, which were bred for many different purposes in different places around the globe, and because of their very long and close association with humans.

The type of dog you choose or most identify with reflects the traits you have or would like to have. And if you know which dog another person chooses — or can sense what type of dog a person is most likely to be — you can better understand them and know how to better relate to them.

You might even consider the system as a kind of "Dogology" personality system, which parallels other systems of learning about oneself and others. For instance, one popular way of learning about people is to ask "What's your sign?" referring to one of the twelve astrological symbols. Or if you're involved with the well-known Myers-Briggs personality system you might ask: "What's your type?" referring to the four dimensions of personality – either you're E or I (extrovert or introvert), S or N (sensor or intuitive), T or F (thinking or feeling) or J or P (judging or perceiving).

Likewise, as a "dogologist" or "dogster" for short, you might ask: "What's your dog type?" to learn more about others. Just asking the question is also a way to break the ice and get others to tell you more about themselves. Once you learn about the different types of dogs and the personality and lifestyle characteristics associated with them, you can give others insights about themselves, too. The process works a little like doing a reading with color, Tarot cards, tea leaves, or Rorschach tests. In effect, you are using your "Dog Sense", like dogs use their sense of smell to pick up information about people. They literally sniff you out.

Here's an example of how it works. While I was in the middle of organizing the dog typing system, a carpet sales rep arrived to help her select carpets for two new rooms she added to her house. After she told the rep about her project, the rep asked her, "What type of dog do you think I am?" As I looked at her for a few moments, seeing a heavy-set, 50-something woman with graying hair, glasses, and a warm, take-charge personality, the image of a Chow Chow came to mind, in part because the woman looked something like a Chow with her broad round face and body shape.

So I told her: "You're a Chow Chow" and described the characteristics associated with the Chow – regal in bearing, a little reserved, very alert, and devoted. The rep smiled broadly and immediately agreed. "Yes. You're right. That's me." She felt she had these same qualities and described how she showed these characteristics in various settings. So the initial dog type insights helped open the doors to a deeper conversation.

Using the dog types is also an easy, comfortable door-opener, because it's a fun and whimsical way of characterizing people. When you ask: "What's your Dog Type?" or someone asks you: "What type of dog am I?" they often ask the question with some amusement, which makes people feel more relaxed and comfortable and therefore, more willing to share information about themselves.

How the Dog Type System Works

The Dog Type System is based on grouping the many different breeds of dogs into 24 to 36 major types based on their personality characteristics. The exact number will vary from country to country, based on the breeds that are most popular there.

The personality characteristics in each group represent a mix of traits divided into four categories:
- individual traits (appearance, demeanor, intelligence)
- social skills (affection, obedience, strength)
- energy (energy level, speed, and indoor or outdoor location)
- power (size, aggression, leadership/dominance)

There are 12 dimensions of personality, which are like 12 spokes on a wheel or the 12 houses in astrology, so they are dubbed "Dog Houses" in the system. Each dog – and by extension each person – can be located along each of these spokes (such as being a very small to a very big dog on the size dimension). After you map the personality traits on each of the 12 dimensions, you come out with a personality profile which looks something like a lopsided star when charted, so these are called "Dog Stars".

While dogs, as well as people, vary in their unique combination of traits, the Dog Star Profile reflects the common characteristics associated with a particular breed or similar breeds.

The write-ups about these major types of dogs (i.e.: Are You a Beagle or Basset Hound?) highlight the major personality traits associated with that group – and by extension, the people who choose that type as their favorite dog or dog they most identify with. Plus each write-up includes a little history about each breed.

Using the Dog Type System

Now that you understand the basics of the system, here's how to use it.

First, keep in mind these two basic principles:
- If a person chooses a particular type of dog – or you think of a person as that type of dog — the person is likely to have these traits or is likely to want to develop them.
- If a person identifies a dog as their least favorite dog or the one they are least like, the person is likely not to have those traits or is likely to want to get rid of them.

You can now apply these basic principles in five major ways:

1) To learn more about yourself and work on personal and professional development along each of the 12 personality dimensions.

2) To learn more about others and use that understanding to better relate for various purposes (i.e.: a better relationship, advancement at work, to better manage a team of people). If the person doesn't tell you this information, imagine what type of dog that person is most like.

3) To gain assistance with whatever you are doing in your everyday life, such as getting help with setting goals, making decisions, solving problems, and resolving conflicts.

4) To have fun, using the different dog types in a variety of playful exercises by yourself or with others

5) To provide others with insights about themselves, such as a guide, facilitator, or counselor.

Here's a brief introduction into how to use the system in each of these areas. You'll find more details on what to do in Part II.

Learning More about Yourself for Personal and Professional Development

To learn more about yourself for personal and professional development, think of what kind of dog you like the most or which you think most represents you, whether you own the dog or not. Think of this as your "Top Dog".

If you have carefully chosen the dog you own, this may well be your favorite. Otherwise, go through the dog photos and profiles and notice which dog you are most drawn to, whether you are already familiar with that breed or not.

Once you choose a particular dog, take time to get more acquainted with that dog and any others in that group by doing the following:

- Look at the list of personality characteristics, and reflect on how you share those qualities.
- Consider how well those personality traits fit what you are doing in your work and personal life.
- Think about how you might further develop some of these qualities.

For example, say you are drawn to a Poodle, a dog that carries itself with an air of pride, dignity, self-confidence, and style. If you already have those qualities, that's a sign you are very much in tune with who you are and have chosen a dog that perfectly reflects you. If you don't have these qualities, think of your choice as a signal to develop them, and use the image of this dog in various exercises to help you.

Then, think about the type of dog you like the least. Consider this your "Underdog". If you already have a clear choice, use that. Otherwise, go through the photos and profiles to pick the breed you like least. Then, take some time to reflect on why you don't like this type of dog. Ask yourself:

- What qualities does it have that I don't like?
- Are there any qualities that I share which I would like to get rid of?

For example, say you chose the Pit Bull as the dog you like least, because you don't like its angry looks and scrappy nature. If you have a usually sunny, outgoing disposition, that choice could be a good match with who you are. Otherwise, if this dog is much like you, this choice might be a signal to change, by finding ways to become more relaxed and not get angry so easily, to better get along with your family and the people you work with.

You'll see a variety of techniques for further exploring and developing or getting rid of these qualities in a future book.

Learning More about Others for Better Relationships

To learn more about others through Dog Profiling, ask them one or two questions. If you can't get the answers directly from them, imagine the type of dog they most seem to be like. The questions to ask are:
- What type of dog do you like the most?
- If you were a dog, what type of dog would that be?

Then, think about the traits associated with that kind of dog and consider the ways in which the other person is like that dog. If he or she is receptive, ask some follow-up questions to learn more. For example, ask questions such as:
- Why did you choose that particular dog?
- What qualities about that dog do you like the most?

Then, listen. These questions may open up a conversation in which the person tells you more about himself or herself and even tells you stories.

Next ask:
- What type of dog do you like the least?
- If you were a dog, what type of dog would you least like to be?

Again, if you can, ask some follow-up questions, such as:
- Why do you like that dog the least?
- What qualities about that dog don't you like?

Again, just listen.

You can ask these questions in a variety of circumstances from having a serious conversation with someone to introducing a fun icebreaker at a party to getting to know your seatmate on a plane.

You can also use these questions and the insights gained about others in different situations and social settings. For instance, use these questions to discover how to better work with your co-workers or boss. Use them to help people get to know each other at a social event. Or use them to select a team, motivate team members, or promote team building.

If you can't ask people questions directly, you can gain these insights after learning the different profiles by using your power of visualization. Simply imagine yourself asking these questions of others and notice what kind of dog immediately comes to mind. Then, think about the qualities you associate with that breed to help you better understand and relate to that person.

You'll see techniques for better understanding and relating to others in another book in this series.

To Gain Assistance in Everyday Life

To apply the Dog Type System in everyday life, think of different types of dogs as companions or advisers who can help you in various ways.

For instance, look to your "Guide Dogs" for advice with setting goals, making decisions, solving problems, and resolving conflicts. To get this advice, get relaxed and imagine your guide dog is with you. Next, ask a series of questions, such as: "What should I do about my problem with the neighbors?" "Where should I go on my vacation this year?" or "What should I do to get that promotion at work?" Then, listen to the answers your Guide Dog provides, using a variety of techniques to get that answer. In effect, you are getting your intuition to speak to you, and imagining that the Guide Dog is giving you this wisdom helps you tap into it.

To improve your abilities and skills, gain confidence, or increase your feelings of power, you can call on your "Power Dogs", that you think of as especially strong and powerful.

If you still need more help, you can call in some "Rescue Dogs" or perhaps use some "Search Dogs" to increase your creativity, again visualizing your Rescue Dog or Search Dog giving you advice.

You'll see techniques for applying the Dog Type System in everyday life in another book in this series too.

To Just Have Fun

The Dog Type system also lends itself to just having fun, using the different dog types in a variety of playful exercises. These activities can be a way to meet and get to know others in a comfortable, light-hearted atmosphere, along with gaining insights. So you can both get to know yourself and others and have a blast doing it.

For example, you can create a game in which you put the name of a breed of dog on someone's back, and he or she has to guess what dog this is. Or organize people into groups based on the type of dog they choose, and then they can participate in a series of games, in which they compete with other groups. For instance, a competition might be between big dog enthusiasts and little dog fans. Or have a "Come as Your Favorite Dog Party", where everyone comes dressed up as the dog they like the most. The possibilities are endless.

You'll see some suggestions to get you started in this next book.

Giving Others Insights about Themselves

Finally, you can use the Dog Type system to give others understanding about themselves, much like a counselor might give someone a personality profile test or an astrological or Tarot card reading. Or give the test in a group, as a facilitator.

To share these observations with others, first learn the Dog Type profiles. After that you can read and analyze someone's "Dog Type", much as I did when the carpet store rep asked her: "What kind of dog do you think I am?"

The way to do this analysis most effectively is to know the system like a salesperson knowing the product line he or she is selling. Then, let your intuition take over, so an image of the person's "Dog Type" immediately comes to mind.

Afterward, share this image with that person and describe the personality characteristics associated with that dog and how they fit that personality type.

Next, encourage the person to share his or her reactions to your assessment. You can give your comments in a spirit of fun or you can use your initial comments to initiate a deeper exchange. For example, you can use the information you gained from your conversation to help the other person set goals, make decisions, or work on developing desired personal qualities.

Still another way to use these techniques is to organize a small informal gathering or workshop where you use various techniques and group sharing for personal development, improving relationships, and applying the techniques in everyday life. Once you plan what you are going to do, invite people to share their experiences for an hour or so, as described in subsequent chapters.

Get Ready, Set, Go

Now start learning about the different types of dogs. You might consider the process a little like going to the dog races where the goal is finding out: "What type of dog are you? What type of dogs are the people you know or meet?"

So, get ready, get set, go, and race on to the next chapter.

PART II: DISCOVERING YOUR DOG TYPE

CHAPTER 2: THE DOG PROFILES

The following 40 Dog Profiles are among the most popular types of dogs in the U.S. They are based on grouping dogs according to their size, breed, personality, and temperament, although the number of profiles varies from country to country, based on the most popular dogs in each country. Each profile includes a picture of the most common dogs in that group and a brief description of their breed's history and personality characteristics.

These profiles have been developed from the 12 trait dimensions on the Dog Star Chart, and they range in the strength of that quality from the inner ring (lowest) to the outer ring (highest). These dimensions are like the 12 spokes of a wheel on an astrological chart which create the four sections called "houses". Similarly, there are 12 Dog Houses on the Dog Star Chart. Each type of dog can be plotted on the chart, using the basic characteristics of that type of dog. You can modify these profiles to reflect your associations with a dog of that type.

To map each profile, assess where a type of dog might fall on each of the 12 dimensions or Dog Houses. Then, trace the dots from each dimension or spoke to draw a profile for that type of dog. While placing a dot on each dimension is subjective, based on individual and common associations for that type of dog, this process will give you an overall profile. You can compare the profiles for different types of dogs by holding these maps side by side.

The 12 Dog Star dimensions or Houses are listed below according to the four major traits they represent, which are like the four divisions used in many systems, such as in the Myers-Briggs personality system (Extroversion-Introversion; Thinking-Feeling; Intuition-Sensing; and Judging-Perceiving), the four quarters in Astrology, the four suits in a deck of cards, and the four directions in many Native American systems. The four dimensions or Dog Houses are Power, Energy, Social Skills, and Individual Traits –

the four key areas to help anyone become a well-rounded successful person.

Power Traits
1. Size: Very Small to Very Large
2. Leadership/Dominance: Follower to Leader
3. Aggression: Very Low to Very High

Energy
4. Energy Level: Laid Back/Relaxed to Active/Intense
5. Speed: Slow to Fast
6. Location: Indoors to Outdoors

Social Skills
7. Affection: Reserved to Affectionate
8. Strength: Tough to Gentle
9. Obedience: Independent/Hard to Train to Cooperative/Team Player

Individual Traits
10. Intelligence: Low to High
11. Appearance: Ugly/Ordinary to Glamorous/Attractive
12. Demeanor: Serious to Playful

You'll see them laid out on the chart on the following page.

DISCOVERING YOUR DOG STAR

To determine your Dog Star, first map the traits on each of the Dog Houses for your chosen type of dog. Then, add in your unique traits that make you and your dog who you each are. Start with the overall pattern for the major type of dog you have chosen and use this as a general guide. You can further modify it to create your personality profile. You can use a different color or different type of line to note any differences. Later, you can use where you and your dog fall on these different spokes as a guide for participating in different exercises – or joining with others who share a similar combination of traits with you.

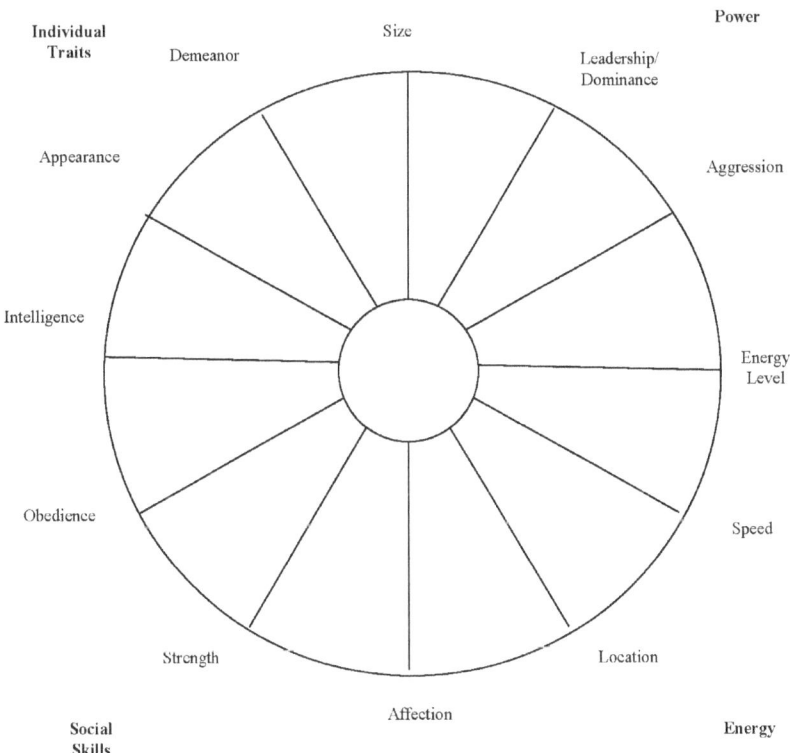

You'll see the Dog Profiles for the major types of dogs commonly known in the United States and Canada on the next 40 pages. Other editions of this book may feature different types of dogs which are relatively popular in these countries.

THE WORKING DOGS

Are You a Siberian Husky, Alaskan Malamute, Samoyed, or Akita?

A Little Bit of History...
In case you chose a Siberian Husky, Alaskan Malamute, Samoyed, or Akita, you have chosen a dog with a close kinship to its wolf ancestors and the Far North.

The Siberian Husky was developed by the Chukchi people of northeast Asia, and was initially used by these nomadic peoples as a sled dog. When the gold rush came to Alaska, these dogs helped the miners carry their gear, and became popular competitors in dog races starting in 1909, when they were first entered in the All-Alaska sweepstakes race. They also gained fame in 1925 when teams of Huskies raced 340 miles from Nenana to bring diphtheria serum to Nome and were honored for saving the town. The current annual Iditarod sled dog race now follows a route from Seward, about 100 miles South of Anchorage, to Nome. Many were recruited in World War II to serve on the U.S. Army's Search and Rescue teams. Now Siberians are a pet as well as a racing sled dog and show dog.

The Alaskan Malamute looks much like the Siberian Husky, except it's larger. They are one of the oldest Arctic sled dogs, and they helped the native Inuit people, known as "Mahlemuts", hunt and haul big game, such as seals and polar bears. When the gold rush arrived, the miners and settlers recruited the Malamutes to participate in weight-pulling contests and races. In the 1920s, they first came to New England, and some gained fame helping Admiral Byrd trek to the South Pole in 1933. They helped during World War II with hauling freight, carrying packs, and search and rescue.

The Samoyeds also originated in ancient times, with the Samoyed people who arrived in northwestern Siberia from Central Asia. These people used their dogs to herd reindeer, protect them from large Arctic predators, and sometimes hunt bears and tow boats and sleds. The Samoyeds first came to England in the late 1800s, and Queen Alexandra helped to promote the breed. In the early 1900s they came to the U.S., and were used on sled teams to Antarctica. They were among the dogs that first reached the South Pole.

The Akita developed in the 1600s in Japan, when a nobleman exiled to the Akita Prefecture, a very rugged, cold area, engaged the landowners in a competition to breed a powerful hunting dog. The result was the Akita, which became renowned for its skill hunting bear, deer, and wild boar. In the 1800s, Akitas were used as fighting dogs, and in 1931, they were honored as one of Japan's national treasures. The first Akitas arrived in America in 1937, and, servicemen also brought them back home after World War II.

What's Your Personality and Style?

If you picked a Siberian Husky, Alaskan Malamute, Samoyed, or Akita, you tend to be **outgoing, friendly, affectionate, playful, fun-loving,** and **adventurous.** You also have a strong **independent, bold,** sometimes **willful, stubborn, tenacious,** and **mischievous** streak, but are still very **loyal** and **devoted** to those you trust and respect, especially family members, and you can be a good **cooperative team player** if you feel so inclined. You are also very aware of **power** in relationships, and either want to be **top dog** or **go along** with whoever is dominant in your group.

Are You a Boxer, Bullmastiff, or Mastiff?

The Boxer dates back to the 1800s in Germany, where it gained early popularity as a contender in the sport of bull baiting. After bull baiting was outlawed, the dog was often used as a butcher's dog to control cattle in the slaughter yards. It also was used by the police and military. Many theories exist about the origin of the breed's name including that the Germans called their butcher's dogs "*boxl*" and because when they fight, they hold their front paws like a boxer. By 1900, the Boxer became a family pet and show dog and since the 1940s its popularity has taken off in the U.S. where it is now one of the most popular breeds.

The Bullmastiff traces its origins to England in the 1800s, where large estates had a problem with game poachers. They needed a strong, tough, courageous dog to quietly wait and attack the poachers without killing them. The result was the Bullmastiff, a cross of a Bulldog and a Mastiff, since Bulldogs were too small and Mastiffs weren't quick enough. They were often called the "Gamekeeper's Night Dog". As the poaching problem declined, Bullmastiffs were recruited as guards and watchdogs, and since the 1920s, have been a show dog and pet.

The Mastiff has ancient roots in England, and when Caesar invaded in 55 B.C., the Mastiffs fought with their masters against the Roman troops. Some of them were brought back to Rome where they were used to fight gladiators, bulls, bears, lions, and tigers. Meanwhile, back in England, they were popular for dog fighting, bull baiting, and bear baiting. Though these activities became illegal in 1835, the fights continued for several decades. Eventually, Mastiffs arrived in the U.S. in the late 1800s, and gradually gained popularity.

What's Your Personality and Style?

If you picked a Boxer, Bullmastiff, or Mastiff, you tend to be outwardly **tough, bold, strong, aggressive, confident,** and **courageous**. Yet, you are **playful**, **loving**, **affectionate, docile, gentle,** and **patient** when you want to be. At times, you can be **stubborn** and **hold your ground**, though you are good at **following instructions** when you want. You commonly have a lot of **energy** and **enthusiasm,** and tend to be very **loyal** and **devoted** to those you trust.

Are You a Doberman Pinscher or Rottweiler?

A Little Bit of History...

If you chose a Doberman Pinscher or Rottweiler, you have picked two of the feistiest fighters.

The Doberman was originally developed in Germany in the late 1890s by Louis Dobermann. As a door-to-door tax collector, he wanted a guard dog to accompany him as he went through unsavory neighborhoods. He crossed a number of breeds to finally get the tough, courageous dog he wanted – a bit of German Shepherd, German Pinscher, Manchester Terrier, Greyhound, and Weimaraner. As the breed spread around Europe and America in the early 1900s, it found a following as a police and guard dog, and later it was recruited to serve in the war effort. Plus it has become popular as a family protector, pet, and show dog.

The Rottweiler traces its ancestry to ancient times, when it was used to drive cattle and guard the herds. The Roman soldiers took the dogs with them on their campaigns, including one to the town of Rottweil in southern Germany, from which it got its name. Later, when the town became the center of cattle sales, the Rottweiler was a butcher's dog. After cattle driving was outlawed in the mid-1800s and the railroad arrived, the breed nearly disappeared. Then some dog fanciers revived the breed in the early 1900s, and it gained a new appeal as a police dog. Since the 1930s, it has grown in popularity as a show dog as well as a pet, and is now considered the 11th most popular breed in the U.S.

What's Your Personality and Style?

If you picked a Doberman Pinscher or Rottweiler, you tend to be very **strong, bold, courageous, feisty, self-assured,** and **confident.** You like being **powerful** and **dominant**, and can sometimes be **headstrong, stubborn,** and **domineering.** You are also a **loyal, devoted protector**, and are on the **alert** and **ready to attack**, should you feel threatened. You tend to be **aloof** and **reserved** with those you don't know very well. You are a **hard, dedicated** worker, like being **active,** and enjoy the **outdoors**.

Are You a St. Bernard, Bernese Mountain Dog, or Newfoundland?

A Little Bit of History...
In case you chose a St. Bernard, Bernese Mountain Dog, or Newfoundland, these are working dogs, known for their ability to thrive in the cold.

The St. Bernard dates back to Roman times where they were used in the farms and dairies to guard, herd, and pull equipment. They got their reputation as rescue dogs when they were brought to a hospice in the Alps in the 1600s to be watchdogs and companions for the monks. Their good sense of smell helped them locate travelers lost during storms, and they saved more than 2,000 people. The reputation as rescue dogs and protectors has endured.

The Bernese Mountain Dogs share a similar background in the farms and mountains of Switzerland, where they were originally brought by Roman soldiers. But by the 1980s they almost died out as a breed until a Swiss enthusiast began breeding them again. Now they have acquired a following on farms, at shows, and as household pets.
The Newfoundland was developed in the 1700s on the coast of Newfoundland as a dog that loved the water and could endure very cold weather. It helped the fisherman haul their heavy nets through the water and saved many people from drowning. On land, it was used for hauling and packing.

What's Your Personality and Style?

If you picked a St. Bernard, Bernese Mountain Dog, or Newfoundland, you tend to be **good natured, gentle, affectionate, hard-working, loyal, dedicated, steadfast,** and **reliable.** You are something of a **protector**, wanting to help and protect those you are close to. You also seek out **approval,** like to **please,** are very much a **people dog,** but in a quiet friendly kind of way, where people look on you with trust and respect. You tend to be **down-to-earth** and **serious**, rather than showy and flamboyant.

Are You a Great Dane?

A Little Bit of History...
Great Danes, as one of the largest dogs, definitely make a statement. In case you chose a Great Dane, here's a little history about them.

Ironically, the Great Dane didn't develop in Denmark but was probably a mix made by German breeders of the Irish Wolfhound and English Mastiff, about 1,300 years ago. Initially, Great Danes were bred for boar hunting by the Germans to be big because boars were powerful, fast, and savage with large, fearsome tusks. Then, in the 1880s and 1890s, fanciers in Germany, England, and America began to show Great Danes, and they became known as the "king of dogs" or "Apollo of Dogs" for their nobility, courage, speed, and endurance.

What's Your Personality and Style
If you picked a Great Dane, you like to **stand out** and be **recognized.** You like being **powerful** and **in charge,** yet you are also **gentle**, **easy-going,** and **affectionate** with others, including children. Just think of the **eager-to-please politician**, and rather than only being a member of a team, you like to **shine** through your **star power**. You're also very **loyal** and **dependable,** and are not normally aggressive, unless stirred to respond, and then you can show great **courage**, since you're not timid. Rather, you're more like the wonderfully **huge friendly father,** who is normally **placid** until threatened, and then you might erupt in anger, but quickly settle down again when the storm is past.

Are You a Giant Schnauzer?

A Little Bit of History...

If you chose a Giant Schnauzer, you have chosen a dog known for being big, outgoing, and playful.

The Giant Schnauzer traces its origins to Germany in the Middle Ages, where it started as a Standard Schnauzer bred big and crossed with a few other breeds to create a powerful dog for driving cattle. Then, for a time these became butcher's and stockyard dogs. In the early 1900s, they were trained as police dogs, and in Germany they continued to be used in that capacity. More recently, they have gained some acceptance as a pet and show dog in the U.S. and other countries.

What's Your Personality and Style?

If you picked a Giant Schnauzer, you tend to be **bold, outgoing, adventurous,** and **playful,** as well as **strong**, **powerful**, and sometimes have a **stubborn, headstrong** streak, yet you are **dependable** and **reliable,** too. You like to be **top dog** and can be **domineering**, but can be willing to **go along** to **get along** with others. You tend to be very **loyal** and **protective** to those you know well, but are more **reserved** with others until you get to know and trust them. You also tend to be very **active** and **outdoorsy**.

Are You a Portuguese Water Dog?

A Little Bit of History...
  In case you chose a Portuguese Water Dog, you have chosen a dog known for being affectionate, fun-loving, and that loves the water.
  The Portuguese Water Dog's ancestors come from the steppes of central Asia. It was brought to Portugal in the 8th century, where it was used to help fishermen herd fish into nets and send messages from one boat to another or to fishermen on the shore. When the old fishing methods ended, a wealthy shipping magnate, Dr. Vasco Bensuade, promoted the breed in the early 1900s. For a time, the dogs were shown in Portugal and briefly in England in the 1950s, before they began to gain popularity in America, where they were recognized by the AKC in 1984. They have been especially popular as a family dog, and have gotten even more attention after becoming the family pet of the Obamas.

What's Your Personality and Style?
  If you picked a Portuguese Water Dog, you tend to be **affectionate, fun-loving,** and have an **easy-going** nature. You are **friendly, adaptable, enjoy being with others,** and make a great companion or **family member.** You also tend to be **adventurous** and **outgoing.**

THE HERDING DOGS

Are You a Collie, Border Collie, or Shetland Sheepdog (Sheltie)?

A Little Bit of History…
If you chose a Collie, Border Collie, or Shetland Sheepdog (Sheltie), these are herding dogs, which are known for their helpfulness, loyalty, and obedience.

Collies date back to the beginnings of history in Scotland and Northern England, when sheepherders first began to use them to herd sheep. Around 1860, Queen Victoria began to sponsor the breed, and they came to the U.S. in the 1870s. They soon gained popularity through literature, such as the stories of Albert Payson Terhune, who celebrated small-town family life in his *Lad: A Dog* books, and in the 1950s the Collie was immortalized on TV as *Lassie*, the ever-loyal farm dog.

The Border Collies similarly trace back to the days of sheepherders, especially in Scotland, and the 18th century Scottish poet Robert Burns celebrated them as a good and faithful dog.

The Shetland Sheepdog, popularly known as the Sheltie, is a miniature working Collie that evolved on the rugged Shetland Islands off the coast of Scotland. They became recognized as a breed in the early 1900s in England and were introduced into the U.S. soon after that.

What's Your Personality and Style?

If you picked a Collie, Border Collie, or Sheltie, you have a great **get-along** personality, as someone who likes being with others. You tend to have a **gentle, mild-mannered** personality, and make a great **follower** and **team player,** because you like to **go along** with what others are doing. You are eager to **please, take directions,** and are good at **following orders.** You tend to be a **very affectionate, loyal,** and **devoted** toward those you know and trust, though you may be more **reserved** with those you don't know very well.

Are You an Old English Sheepdog, Bearded Collie, or Bouvier des Flandres?

A Little Bit of History...

If you chose an Old English Sheepdog, Bearded Collie, or Bouvier des Flandres, these are all very hairy, lovable dogs, best known for herding sheep.

The Old English Sheepdog was developed 150 years ago in the English countryside, where it was mainly used to drive sheep and cattle to the city markets. Sheepdogs were developed with a long coat to insulate them against the cold, damp English climate.

The Bearded Collie gained their popularity in Scotland in the 1500s to late 1700s, where they were used to drive sheep and cattle. In the 1950s, they spread to England as show dogs, and arrived in the U.S. in the late 1960s.

The Bouvier des Flandres developed in the 1600s and was used for herding cattle in the farmlands of Flanders and in northern France. In fact, "bouvier" means cowherder or oxherder in French.

What's Your Personality and Style?

If you picked an Old English Sheepdog, Bearded Collie, or Bouvier des Flandres, you tend to be a **light-hearted**, **fun-loving**, **affectionate** person who loves **being with people.** You tend to be **high-spirited, playful**, and sometimes even **rambunctious.** You are also very **loyal, faithful**, and **protective** of those you like and trust. You're very **down-to-earth**, not at all arrogant, and don't care much for style or show.

Are You a Pembroke Welsh Corgi?

A Little Bit of History…

If you chose a Pembroke Welsh Corgi, you've chosen a dog known for its long body, short legs, and perky disposition.

The Corgis got their start in 12th century Wales, where they were used for herding cattle. Their style was to nip at the cows' heels and then duck quickly under their hooves. They were also used to herd sheep and Welsh ponies. Despite their very different breeding as herding dogs compared to the hunting Dachshund, they have much the same look and personality. They, too, since the 1960s, have become very popular pets, especially in Britain, where they were favorites of King George VI and Queen Elizabeth II.

What's Your Personality and Style?

If you picked a Pembroke Welsh Corgi, you tend to be **clever, energetic, perky, bold,** and **courageous.** At the same time, you are **loyal, devoted,** and **very affectionate** and **friendly**; a real **people person.** You like to **please** others and make a great **companion.** You have a great sense of **playfulness** and **fun.**

Are You a German Shepherd or Belgian Malinois?

A Little Bit of History…
If you chose a German Shepherd or Belgian Malinois, you've picked a dog known for its strength and courage, as well as being a popular police dog.

The German Shepherd was developed in Germany in the 1800s to herd and guard sheep. In 1899, the Verein fur Deutsche Scharferhunde SV was formed to improve the breed, so it not only made a great herding dog, but could be very courageous, athletic, and intelligent, making it an ideal police dog. It became a war sentry during WWI. For a time, its name was changed, so it wouldn't be associated with its roots in Germany, but in 1931, its original name was restored. It also gained movie fame as Rin Tin Tin from the silent movie first released in 1922 and then produced as a series of films and TV series, including a 1947 film with child actor Robert Blake and the 1950s TV series *The Adventures of Rin Tin Tin,* thought different dogs were used over the years. It has since been a popular police dog, and has helped in search and rescue operations and detecting explosives, as well as being a popular pet.

The Belgian Malinois developed in Belgium in the 1800s and was also used to herd stock. They became popular in the U.S. after 1911 until World War II and then declined in popularity, though in recent decades have become renowned as police dogs around the world.

What's Your Personality and Style?

If you picked a German Shepherd or Belgian Malinois, you tend to have **lots of energy**, and are very **alert, intelligent,** and **serious.** You can be **stand-offish** when you first meet someone, and tend to be **strong,** and even **domineering**. You are very **protective** of those you are close to, and are very **devoted** and **faithful**. You also have a strong sense of **mission** or **purpose.**

Are You an Australian Cattle Dog?

A Little Bit of History…

If you chose an Australian Cattle Dog, you've chosen a dog known for its ruggedness and endurance.

The Australian Cattle Dog was developed in the 1800s in Australia, when cattle were introduced to the newly opened lands for grazing stock. But the cattle became so wild that the traditional herding breeds didn't have the strength or stamina to deal with them. As a result, through the 1800s, breeders worked to develop a new breed by crossing a variety of breeds including Bull Terriers, Dalmatians, Kelpies, and Dingos. The goal was to create a dog that didn't bark and combined herding instincts with endurance, ruggedness, and protectiveness. The Australian Cattle Dog was recognized in 1897, though it took some time to gain popularity in America, and was finally recognized by the AKC in 1980. It has become a pet and show dog, as well as a herder.

What's Your Personality and Style?

If you picked an Australian Cattle Dog, you tend to be **full of energy, strong,** and **tenacious** as well as **feisty, independent** and sometimes **stubborn.**

THE HOUNDS

Are You a Beagle or a Basset Hound?

A Bit of History...
If you chose a Beagle or Basset Hound, here's a little history about them.

The beginnings of the Beagle are lost in ancient history, though the Beagle was one of the small hounds bred for hunting – especially fox hunting in England. Beagles came to the U.S. in the mid-1850s as a popular hunting dog. While some people still use them for hunting individually or in packs, they have become warm, gentle, trustworthy pets.

The Basset Hound originally came from France several centuries ago and thrived in Europe, especially in France and Belgium, where they were used for trailing rabbits, deer, and other small game. When the Basset Hound came to the U.S. in the 1800s, hunters mostly used them to hunt rabbits and some birds. Like Beagles, they can hunt in packs and alone, and have a friendly, warm personality.

What's Your Personality and Style?
If you picked a Beagle or Bassett Hound, you tend to be **friendly** with a **gentle**, **easy-to-get along with** temperament, just like these dogs. You are normally **loyal** and **devoted** to others. You tend to be a fairly **low-maintenance** person, not overly concerned about beauty and grooming, just as these dogs don't require much coat care or trimming. You tend to be **relaxed, laid-back**, and like **lounging around.** Yet you love being **sociable** around people and love to be loved. Your style is **casual** and **informal,** especially if you chose the Basset Hound.

Are You a Dachshund?

A Little Bit of History…

If you chose a Dachshund, you've chosen a dog known for its long body, short legs, and perky disposition.

The Dachshund dates back to the 1500s in Germany, where it was originally used to flush out badgers. In fact, its name means: "badger hound". The dachshund would chase the badger to its burrow, dig into it, pull it out, and quickly kill it. While the original Dachshund had smooth coats, they were bred in two sizes – standard and miniature – and three coats – smooth, longhaired, and wirehaired for different types of hunting, including chasing foxes and other small mammals. Now they have come into their own as a popular family pet.

What's Your Personality and Style?

If you picked a Dachshund, you tend to be **clever, energetic, perky, bold,** and **courageous.** At the same time, you are **loyal, devoted,** and **very affectionate** and **friendly**; a real **people person.** You like to **please** others and make a great **companion.** You have a great sense of **playfulness** and **fun,** too.

Are You a Greyhound or Whippet?

A Little Bit of History…
    If you chose a Greyhound or a Whippet, here's a little history about them. Both are hunting dogs that are best known for being fast – whether on the hunt or in a race.

    The Greyhound has a long history, back to the pyramids of Egypt, where it was a dog of the pharaohs. After further development in the ancient Greek and Roman empires, the Greyhound became popular in England for hunting all types of small game, especially the hare. They were not uncommon in colonial America, too. Greyhounds became track racing dogs in the 1920s, and their popularity races on today.

    The Whippet is a miniature English Greyhound, developed in England about 100 years ago. They were used by the gentry to chase rabbits in a sport that became known as "snap-dog coursing", since the winner was the dog who snapped up – that is caught – the most rabbits. Whippets are still used for racing on a straight course, while their handlers wave towels or rags to encourage them on.

What's Your Personality and Style?
    If you picked a Greyhound or Whippet, you like to do things **fast.** You are **quick-moving,** with lots of **energy** and **enthusiasm**. You can be very **intense** and **focused**, when doing something that's important to you, as you **race** to accomplish whatever it is. You also tend to have a very **friendly, gentle** disposition, are **warm** and **affectionate** and like to **please.**

Are You an Afghan Hound, Borzoi, or Saluki?

A Little Bit of History...

    If you chose an Afghan Hound, Borzoi, or Saluki, these are all hunting dogs with a touch of class, royalty, and elegance.

    The Afghan dates back to pre-Christian times, possibly to Egypt, and they were raised by the kings of Afghanistan for hunting. In the late 1800s, British officers who had fought in the Indian-Afghanistan wars brought Afghans back to England, and they came to the U.S. in the 1920s and '30s.

    The Borzois gained their aristocratic heritage in Russia, where they were bred by the Russian aristocrats for many centuries. They were raised on large country estates where hundreds of serfs helped breed and train them. Even some Mongol Rulers, including Genghis Khan in the 13th century, raised these dogs for hunting. The wolf was the typical target of the chase. In the late 1800s and the turn of the 20th century, they came to England and America.

    The Saluki's noble heritage dates back to the beginnings of ancient Egypt around 6000-5000 B.C. before the dynasties of pharaohs and possibly even to the Sumerian empire from around 7000-6000 B.C. They are possibly the oldest known domesticated breed of dog. In fact, their noble status was so great, that the Moslem considered the Saluki to be sacred. They arrived in England in about 1840 and came to the U.S. in the early 1900s.

What's Your Personality and Style?

If you picked an Afghan, Borzoi, or Saluki, you tend to have an **aristocratic** demeanor. You tend to be **aloof, dignified,** and **reserved**, yet reveal a **sunny, cheerful** disposition when you are with others you are close to. You also show great **loyalty, affection,** and a willingness to **please** those you feel worthy of your commitment and trust. Generally, you are **calm** and **even-tempered.** You might think of yourself as the **benevolent ruler**, eager to help your trusted subjects.

Are You a Bloodhound or Coon Hound?

A Little Bit of History...
If you chose a Bloodhound or a Coonhound, here's a little history about them. Both are best known for trailing a scent – whether helping an English detective or a good old boy in the South.

The Bloodhound dates back thousands of years to the earliest scent hounds, and showed up in Europe by the 8th century. William the Conqueror brought them to England in 1066, and many Church officials and monks used them to help in the hunt. They became famed in England and America for trailing suspects, and are frequently used now by Search and Rescue clubs.

The Coonhound developed in the U.S., probably from crossing the Bloodhound and Foxhound in the 1700s. They became most well-known in the southern U.S., most notably in the Appalachians, Ozark, Blue Ridge, and Smoky Mountains, where they were used to trail raccoons, opossums, and bears.

What's Your Personality and Style?
If you picked a Bloodhound or Coonhound, you tend to have a **relaxed, laidback, calm** nature, though you enjoy being **active** and **playful** at times. You tend to have a strong **independent** and **stubborn** streak, so you may enjoy **going off on your own** and really **sticking to things** you like to do. Yet, while you are generally **warm** and **gentle** with those you consider friends and family, you are more **reserved** or **shy** with strangers.

Are You an Irish Wolfhound or Otterhound?

A Little Bit of History...
      If you chose an Irish Wolfhound or Otterhound, you've chosen a big gentle hunting dog with lots of hair.
The Irish Wolfhound dates back to ancient times in Ireland, possibly brought by the Greeks in 1500 B.C. They were acclaimed for their ability to fight wild animals and were used by the Irish chieftains to hunt wolves, elk, and other game. Ironically, they nearly died out in Ireland after the wolf went extinct, because so many were given to foreign nobles. But they were revived in the late 1800s and have gained increasing popularity for their easygoing, gentle nature that has led them to be dubbed "the gentle giant".
      The Otterhound dates back to the 13th century and maybe earlier in England, where they were used for hunting – especially for finding otters that were preying on fish in the local streams and rivers: hence its name. It became especially popular as a hunting dog from the middle to the end of the 19th century in England, and the first Otterhounds arrived in the U.S. around 1900. But while one of the most ancient of breeds, it is relatively unknown today.

What's Your Personality and Style?

If you picked a Wolfhound or Otterhound, you tend to have a **gentle, mellow** nature, though you like to be **active** and love the **outdoors**. You are generally **calm, sensitive, patient,** and **easygoing**, with a **sweet, loving, affectionate** disposition. Though you may be **reserved** with those you don't know, you are **very warm** with those you know and trust. When necessary, you can show **courage** and **independence**, though you are usually **gracious** and **eager to please.**

THE SPORTING DOGS

Are You a Labrador or Chesapeake Bay Retriever?

A Little Bit of History…

If you chose a Labrador Retriever, including a Black, Chocolate, or Yellow Lab, or a Chesapeake Bay Retriever, you've chosen a dog known for retrieving game that has become a very popular family pet.

Ironically, the Labrador Retrievers didn't originate in Labrador, but in Newfoundland in the early 1800s. There they retrieved not only game but fish, and they pulled small fishing boats through the water by swimming. Though the Labradors died out in Newfoundland because of a steep dog tax, some retrievers were taken to England, where they became known for retrieving upland game. At first they were just black, but soon chocolate and yellow labs were developed, and by the early 1990s, the Labrador had become the most popular breed in the U.S., including being owned by President Clinton, who chose a Chocolate Lab and named him Buddy.

The Chesapeake Bay Retrievers were developed in the U.S. in the 1800s after an English ship went down off the coast of Maryland, and sailors on an American ship rescued their cargo and crew, which included two Newfoundland pups that some rescuers adopted. They turned out to be great water retrievers, and after they were bred with several other dogs, including the Irish Water Spaniel, Newfoundland, and Bloodhound, they became known for their ability to retrieve ducks in the icy Chesapeake Bay Waters – hence their name.

What's Your Personality and Style?

If you picked a Labrador Retriever or a Chesapeake Bay Retriever, you tend to lead a **well-rounded, active** life. You tend to be a good **people person,** someone who is generally **amiable** and **friendly.** You enjoy **pleasing** others, have an **upbeat, positive outlook,** and tend to be very **devoted, dependable**, and **obedient,** because you want to do what it takes to **get along with others**. You tend to be **gentle, non-aggressive,** and **adaptable,** ready to **conform** and be a **good team player**.

Are You a Cocker Spaniel or a Golden Retriever?

A Little Bit of History...
In case you chose a Cocker Spaniel or a Golden Retriever, these are both sporting dogs which are among the most popular family dogs.

Cocker Spaniels date back to the 1360s in England, where they were divided into land and water spaniels. The cockers were the smallest of the sporting dogs, and they initially helped hunters by flushing out game, generally small birds. They first came to the U.S. in the 1880s and quickly became beloved as a family companion, because of their energetic, friendly, affectionate personality.

The Golden Retrievers were developed in Scotland and England in the early 1800s to help with retrieving game from the water as well as on land, and they came to the U.S. in the 1890s. They are especially known for their obedience, and have become popular as guide dogs for the blind, as well as good at detecting narcotics for the police, because of their sensitive smell ability.

What's Your Personality and Style?
If you picked a Cocker Spaniel or a Golden Retriever, you tend to be a **very affectionate, warm, outgoing, extroverted people-person,** with **lots of energy**, just like these dogs. You are often **playful,** and can be very **charming,** but you're **down-to-earth,** even **humble** in your nature, not showy or ostentatious. You have an **optimistic, cheery** outlook, and are **loyal** and **devoted** to others. No wonder you are likely to be **popular** and enjoy **socializing** with others, just like these dogs.

Are You an English Springer Spaniel or a Brittany?

A Little Bit of History…

If you chose an English Springer Spaniel or a Brittany, you've chosen a dog known for both being game dogs and a family pet, with a sense of class.

The English Springer Spaniel traces its roots to the Cocker Spaniel, and was originally distinguished for its larger size in the early 1900s. Like the Cocker Spaniel, it was popular as a gundog for hunters, and used to both flush and retrieve game. It also boasts a royal heritage, since the Duke of Norfolk in England bred some of the early Springers. Now it has become both a popular show dog and pet, and still retains its sense of royal class. President George W. Bush chose an English Springer Spaniel as one of his dogs.

The Brittany was developed in the mid-800s, when French sportsmen crossed English Setters with their own small land spaniels. Soon the Brittany became popular with the French gentry, who liked their ability to both point and retrieve, combined with an eager desire to please and be obedient. These dogs were also popular with the French artists, and many appear in 17th century paintings and tapestries. They became a recognized breed in the early 1900s. After coming to the U.S. in the 1930s, they grew in popularity as a hunting dog, especially for birds. Plus the Brittany has become a popular city dog, too.

What's Your Personality and Style?

If you picked an English Springer Spaniel or a Brittany, you tend to be **friendly, cheerful, enthusiastic, energetic,** and **eager to please.** You can be very **playful** and **ready for fun,** and you enjoy both being **active outdoors,** as well as **relaxing at home.** You also tend to be good at **following orders, conforming** to what others want, and being **obedient,** though you have a **curious, independent** nature, too. But generally, when asked, you'll give up your independence to **follow the rules.** Plus, you have an air of **dignity** and **elegance.** No wonder people love to have you around.

Are You a Weimeraner or Vizsla?

A Little Bit of History...

If you chose a Weimeraner or Vizsla, you've chosen a dog with a touch of nobility.

The Weimeraner is a relatively recent breed, developed in the early 19th century, possibly from a line of Bloodhounds, to become one of the hunting breeds in Germany. He became a favorite with the nobles in the court of Weimar, who took him out to hunt game – and hence the name. The nobles particularly liked the Weimeraner's good sense of smell, speed, intelligence, and courage. While he was initially used to hunt big game, he was trained to hunt birds and upland game. Eventually, he arrived in America in 1929, and has since become a popular pet. He has also gotten a reputation as a sensitive artist's model, used to pose in human-like shots by artist William Wegman, and he was portrayed as the neurotic, high-anxiety dog in the movie *Best of Show*.

The Vizsla's roots date back to the Magyars who came to Europe and settled in Hungary over 1,000 years ago. Hunters used Vizslas to point and retrieve birds and track other game through the woods and underbrush, and by the 18th century, the breed had become a favorite with the barons and warlords of the day. After World War II, as the Hungarians fled from the Russian troops, they took their dogs to other countries, including the U.S.

What's Your Personality and Style?

If you picked a Weimeraner or Vizsla, you tend to combine a lot of **energy** and **enthusiasm,** even a **rambunctious exuberance,** with a **sensitive** and sometimes **stubborn** and **shy nature.** Still, you can be **friendly, courageous,** and willing to **conform** when you want to. Plus you usually have a **gentle**, **affectionate** manner, and you can be particularly **devoted** to those you trust. Additionally, you tend to have a **proud, dignified** manner, as if you have a little **royalty** in your veins.

Are You an English or Irish Setter?

A Little Bit of History...
If you chose an English or Irish Setter, these are bird and gaming dogs, developed in England and Ireland.

The English Setters were developed in 14th century England, and trace their ancestry to the Springer Spaniel, Water Spaniel, and Spanish Pointer. They were especially popular as bird dogs and excelled at finding and pointing out game in the countryside. They were first shown in the 1850s and from there spread to the U.S.

The Irish Setter developed out of the English Setter and possibly the Spanish Pointer and another less well-known setter from Scotland, the Gordon Setter. They are especially known for their mahogany red coat, thought some have white coats. Like the English Setters, they also became popular bird and game dogs.

What's Your Personality and Style?
If you picked an English or Irish Setter, you tend to be **very active,** enjoy **physical activity,** and are drawn to the **outdoors.** You tend to be very **friendly, amiable, outgoing,** and **easy-going,** a good **people person** who gets along well with others. You tend to be **calm,** with a **mild,** "it doesn't bother me" **disposition.**

Are You a Pointer?

A Little Bit of History...
    If you chose a Pointer, including the German Shorthaired or Wirehaired Pointer, you gained your reputation pointing out hares. The first Pointers originated in England in the 1600s, probably from a mix of Greyhounds, Foxhounds, Bloodhounds, and Spaniels. Their primary job was to point out hares, and once they did, Greyhounds were sent out to pursue the prey. In the 18th century, when wing-shooting became popular, the Pointers were called on to locate birds. They gained their name and fame because on finding the game, the dog would indicate its location by remaining still and pointing at it, while the hunter got ready to shoot.
    The German Shorthaired Pointers go back to Germany in the 1600s, with a mix of English Pointer and a few other strains, including a bit of hound. They were especially well known for not only pointing but retrieving, trailing, and even killing game. They were recognized as a show breed in Germany in the late 1800s and arrived in the U.S. in 1920.
    The German Wirehaired Pointer was developed in the 1800s as a general hunter from the Shorthaired Pointer mixed with some other breeds, including the Polish Water Dog, which contributed the more furry look. They were bred for their versatility in not only pointing, tracking, and retrieving game, but also acting as a companion and watchdog. The rough wiry coat was developed to help the dog get through thick brambles when hunting. They gained their recognition in the show world in the 1920s, and came to the U.S. then, too.

What's Your Personality and Style?

If you picked a Pointer, including the German Shorthaired or Wirehaired Pointer, you tend to lead an **active** lifestyle, enjoy **physical exercise**, and like the **outdoors.** You also tend to be very **focused, direct,** and **to-the-point** in your style; you might consider yourself a real **straight-shooter** and have a sense of **serious dignity** about you. You're a **good, hard worker,** too, with your intense **concentration** and **focus** – your **nose to the grindstone**, so to speak. You are also especially **loyal** to friends and family and like to **please,** though you may tend to be **aloof** and **reserved** with strangers.

THE TERRIERS

Are You a Bull Terrier, American Pit Bull, or Staffordshire Bull Terrier?

A Little Bit of History...

In case you chose a Bull Terrier, American Pit Bull Terrier, or Staffordshire Bull Terrier, you chose a dog originally raised for dog fighting, yet very lovable and affectionate. They all include a mix of Terrier and Bulldog.

The Bull Terrier dates back to the 1800s in England where it was originally developed as a fighting dog for bull-baiting. When dog fighting was outlawed in the mid-1800s, some owners turned to showing their dogs, and when one owner, James Hinks, crossed the Bull and Terrier with a White English Terrier and a Dalmatian in 1860, the first white Bull Terrier was born. Gradually, with some more breeding, the Bull Terrier gained its longer head and some color, too. Most recently, the Bull Terrier has gained fame as a film and advertising personality, such as in ads for Target stores.

The American Pit Bull was brought to America in the late 1800s, where it became bigger than its English cousin and was the most popular dog fighter. Yet, while a fighter in the pits, the dog was bred to be docile and obedient, too, to respond to its owners. Recently, though, the Pit Bull has gotten a bad reputation from being used for illegal fighting and being involved in vicious attacks in the inner cities, though it is popular among other pet owners as a fun-loving, sweet-natured dog.

The Staffordshire Bull Terrier was also developed in England in the 1800s, where it was popular for dog fighting, but friendly toward people when not fighting. After dog fighting was banned in England, it became mainly a show dog, though some enthusiasts still fight their dogs in secret gatherings.

What's Your Personality and Style?

If you picked a Bull Terrier, Pit Bull, or Staffordshire Bull Terrier, you can be an **aggressive fighter** when provoked, in a competitive situation, or when being **protective** of others. But at other times, you can be very **docile, sweet-tempered, loving, affectionate**, and **devoted** to those you are close to. You also tend to be **stubborn, tenacious, strong-willed, courageous**, and **assertive.** You commonly have lots of **energy,** like **action,** and may be even somewhat **exuberant** and **rambunctious.** If you picked a Bull Terrier, you tend to have a **comical, mischievous** side, as well.

Are You a Cairn, Norfolk, or Scottish Terrier?

A Little Bit of History...
If you chose a Cairn, Norfolk, or Scottish Terrier, you chose one of the classic terrier types, known for their fearless and feisty character.

The Cairn Terrier dates back to the Middle Ages in Scotland, where it was developed on the Island of Skye, originally for hunting badgers, otters, and foxes. It is closely related to the Dandie Dimont and Skye Terrier, but was eventually distinguished as a separate breed in the early 1900s. It gained fame in the 1940s as the dog that played Toto in *The Wizard of OZ, which was released in 1939.*

The Norfolk Terrier was developed in the 1800s in England. It was originally used for going after rats and foxes, and then gradually developed as a separate breeds in the early 1900s.

The Scottish Terrier was developed in the 1800s in Scotland, originally for hunting vermin, and is closely related to the Skye Terrier. By the 1880s, it was distinguished as a separate breed and came to America. It grew in popularity in the U.S. after World War II, and one Scottie, Fala, became especially well known as Franklin Roosevelt's constant companion.

What's Your Personality and Style?
If you picked a Cairn, Norfolk, or Scottish Terrier, you tend to be **bold, feisty, spirited,** and **strong-willed,** have an **independent** nature, and can be **stubborn** and even **scrappy.** You also tend to be very

inquisitive and **curious,** and are eager for **adventure** and **excitement.** You can become very **devoted** and **loyal** to family members and try to **please** those you care about, but you tend to be more **reserved** and show your **independence of spirit** with others.

Are You an Airedale Terrier?

A Little Bit of History...
     In case you chose an Airedale Terrier, you have picked a dog known for being big, outgoing, and playful.
     The Airedale is the largest terrier, sometimes called the King of Terriers. They originated in the 1800s in England, where they were originally bred to hunt badgers, otters, fox, and other small game. It arrived in the U.S. in the early 1900s, where it continued to be used in hunting, even for big game, and was tapped to work with the police as well.

What's Your Personality and Style?
     If you picked an Airedale Terrier, you tend to be **bold, outgoing, adventurous,** and **playful,** as well as **strong, powerful,** and sometimes have a **stubborn, headstrong** streak, yet you tend to be **dependable** and **reliable,** too. You like to be **top dog** and can be **domineering,** but can be willing to **go along** to **get along** with others. You tend to be very **loyal** and **protective** to those you know well, but are more **reserved** with others until you get to know and trust them. You also tend to be very **active** and **outdoorsy.**

Are You a Bedlington Terrier, West Highland White Terrier, or Soft Coated Wheaten Terrier?

A Little Bit of History...

If you chose a Bedlington Terrier, West Highland White Terrier, or Soft Coated Wheaten Terrier, you chose dogs known for being gentle and loving.

The Bedlington Terrier, which looks a little like a lamb, was developed in the 1800s in England and got its name from the mining shire where it was developed. Originally it was used for killing rats, badgers, otters, fox, rabbits, and other small animals. In the late 1800s, the English elite took a fancy to it, and it became a show dog and pet.

The West Highland White Terrier goes back about 300 years, where they developed in Scotland to chase down fox, badgers, and other vermin. They were first recognized as a breed by the AKC in 1908.

The Soft Coated Wheaten Terrier got its start in the 1700s in Ireland, initially to help with various farm chores, including rounding up stock and guarding the home. It was late in becoming a show dog, since it only gained recognition in the late 1930s in Ireland and in the mid 1940s in England and the U.S.

What's Your Personality and Style?

If you picked a Bedlington Terrier, West Highland White Terrier, or Soft Coated Wheaten Terrier, you tend to be very **affectionate, gentle, friendly, warm, easy to get along with, playful,** and **fun-loving.** You tend to have a **sunny, happy** disposition. You also are generally **loyal** and **obedient**, willing to **do what's asked**, and enjoy **taking it easy** and **being pampered.** Normally, you are **not aggressive** and tend to **avoid confrontations** but will snap back if provoked enough.

Are You a Jack Russell Terrier or Fox Terrier?

A Little Bit of History...

In case you chose a Jack Russell Terrier or a Smooth or Wire Fox Terrier, you chose a live-wire dog primed for excitement and adventure.

The Jack Russell Terrier hails from England in the 1800s, where it was originally used for fox hunting. The breed was initially bred by a Parson named John Russell from Devonshire, England, who loved fox-hunting and wanted a fast-moving terrier that could keep up with the horses and bolt the foxes out of their dens. This Terrier first came to the U.S. in the 1930s, and in the 1990s, they became a popular breed featured in the media as a kind of lovable scamp, resulting in their growing popularity as a pet.

The Smooth Fox Terrier dates back to England in the 1700s, where they were first used to hunt down vermin and find and bolt foxes. They were the first of the Fox Terriers to become show dogs, and for a time, they were crossed with the Wire Fox Terrier, but by the late 1900s, the crossing stopped, and the two types of terriers were classified as separate breeds in 1985.

The Wire Fox Terrier was developed in England in the 1800s, and like the Smooth Fox Terrier, was used for hunting vermin and bolting foxes. It became a show dog about 15 to 20 years after the Smooth variety, and was identified as a separate breed in 1985, too.

What's Your Personality and Style?

If you picked a Jack Russell Terrier or a Smooth or Wire Fox Terrier, you are a real **live-wire**, who loves **action** and **adventure** and has lots of **energy**. You are very **playful, bold, outgoing, friendly,** and **affectionate,** though you may be **reserved** with those you don't know. You also tend to be **inquisitive** and **curious,** and have an **independent, feisty,** and **mischievous** streak that sometimes gets you into trouble. At times, you can be **scrappy**, too. No wonder you are sometimes considered a **lovable rascal** or something of a **clown** and a **scamp.**

Are You an Irish Terrier, Kerry Blue Terrier, or Schnauzer?

A Little Bit of History...
If you chose an Irish Terrier, Kerry Blue Terrier, or Schnauzer, you chose one of the long-legged, fun-loving terriers.

The Irish Terrier originated in Ireland in the 1700s, where it was originally used for hunting foxes, otters, and other small game. It may have a bit of Irish Wolfhound mixed in. It is the fastest of the terriers, with the longest legs and longest body. It became very popular in England in the 1870s and 1880s, and then spread to America. During World War I it was drafted as a messenger and guard dog, but has declined in popularity today.

The Kerry Blue Terrier also originated in Ireland in the 1700s, and was used for hunting rats, as well as foxes, badgers, and even birds. But it was late coming to the show scene, since it was first shown in the 1920s in England and the U.S. It has also been used in police work and training.

The Schnauzer developed in Germany in the Middle Ages. Though it is now classified as a working dog, it was initially considered a terrier, as is the Miniature Schnauzer. It includes a mix of terrier and was originally bred for catching rats, as well as being a guard dog. During the 12th century, the Schnauzer was used to guard farmers' carts in the marketplace. In the late 1870s, it was first shown in Germany, and it came to America in the 1900s. Schnauzers have been used in police work, too.

What's Your Personality and Style?

If you picked an Irish Terrier, Kerry Blue Terrier, or Schnauzer, you tend to be **brash, bold, eager for action** and **adventure,** and like the **outdoors.** You also have an **independent, strong-willed** nature, are very **inquisitive, playful, lively,** and **fun-loving** and tend to be **assertive,** even **aggressive**, or **reserved** with others, though you are **loyal** and **devoted** to those close to you. You may have a streak of **mischievousness** in you, too.

TOY DOGS

Are You a Pomeranian, Kings Charles Spaniel, Papillion, Yorkie, or Silky Terrier?

A Little Bit of History…

In case you chose a Pomeranian, King Charles Spaniel, Papillion, Yorkshire Terrier (Yorkie), or Silky Terrier, these are all feisty, almost catlike Toy Dogs, that make great companions.

The Pomeranians are descendants of the Nordic sled dogs and at one point they were sheep dogs before they were recognized in their diminutive form in the 1870s as a pet and show dog. It is believed they were miniaturized in Germany, particularly in Pomerania, where they got their name. Their popularity spread after Queen Victoria brought a Pomeranian home from Italy, and they were bred in her royal kennels.

The Papillions gained their fame in the 16th century, where they were known as "dwarf spaniels". Initially, they were raised in Spain, then spread to Italy and to France, where they were raised in the court of Louis XVI and became beloved by the artists of the day who included them in many paintings of nobility. After being shown in French dog shows, they spread to England and America in the early 1900s.

The King Charles Spaniel (officially known as the Cavalier King Charles Spaniel) resulted from breeding small spaniels to small Oriental dogs, and the breed became popular in England in Tudor times as lapdogs and foot warmers, and was a favorite of King Charles II. They became very popular in England in the 1900s and later gained recognition in the U.S.

The Yorkshire Terrier was a much later arrival, coming from the working class area of Yorkshire England in the 1800s, where breeders developed many of the Terrier varieties. Despite the Yorkie's lowly origins, the wealthier fanciers were soon attracted to the breed and began showing them. By 1900, the Yorkies had come to America.

The Yorkies played a role in the development of the Silky Terrier in Australia, where breeders combined Yorkies with the Australian Terrier in the late 1800s. By the early 1900s, voila, this new breed was created and came to the U.S. in the 1950s.

What's Your Personality and Style?

If you picked a Pomeranian, King Charles Spaniel, Papillion, Yorkie, or Silky Terrier, you have picked a small but **feisty** toy dog, that is **very alert, vivacious, joyful,** and brimming with **high-energy.** You're also very much the **extrovert**, a real **people-person,** who loves to be with others, and makes a **warm, loving, affectionate** companion. You're usually **obedient, docile,** and **eager to please** others, and you spread your **love** and **affection** around. You love **looking good** and appreciate **good grooming,** and have a high confidence that comes with **knowing you look good**. In fact, your confidence sometimes gets you in trouble, since you're sometimes ready to challenge the "big dogs", using your **cleverness** to outwit and outplay.

Are You a Chihuahua, Chinese Crested, or Pug?

A Little Bit of History...

    In case you chose a Chihuahua, Chinese Crested, or Pug, these dogs are best known for being playful, affectionate companions.

    The Chihuahua's ancestry dates back to the Toltecs in the 9th century and then to the Aztecs in what is now Mexico. They are steeped in legend, and the Aztecs believed the Chihuahua helped guide the soul through the underworld and fight off evil spirits. When Cortes conquered the Aztecs in the 16th century, the dogs were abandoned for a time and ran wild, until a few were discovered in 1850 in Chihuahua – hence the name. After the popular rumba bandleader Xavier Cugat showed off a Chihuahua, their popularity spread in the U.S. and they have gained some fame in the movies, such as in Beverly Hills Chihuahua and Beverly Hills Chihuahua 2, and in commercials, such as the talking dog in the Taco Bell commercials ("Yo quiero Taco Bell).

    The Chinese Crested dates back to 13th century China, when Chinese seamen used them on the ships to get rid of rats and to trade them with the local merchants. Gradually the breed spread to the rest of Asia, Africa, and even Central and South America, where it might have contributed to the Chihuahua. It arrived in Europe in the 1800s and to America in the early 1900s. Though the Hairless Chinese Crested is best known, there is a Powderpuff breed that is covered by a puff of long hair.

    The Pug initially developed in China around 400 B.C. and became a pet for the monks in Buddhist monasteries. From there it spread to Japan and Europe, where it became a popular pet in the royal courts. It even became the official dog of the House of Orange in Holland in the 16th century, after one pug saved the life of William of

Orange by barking at the arrival of the Spaniards. It arrived in England in 1860, after the British raided the Imperial Palace in Peking, and soon after spread to the U.S.

What's Your Personality and Style?

If you picked a Chihuahua, Chinese Crested, or Pug, you picked a dog that is characterized by **playfulness** and **charm**. You are **outgoing, loving,** and make a great **companion,** since you're **devoted** and **eager to please.** You also enjoy **standing out**, **being unique**, the **center of attention**, and the **life of the party.** You have **lots of energy**, too.

Are You a Miniature Pinscher, Italian Greyhound, or Toy Terrier?

A Little Bit of History…

In case you chose a Miniature Pinscher, Italian Greyhound, or a Toy Terrier (either the Toy Manchester Terrier or Toy Fox Terrier), these are small, lively, sometimes scrappy dogs.

The Miniature Pinscher, sometimes called "king of the toys" or Min Pin is a scaled down version of the large German Pinschers, with a mix of Dachshund and Italian Greyhound. The name "pinscher" means terrier. They were developed in the 1600s in Germany and were used to chase down rats in the stables. They gradually spread around Europe in the late 1800s and arrived in America in the early 1900s.

The Italian Greyhounds have a long, ancient history, dating back to the tombs of the Egyptian pharaohs, and they are thought to be the first dogs that were bred to be strictly companions. By the Middle Ages, they had spread throughout Southern Europe, and were especially popular with the Italians in the 16th century, which is how they came to be known as "Italian Greyhounds". Then, they continued to be favorites of powerful nobles and rulers throughout Europe.

The Toy Manchester Terrier (also called the English Toy Terrier) comes from England, where it was first developed in the 16th century, possibly with a little input from the Italian Greyhound. It was especially valued for its ability to kill rates, and it even became a contender in contests to see which dog could kill the most rats in a given time period. Later, it became popular with Queen Victoria.

The Toy Fox Terrier (also called the American Toy Terrier) is a later development by American breeders, who created a new breed from a mix of Fox Terrier, English Toy Terrier, and a little bit of Chihuahua.

What's Your Personality and Style?

If you picked a Miniature Pinscher, Italian Greyhound or English or American Toy Terrier, you tend to be **lively, playful**, **feisty, energetic,** and sometimes **scrappy.** You tend to be **confident** and **self-assured,** even **bold and brash.** You generally are very **loyal** and **devoted** to family members and those you choose as friends, yet more **reserved** with others, until you develop trust in them. You also have an **inquisitive, curious** nature, and can be **stubborn** and **independent.**

Are You a Pekingese, Maltese, LlasaApso, Havanese or Shih Tzu?

A Little Bit of History...

If you chose a Pekingese, Maltese, Havanese, or Shih Tzu, you have chosen a Toy Dog, known for its companionship and noble lineage.

The Pekingese comes from the royal courts of China, dating back to the Tang Dynasty of the 8th century, where they were considered sacred dogs. They were bred and kept in the sacred Buddhist temples and would enter the temples before the emperor to announce his arrival. Should someone steal a sacred Pekingese and be caught, death by torture was the punishment. They arrived in England in 1860 after the British looted the Imperial Palace, and from there spread to the U.S. as a regal lapdog.

The Maltese's aristocratic heritage dates back to ancient Greek and Roman times, when the dogs were bred on the island of Malta, which was an early trading port. In the 14th century, they were brought to England, where they charmed the upper-class ladies, and by the late 1800s, they spread to the U.S.

The Lhasa Apso comes from the villages and monasteries of Tibet, where it was believed the souls of the lamas entered their bodies upon death. It first came to England in the 1930s, and has been assigned to AKC's Non-Sporting group, though it looks much like a toy.

The Havanese are one of the rarer breeds, whose heritage traces back to the Mediterranean and Spain. The Spanish traders brought some Havanese to Cuba where they gave them as gifts to wealthy Cuban women. There they became both pets of the wealthy and performing circus dogs, and after almost becoming extinct, some Cuban families brought them to the U.S. in the 1950s.

The Shih Tzu, sometimes called the "Chrysanthemum Dog", was developed in China, where they were especially popular with the Chinese emperors. They were bred in the royal courts by the court eunuchs, who competed to produce the dogs the emperors would like the most. They were frequently pictured in art as hangings or tapestries, and the Buddhists called them "Lion" dogs, which is what the word "shih tzu" means.

What's Your Personality and Style?

If you picked a Pekingese, Maltese, Lhasa Apso, Havanese, or Shih Tzu, you tend to have an **outgoing, friendly, affectionate, happy,** and **trusting** personality. You like the **companionship** of others, and have a **gentle, warm** nature, but combined with a sense of **regal bearing, dignity** and **self-assurance** that befits your royal heritage. You also tend to balance being **playful** and **active** with being very **relaxed** and **laid back.**

NON-SPORTING DOGS

Are You a Chow Chow or Chinese Shar-Pei?

A Little Bit of History…

In case you chose a Chow Chow or Chinese Shar-Pei, these are non-sporting dogs developed in China.

The Chow Chow dates back at least to the Han Dynasty in 150 B.C. when it was developed as a hunting dog. For centuries, the rulers made him their main sporting dog, and one of the T'ang emperors in the 7th century had more than 2,500 of these dogs and 10,000 hunters in his retinue. The dogs were imported from China to England in the late 1700s. Queen Victoria's interest in these dogs helped to increase their popularity in the late 1800s and they came to America in the early 1900s. Since the 1980s, they have become very popular – the 6th most popular U.S. breed according to some accounts.

The Chinese Shar-Pei's heritage dates back to southern China, where it was first raised in a small village, Tai Li in the Kwantung Province, around the time of the Han Dynasty in 200 B.C. Its name: "shar-pei" refers to its rough, short, sandpaper-like coat. Unlike the royal Chow Chow, these dogs were used by peasant farmers as guard dogs, wild boar hunters, and dog fighters. Most of them were eliminated from China when the Communists took over in the early 1920s, but a few were bred in British Hong Kong and Taiwan. Then, in the 1960s, a few Shar-Peis arrived in America, and the breed took off in 1973, when an article referred to them as the "world's rarest dog".

What's Your Personality and Style?

If you picked a Chow Chow or Chinese Shar-Pei, you tend to be somewhat **reserved, aloof**, and **serious,** with a **quiet self-assured dignity.** You might even characterize yourself as **regal** or **lordly** in your bearing. You also tend to be **independent,** sometimes **stubborn,** and while you may show **reserve** to those you don't know, you tend to be very **devoted** and **protective** to family members and those you care about.

Are You a Bichon Frisé?

A Little Bit of History…

In case you chose a Bichon Frisé, these dogs were developed in the Mediterranean in ancient times when a large water dog called the Barbet was crossed with a small white lapdog. One of the dogs in this family, called the Tenerife, developed in the Canary Islands, probably taken there by Spanish sailors. In the 14th century, Italian sailors brought a few of these back to Italy, where they became popular as pets with the upper classes. After the French invaded in the 1500s, the dogs were taken to France, where they became popular with the French kings, Francis I and Henry III. Then, for a time the breed declined in popularity and became a common street dog. However, peddlers and organ grinders found the dogs were good at performing tricks and featured them on the streets and fairs. The breed nearly disappeared during World War I and again due to World War II, but some French breeders helped to keep the breed going, and it came to the U.S. in the 1950s. Finally in the 1960s it gained a new popularity after its hair was cut with the distinctive look it wears today.

What's Your Personality and Style?

If you picked a Bichon Frisé, you tend to be somewhat **fun-loving** and **playful.** You are **lively, high-spirited, bouncy,** and very **friendly** and **outgoing.** You also are **warm, sensitive, affectionate**, and **attuned to others.** And you are usually **happy, carefree,** and have an **optimistic** attitude toward life generally.

Are You a Dalmatian?

A Little Bit of History...

If you chose a Dalmatian, these are non-sporting dogs that got their name from a region in western Yugoslavia called Dalmatia, though they date back to even earlier times, since their images have been found on Greek friezes and tablets dated back to 2000 B.C. They played many roles, including being a war dog, shepherd, draft dog, ratter, retriever, bird dog, and circus dog. However, in Victorian England, the Dalmatian gained its fame as a coach dog, which both protected the horses from other dogs and looked stylish as they paced before or alongside the coach. They were adopted by fire departments in the 1800s because they were good with horses. Then, with the development of the automobile, they dropped out of being a high society dog though they remained as a coach dog on the fire-engines drawn by horses, and eventually became adopted as a fire-dog by modern fire engine companies. Its distinctive colors helped it become a popular pet and show dog, and after being featured in several children's movies, such as *101 Dalmatians*, it has become even more popular today.

What's Your Personality and Style?

If you picked a Dalmatian, you tend to be **enthusiastic** and **playful,** and full of **energy**. You love to be **active**, like the **outdoors,** and are sometimes **aggressive** or **reserved** with strangers, and may have a **stubborn streak.** However, you are **outgoing** and **friendly** once you know and trust others, and you are very **dedicated**, **loyal**, and **love to please**.

Are You a Poodle?

A Little Bit of History…
    If you chose a Poodle, these are non-sporting dogs developed in central Asia, though they are most commonly associated with France.
    The ancestors of the poodle had curly coats and helped with herding. From central Asia they spread to France, Russia, Hungary, and other places in Europe in the 1500s. The Poodle got its name from its German version, where it was called a "pudel", due to its ability to splash in the water. It was also used for hunting ducks and herding in France, as well as being a military dog, guide dog, guard dog, and wagon puller for actors and circus performers. Eventually it became a circus dog, and it got its distinctive pulls of hair on its legs and tail as a result of its role as a performer, though some have claimed these clips helped to keep their joints warm when they were in cold water. Then, in 1700s and 1800s, it was adopted by fashionable ladies and gained favor with the French aristocracy, which led to it becoming the national dog of France. By the late 1800s, it was entered in the show ring, and in the 1900s it nearly died out in America. But in the 1930s, it regained its popularity and became one of the most popular U.S. dogs.

What's Your Personality and Style?
    If you picked a Poodle, you tend to be **playful, friendly**, **smart,** and a real **people pleaser.** You like to be **sociable** and like **get along with others,** though you might be **reserved** when you first meet people. You are good at **following directions**, and tend to be **very loyal** and **devoted** to one person. You also tend to be **optimistic** and full of **enthusiasm.** You thrive on **getting attention,** and may tend to be **very self-confident, assured,** sometimes even **arrogant,** because you are used to being admired and shown off for your good looks.

Are You a Boston Terrier?

<u>A Little Bit of History…</u>
       In case you chose a Boston Terrier, these are non-sporting dogs that developed in the United States. Starting about 1865, they were bred by the coachmen of some wealthy people in Boston from their dogs, resulting in a cross that combined an English Terrier, Bulldog, and French Bulldog with the dog's distinctive markings, making it look a little like a gentleman in a tuxedo. Interestingly, the dogs they were bred from were at one time fighting dogs. By 1893, they were recognized by the AKC, and by the early 1900s, their popularity spread.

<u>What's Your Personality and Style?</u>
       If you picked a Boston Terrier, you tend to be somewhat **playful** and **feisty,** though you are comfortable being **formal** and **business-like** with a sense of **elegance** and **self-importance.** You're also **smart, clever,** and a **fast learner**. You can be very **determined** and **persistent**, and sometimes even **stubborn**. You are quite **sensitive** to others, **devoted** and **loyal** to those you are close to, but you can be **reserved** and **aggressive** to others.

Are You a Bulldog?

A Little Bit of History…
If you chose a Bulldog, these are non-sporting dogs developed in England in the 1200s.

The bulldog was originally developed to bait bulls by attacking and grabbing the nose, making the bull angry, mainly for entertainment, though some thought the bull's meat tasted better as a result of the baiting. Some bulldogs were also used to bait bears, and owners highly valued the dog's aggressiveness. However, after 1835, when bull baiting was outlawed, the breed lost it reason for being, and its popularity declined. But some fans decided to rescue it by selectively breeding to keep its unique physical features while selecting against its aggressiveness. The result was that the bulldog became a very friendly, even clownish dog, though with a tough steadfast persona, that led it to become a show dog starting in 1860, and eventually it became the national symbol of England.

What's Your Personality and Style?
If you picked a Bulldog, you tend to be very **friendly, comical, docile,** and **sociable.** You tend to be very **relaxed, mellow,** and **easy-going,** along with a sense of **modesty** and **humility.** You love to **please others**, but you sometimes can get **stubborn**. You also are characterized by **determination, boldness,** and **loyalty.**

CHAPTER 3: GAINING INSIGHTS INTO OTHERS

The Dog Profile System is a great tool for understanding others, and using these insights to have better relationships at work and in your personal life. The result? More enjoyable relationships by understanding others better, and you can up your chances for success.

Say you have trouble getting along with that cranky aunt when she comes to visit, and each visit usually ends in an argument. By gaining advance insights, you can better know what to say and how to act to get along. Additionally, as you'll discover in other books in the Dog Type series, you can call on your Top Dog or a Power Dog to help you control any angry feelings and hold back from saying or doing anything that might trigger a conflict.

Or say you are going on a job interview. The more you know about how your interviewer thinks, the better you can present yourself. You can use the Dog Profile system, along with visualizing alternate scenarios to help you make a better self-presentation.

This system can also help you tune into the veracity and intentions of the person you are dealing with, so in a business deal, you can use your insight to determine if you can trust and effectively work with a prospective associate. Additionally, the Dog Profiling approach can help you better understand customers or clients, so if you are selling a product or pitching a service, you can better sense what message your prospect would most like to hear. Then, you can tailor your presentation accordingly. The advantages are endless.

How the Dog Profiling System Can Up Your Inner Radar

A key reason that the Dog Profiling approach works well is that it makes your inner radar to others more sensitive by giving you visible symbols to enhance vague feelings and impressions. Then, too, this approach provides you with inner advisers, called Guide Dogs, who can help you through self-talk and dialogue to better evaluate someone or decide your best approach to that person or situation. Other dogs that can help include Power Dogs and Top Dogs you can call on to feel more power and confidence.

This Dog Type method builds on the intuitive approach to understanding others which I first wrote about in *Mind Power: Picture Your Way to Success*. Then, it adds in using Dog Profiles, along with Guide Dogs and Power Dogs, so you can gain more insights to better understand and relate to others.

For instance, when you meet someone, notice what type of dog comes to mind to give you an idea of what that person is like. Or if you are making a decision about whether to work with someone, call on one of your Guide Dogs to help you access your inner knowing or gut level feelings of whether you really want to work with this person.

In effect, consider different types of dogs as amplifiers to help you tap into your inner wisdom in working with others. And the more you access this inner knowledge for one purpose, the more you can apply it in other contexts, such as in resolving problems, making decisions, and setting goals.

Here's an example of how it can supplement this inner wisdom. In this case, Debbie, an artist and designer, used her inner knowing to steer clear of several partnerships that could have been a disaster. Previously, she had gotten into several arrangements with business people, who had taken advantage of her lack of business acumen, and she had unwisely trusted their claims about what they could do, until she later realized these people didn't have the skills or contacts they said. One man who promised to set

Debbie up in a design studio was more interested in a romance with her. A financier talked grandiosely about the financing he could arrange to get Debbie's cards and posters on the market. But then he reported that his business partner had been embezzling from the company, so he had to cancel any new business deals. And Debbie had several other aborted business arrangements.

However, once she discovered how to access her inner impressions to get valid insights into people, she was able to steer clear of the business flakes who made empty promises, and she discovered people who were genuine and sincere. While she used simple visualization exercises to tap into these impressions and feelings, she could have used the advice of her Guide Dogs and the Dog Profiling system to make these insights even stronger and clearer.

In one case, Debbie met a promoter who wanted to start a travel club. He said all the right things to entice her, such as telling her she could design all of the club's materials, get an excellent salary, have travel perks, and even get shares of company stock. So Debbie was enthusiastic about doing some preliminary work on speculation, while funds from a stock issue came through.

But just as they ended their conversation, Debbie's inner radar picked up some danger signals, such as a knotted up feeling in her stomach, which the Dog Profiling system could help her interpret by asking one of her inner Guide Dogs for advice. Or she might get a visual image of a dog associated with that knotted up feeling. Then, if she had negative associations with the dog that appeared – say she thought of a Chihuahua as a sneaky, deceptive dog, like some of the workshop participants did in one of my workshops, that would be a clear message that this person probably had those characteristics, too.

In Debbie's case, her inner warning signal led her to tell the man she would have to think about his proposal (though the Dog Type system might lead to a quicker and surer response, given the strong, clear message). Then, when she did some checking, she learned that this so-called successful promoter was operating his business out of his bedroom. He only had promises of backing, and several people who had worked for him before on spec had ended up with nothing.

Similarly, Debbie used her inner powers a few weeks later when an associate introduced her to a man with extensive video and film credits, and invited her to design some dolls for him.. Yet, as he bragged about what he could do, while dropping many names of well-known people, Debbie heard her inner voice repeating the warning: "Beware...Beware. This man isn't what he seems." Here a Dog Profile could supplement this inner warning with an image of the type of dog representing this man, and the traits associated with this dog could provide more insights into what this man was really like. And questions to a Guide Dog could provide further insights into why the man might not be what he seemed to be.

In any case, the message that this man was trouble came through loud and clear, so Debbie diplomatically explained she was busy with other projects; and later her intuitions were confirmed, when others told her the man was difficult to work with, unrealistic in his expectations, unwilling to listen to reasonable suggestions, and ready to blow up if challenged.

Unfortunately, sometimes it's easier to miss or dismiss these early inner rumblings or not know how to understand their meanings. That's where the Dog Type system could be especially valuable, because it helps to amplify and give these vague impressions more meaning. Then, too, if you work with the Profiling System and your Guide Dogs on a regular basis, your first sign of concern, such as a feeling of anxiety or tension in your stomach, can trigger a review of what's wrong. To conduct this review, you might think about the traits of the type of dog you associate with this person. Additionally, you can ask your Guide Dog for advice on how deal with this person based on your associations about the person based on the dog he or she is like. Then, if you don't like that dog or have negative associations with it, that's an even clearer indication that there's a problem in working with that person or you can act accordingly to work around the problem.

Using Dog Types to Make Good Decisions about People

As Debbie's example illustrates, the Dog Type system is ideal for tapping into your inner knowing to make some quick decisions about people when you first meet. You can ask your Guide Dog for a quick assessment, imagine what kind of dog this person might be, or do both. Then, use that information to decide how to better relate to that person and determine what type of relationship you want, if any, with that person.

Say you meet someone briefly to discuss a possible business venture, and the first image which comes to mind is a Golden Retriever, which is a gentle, friendly, warm, sensitive dog, which likes being around people. It might be good to be open and friendly with this type of person and maybe spend more time engaging in small talk. You might even ask that person about his or her family and share a little bit about yours. By contrast, if the image that comes to mind is a German Shepherd, which is a tough, stern, aggressive dog, which is good at being obedient and following the rules, take a more reserved, strict business approach. Be more direct and get to the point; don't try to schmooze; and keep your approach more business-like and formal.

Or say you are interviewing people to rent a room in your house. You can use the insights you gain from imagining what type of dog each person might be, or you can ask your Guide Dog for advice which might help you decide if you want that person to be your roommate. If you are in sales or pitching or promoting anything, the system is ideal for getting a quick read on someone. Then, you use this information to know how to best approach that person to get a positive response to whatever you are pitching or promoting.

Here's how Paul, who markets health and food products through direct-sales, might use these techniques to custom tailor his presentations and increase his chances of closing a deal. While Paul has dozens of products to show people and a list of over twenty benefits his products offer, he can use this system to select a few products and benefits to emphasize, depending on the insights he gets about a person.

He can begin getting these intuitions with his first phone call. As he asks a few preliminary questions to determine if the person would be a good customer, he can form an image of the type of dog this person might be. Then, the personality traits associated with this type of dog would give Paul an intuitive sense of the person's personality and preferred way of perceiving and receiving information.

When he meets the person, Paul can use this preliminary picture to shape his opening remarks. As they talk further, he can continue to refine this image to better know this person.

The result of this approach is that Paul will have a better rapport with his prospects. Why? Because pre-visualizing who the person is based on the type of dog associated with him helps sense what this person is like and type of approach he or she will be most receptive to. Then, Paul can relate to that person from that person's own perspective. As a result, at their first meeting, after a minute or two to build rapport, Paul can emphasize those features of his products and business he thinks will have the most appeal based on his assessment of that person.

The Type of Information Gained Through Dog Type Techniques

These Dog Type techniques provide insights into others, because they enable you to tune into the other person's inner essence or self, much like you might get a gut level feeling about someone and use that to decide whether to trust him or not. Then, you become more sensitive to what these inner feelings or gut sensations are telling you by associating them with an image or symbol, in this case a Dog Profile or advice from your Guide Dog. As you work with these images and associations, you become more in touch with and better able to recognize what your intuitive feelings are telling you, so you can use them to gain more precise information.

The process works like learning a language. As you gain more vocabulary and are better able to combine words into sentences with layers of meaning, you can more clearly express your thoughts and feelings.

Another way to think of this process is that you first see something normally when you look at it with your eyes. Then, you can see a clearer, larger image when you look through a pair of glasses and can see even better when you use a telescope to bring the faraway image closer. Thus, by adding the glasses and telescope, you see what you want to look at more clearly. It's sharper and larger, so you can see much more detail than with the naked eye.

Similarly, when you visualize images for the types of dogs or use a Guide Dog to express your thoughts and feelings, you magnify and clarify them.

Likewise, you can develop your facility to call on these images to better access your inner abilities and insights. Then, whether you get this information through reflection before you meet, when you first meet, or later interact with someone, you have more detailed and more accurate information to go by in assessing this person.

To complement this inner process, work on become more sensitive to people from external cues, too. As you do, you can call on your Guide Dogs to help and support you by providing you with advice. In turn, your invitation to be there serves as a trigger to be more attentive and observant, much like saying a chant can help you get in a more centered, meditative state, so you become more receptive to the information you receive.

Some ways to become more attentive and receptive to external cues are these:
- Train yourself to become more sensitive to ordinary outer cues, such as clothing, gestures, and facial expressions, because you can learn much about a person's character through his or her outward appearances and behaviors. For

instance, a woman who wears a lot of bright colors to work is probably a more outgoing, friendly, dramatic person than someone who wears blues and browns or soft pastels.
- As you look at a person, ask yourself: "What kind of dog most fits how this person looks or what he or she is doing?" Then, keep on observing and don't try to direct the answer you get. Just let the image of a dog come to you or hear a voice in your head telling you the answer. Then, keep looking, and ask yourself: "In what ways does this person have the qualities of the dog I have associated with him or her?"

You can then go even deeper to discover more about a person's character, sense of integrity, perspective, and preferred way of receiving information and communicating with you. Your Guide Dog can help you learn about someone in four ways:

- To get a quick first impression when you meet someone new (i.e.: listen to what your Guide Dogs tell you, or see a dog representing that person suddenly appear);
- To get an advance impression when you set up a meeting with someone in order to have a better first meeting (i.e. review the Dog Profiles to see which type of dog best fits that person in order to adapt how you act before that meeting;
- To gain a more in-depth understanding of a person (i.e.: have an extended conversation with that person in your imagination or discuss who they are with your Guide Dog, so you can communicate better when you meet);
- To reflect on your meeting and decide how to best follow-up (i.e.: review your meeting in your head through a dialogue with your Guide Dog and ask questions like: "What do you think that person thought of my presentation?" and "How can I make a better presentation in the future?" Then listen as your Guide Dog gives advice).

Recognizing Different Personality Types and Behavioral Styles

Using the Dog Type system can give you these insights, because sensing what dog best matches that person makes you more aware of the person's personality type and behavioral style. Then, you can use this information to make any interaction go more smoothly or decide if you want to interact, continue an interaction, or interact more closely with a person.

The different dogs also provide a more nuanced way of understanding other people that can build on other personality systems which divide people up into a small number of major personality types. These other systems provide a good starting point. Then, incorporate the insights you gain from your associations with different dogs to fill in additional details about a person, so you can better communicate and interact with that person if you wish.

You'll see some examples of these broad personality groupings in the Charts, which I adapted from *Mind Power.* In the Personality Types and Personal Characteristics Chart, each personality type is characterized by certain traits, ways of viewing the world, and preferences in relating to others.

In the Ethical Styles Chart, every person, whatever their personality style, has their own approach to making ethical choices and their own way of relating to the world and others.

There are all sorts of ways of categorizing people in different systems. For example, the DISC theory, developed by William Marsten, who researched the emotions of normal people, categorizes people based on their four major drives into four primary types, which is where the DISC term comes from.(And if you think of a person as a certain type of dog, you can fit them into these four categories, as noted).

- (D) high dominance and directness (Mastiff, Great Dane)

- (I) high influence and interest in people (Pomeranian, Golden Retriever)
- (S) high in steadiness and stability (German Shepherd, Pointer)
- (C) high conscientiousness and competence (Collie, Shetland Sheep Dog).

The psychologist Carl Jung divides people into those who are combinations of thinking and feeling or knowing and sensing, while Katherine C. Briggs and Isabel Briggs Myers, developers of the Myers-Briggs system, added two additional dimensions – extroversion-introversion and judging-perceiving. Other groups use other categories and terms. Whatever the system, you can plug different dogs into those categories, so you can then use the principles from that system.

For example, to take the popular Myers-Briggs system, here's how some of the most well-known dogs might fit in. (Since these are subjective associations, what's most important is the associations you make with different dogs, because you will use the system to first sense what type of dog characterizes this other person. Then, you will look at what this association tells you about this person's personality.) Here are my own associations:

- Extroversion (Pomeranian) – Introversion (Afghan Hound)
- Intuitive (Siberian Husky) – Sensing (Blood Hound)
- Thinking (German Shepherd) – Feeling (Pug)
- Judging (Weimaraner) – Perceiving (Chow Chow)

If you combine the way people primarily look at the world (their perceptual style) with the way they are likely to act and respond (their behavior style), you come up with four major categories of people, which can be a good starting point for creating further subcategories of people. You can associate different types of dogs with each category as in the examples below:

- The Take-Charge Personality (German Shepherd, Mastiff, Pit Bull)

- The Analyzer/Explorer (Siberian Husky, Norwegian Elkhound)
- The People Person (Pomeranian, Pug)
- The Conscientious Planner (Collie, Shetland Sheepdog).

The take-charge person tends to have a strongly developed ability to take in information by hearing it; the analyzer/explorer has a well-developed visual sense; the people person tends to experience sensations and respond emotionally or expressively; and the conscientious planner often has a feeling of knowing or certainty about how things are or will be. Many people may be a mixture of different types.

Whatever personality type system or terminology you use, what's most important is recognizing that people have different perceptual and behavioral styles. To most effectively relate to them, you need to be aware of their perspective, as people are most responsive to someone who relates to them in terms of their point of view. Accordingly, when you associate a person with a particular dog, you can use the qualities associated with that dog to help you pick out a person's major personality traits and behavior style.

Then, use this awareness about this person to better understand and relate to him or her. For example, an employer using this awareness can better manage his employees; an employee can make things go more smoothly with her boss; and a salesperson is more likely to have a receptive customer and close a sale. Likewise, you can use this information to make your personal life go more smoothly, such as understanding how to best interact with your partner, mother, cousin, or finicky aunt.

The major characteristics of people with the four different personality types are illustrated in the Personality Types and Personal Characteristics Chart.[3] This chart also indicates how these people prefer to interact with others. As you pick up information

---

[3] Gini Graham Scott, *Mind Power: Picture Your Way to Success in Your Work and Personal Life*, Changemakers Publishing, 2011, p. 109

from the dog you pick for a person and your associations with that dog, you will improve your abilities to interact with that person (or decide not to interact with them) by keeping these characteristics and preferences in mind.

Personality Types and Personal Characteristics

Personality Type	Major Characteristics	Preferred Types of Response
The Take-Charge Personality	Assertive, aggressive, direct, energetic, organized. Interested in broad overviews, trends. A leader type.	Likes someone to be direct, to the point. Likes someone to get behind his or her ideas, plans, and support them.
The Analyzer/Explorer	Cool, calm, detached, independent. Curious, an explorer. Concerned with seeing how things fit together. An evaluator/analyzer type.	Likes someone to be clear, organized, provide a full picture. Likes someone with an analytical mind.
The People Person	Sensitive, emotional, dependent on others. Concerned with details. Very aware of and responsive to people. Concerned with making things go smoothly. Often a follower or helper type.	Likes someone to provide details. Likes someone to be warm, feeling, responsive.
The Conscientious Planner	Very perceptive, quick to know something. Often critical, judgmental, or feels he or she knows it all. Frequently opinionated, righteous. A good sense of what will happen, how things will turn out. A planner, organizer type.	Likes someone to be agreeable, receptive to his or her ideas. Likes someone to be organized, self-assured, and confident.

The major types of ethical styles based on a person's morality and sense of integrity are described on the Ethical Styles Chart.[4] This will help you decide how far you want to trust the person with whom you are interacting, whatever the personality type.

For example, you might think of a person you associate with a Siberian Husky as something of a pragmatist, who thinks, "What's in it for me?" in deciding whether to follow instructions or not. Such a person might also be ready to head out the door if given the opportunity. By contrast, you might think of the Collie a very steadfast, loyal, and trustworthy dog, always ready to patiently wait, so that a person you associate with a Collie similarly has those qualities.

To gain more insights about ethical considerations and how well to trust someone, get relaxed and ask yourself some questions about that person and how to best deal with him or her, by calling on the wisdom of your Guide Dog. Then, listen for the answers as they come to you.

---

[4] Ibid., p. 110.

ETHICAL STYLES

Ethical Style	Major Characteristics	Considerations When Interacting
The Complete Moralist	Completely honest and expects total honesty and integrity from others. May sometimes be very righteous or have a strong religious base for this morality.	Expect to be very honest and straight with this person. Feel confident that you can trust this person completely.
The Situational Moralist	Adapts his or her ethical response to the situation or person. If others in the situation are behaving morally and ethically, he or she will, too.	Be very honest and straight with this person, and he or she will be honest and straight with you. Also, make sure this person is aware you are doing this, for if this person has any reason to distrust you, you may find he or she is no longer being straight with you, but instead is acting like a pragmatic moralist.
The Pragmatic Moralist	Totally amoral. Acts honestly and ethically when it is to his or her advantage to do so. But can engage in dishonest or unethical activities at any moment, if it seems profitable to do so, and there is a low risk of getting caught.	Be wary in any dealings with this individual. As long as he or she thinks there is some personal gain in it, he or she will be straight with you. But if you lose your value, this person will have no qualms about acting unethically toward you.

Summing Up

By keeping these personalities, behavioral, and ethical styles in mind, you can gain insights about others through the dogs you associate with them and the qualities you associate with those dogs and therefore that person. The process looks like this:

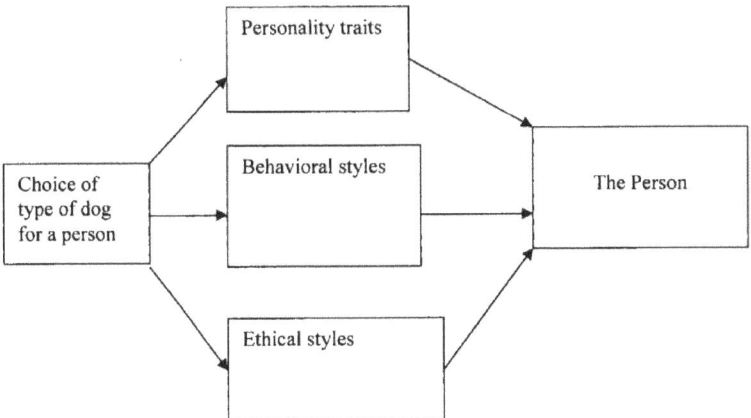

Besides learning about the person and how to better interact based on the dog associated with that person, you can gain further insights by asking your Guide Dogs for guidance. At first, you may need to take time to get relaxed and reflect in a quiet comfortable environment. But as the process becomes more familiar, you can ask a question and get information in response wherever you are.

Other books in this series describe different techniques you can use to get information about others, such as gaining advance impressions before you meet, getting a quick first impression, and gaining more in-depth insights into others. These books also discuss ways to improve your relationships, such as improving your communication, creating a warmer relationship, and increasing your power and influence in a relationship. Plus you can use the 4-Dog Type method to better communicate and work with people in the workplace and in business situations, such as to build teams and more effectively promote and sell your products and services to customers and clients.

PART III: GETTING HELP FROM YOUR DOGS

INTRODUCTION TO PART III

The basic Dog Type system is based on understanding more about yourself and others based on the type of dog you and others like most or least. Or you can imagine what type of dog other people might be if you don't know their choices for what they like or don't.

It can be helpful to know about these different types of dogs in getting help from your dogs, as described *Discovering Your Dog Type*. This knowledge gives you a greater range of choices and more information about the qualities of these dogs.

However, you can still gain help from different dogs based on what you already know about the most popular dogs. For example, you probably already know about Beagles, Dachshunds, German Shepherds, Golden Retrievers, Boxers, Pit Bulls, Collies, Labradors, Poodles, and other dogs you read about every day, and if you own a dog, you certainly know a lot about that breed or mix, and other dogs you may have learned about before deciding on the pooch you finally got.

The way to get help is to use your power of visualization to call on different types of dogs for different purposes. The process is similar to using meditation, hypnosis, journeying, or other techniques to tap into your intuition or creative force within you – however you want to call it. In the course of using these techniques, in different systems you may call on teachers, guides, helpers, mentors, coaches, gurus, heroes, wise men or women, spirits, or the image of actual people you know or admire. The difference here is that you are calling on different types of dogs you associate with different abilities and powers for their help.

The Main Categories of Helpers

There are six main categories of dogs you can call on – and you choose the particular breed of dog to provide that kind of help. These are:

Guide Dogs, who are like mentors or wise men or women in that they provide you with advice.

Power Dogs, who you imagine as being very strong, assertive, and powerful, and you gain power and confidence from them.

Top Dogs, who are your favorite dogs, and you can look to them as friends, parents, relatives, or other family members, who can share their insights, wisdom, and support with you.

Watch Dogs, who provide you with protection, such as if you are in a scary situation, to help you overcome your fears and warn you to stay away from danger.

Underdogs, who represent things you don't like, including your weaknesses or lack of abilities in some area; you may either want to acknowledge them or work on changing and improving them, so they may turn into some other kind of dog.

Rescue Dogs, who can help you out of very difficult situations, when you need some extra help.

The Development of this System

As described in more detail in *Discovering Your Dog Types,* this approach of calling on your dogs developed out of a series of workshops I conducted based on using the dog profiles to look to different dogs for these six types of help. Or you can use the dogs you already know about in deciding what dogs to call on different types of help.

I have included examples of these workshops to illustrate how participants used the Guide Dogs, Power Dogs, Top Dogs, and other types of dogs to help them in everyday situations. As these examples show, this can be a powerful, helpful system which you can use regardless of any other spiritual, religious, or self-help system you might be involved in. Just think of this as an alternate source of help you can draw on in your personal or work life. Also, it is a system you can use in a group to gain insights about yourself and gain help from your dogs and from others who are experiencing the process with you.

This approach is not only designed to provide you with the help you need when you need it, but it is designed to be fun. It is designed to be a lighthearted way to use these techniques to get the information and help you need every day. So feel free to supplement these exercises and visualizations with fun objects, or combine seeking insights with other things you enjoy doing, such as calling on your dogs while you are taking a walk in your neighborhood, hiking on a nature trail, paddling in a kayak, enjoying a cruise, or having a meal in a trendy restaurant overlooking the city.

In other words, this is a system you can use anywhere and at any time. For example, if you are at a social gathering or at a meeting, you can take a few moments to call on your Guide Dog for advice about what to do or what to say in a particular situation. If you are going to a job interview or important meeting, you can call on your Power Dog to watch over you to give you an infusion of power or confidence. If you are nervous about doing something you haven't done before – such as speaking to a large audience – you can ask your Rescue Dog to help you overcome your fear and anxiety.

And so, get ready, get set. And learn how the different kinds of dogs can help you succeed at whatever you are doing, and if you wish, use the Dog Profiles to help you choose the dogs to help you – or just select from the dogs you already know about.

CHAPTER 4: WHAT'S YOUR DOG?

Just as the expression: "What's your sign?" refers to one of 12 astrological signs and "What's your type?" refers to one of 16 Myers-Briggs personality types, "What's your dog type?" refers to the dog profile you most identify with.

The dog you like the most or feel the most connection with is your "Top Dog." Your second favorite is your "Watch Dog" or "Guard Dog," since it's next in line, like a body guard to the Top Dog. These two dogs represent who you are now or would like to be.

Last, and in this case least, is the dog you like the least or feel the least connection with. This is your "Underdog," which has the traits you don't have – or don't want to have.

You can use the Dog Profile descriptions in *Discovering Your Dog Type* as a guide with more information on different breeds of dogs. Or select from the dogs you already are familiar with. It doesn't matter if you own a dog or not.

Determining Your Top Dog, Watch Dog, and Underdog

If you already own a dog, this may turn out to be your Top Dog or Watch Dog, particularly if you have given much thought to choosing the dog you own, which is the case for many people who show their dogs at dog shows. They spend hours poring through dog books, visiting dog breeders, talking to other owners of that breed, and carefully selecting the breed they want to raise and show. After joining the dog show circuit, they become part of a close community of owners of that breed. So commonly, their Top Dog choice is already clear.

In other cases, the dog you own may not necessarily be your Top Dog or Watch Dog, such as if you got your dog as a gift or adopted a dog that wandered into your yard. Also, your dog might be an unlikely contender, if your dog is very unlike you, such as if you are a high-energy go-getter, and your dog grows from a playful pup into a lazy dog that loves to spend the day curled up on your couch.

How do you determine your Top Dog, Watch Dog, and Underdog? The following chapter describes the process and how to use that information to learn more about yourself and for personal and professional development. You can additionally use that information to better understand and relate to others and achieve greater success.

So let's get started on the "Dog Trail", so to speak, to learn more about you.

Discovering Your Top Dog and Watch Dog

There are several ways to determine your Top Dog and Watch Dog. Use whichever method is most applicable for you, or use two or more methods to help confirm your choice. You can repeat the process from time to time, since your choices can change over time, as you change your dog type preferences or identifications. Such changes often occur when you work on personal and professional development. In fact, to make changes in your life, change your Top Dog to help you refocus on the traits you want to develop – and gradually you will become more like that dog.

If your first and second choices have the same Dog Type Profile, such as if a Beagle is your first choice and a Basset Hound is your second choice, that's like having one astrological sign — say Gemini — for both your birth and rising sign, which makes you a "Double Gemini." The same goes for choosing your dog type. If your choices are similar, that shows that this profile is even more clearly your type.

Here are the major ways to identify your dog choices.

1) <u>You already own a dog and know that's the dog for you</u>. So that's your Top Dog. Then, go on and choose your Watch Dog.
2) <u>Review the Dog Type Profiles</u> and choose the one you might like or most identify with as your Top Dog; your next favorite is your Watch Dog. If you have already chosen your Top Dog, review the dog profiles again to make your second choice. As you glance through the pictures, make your choice based on your first impression or "top of mind" reaction. Later, you can read through the "What's Your Personality and Style?" or "Little Bit of History" section to get more acquainted with that breed. As you learn more about these different types of dogs, feel free to change your Top Dog or Watch Dog. (For example, say you decide that a gentle herder like an English Sheep Dog is too soft and cuddly, and you prefer to identify with a more aggressive hunter dog. Make the change.)
3) <u>Use a guided meditation or visualization to choose your dog</u>. To use this method, you will get very relaxed and meditate or take a journey by yourself, with a partner, or in a group. Before doing so, review the Dog Type Profiles on your own or in a group for an overview of the different dog types. Or make a list of the different dogs you are familiar with. Then, use meditation or a visualization to make your final choice, based on strongly feeling a preference, identification, or connection with your favorite dog.

Whichever method you choose, first select your Top Dog, and then your Watch Dog. Should you use a guided meditation or visualization to make your choice, here are a few approaches you might use. Choose the method that feels most comfortable for you.

Using Guided Meditation or Visualization to Discover Your Top Dog or Watch Dog

Take some time to think about the different types of dogs, before beginning to meditate or visualize, unless you are confirming a choice you have already made. It's best not to make a choice in advance, since doing this can skew your experience, so you are drawn to an already made choice. Rather, use this initial review to think about the range of dogs that exist.

When you review the breed profiles or make a list of familiar breeds, don't expect to remember all of the dogs in detail, since your conscious mind normally cannot process and categorize so much information. But as you do your review to find your Top Dog and Watch Dog, your unconscious mind will pick up the types of dogs you feel especially drawn to. Then, when you meditate or use visualization, this unconscious information will be available to you, since you are in a very relaxed, focused state of mind where you can tap into your unconscious.

To get acquainted with the different types of dogs, spend about 10-15 minutes doing a Dog Type Profile review or making your list of familiar dogs. Look at the profiles or your list. If you use the profiles, notice the dog names and photos and read the profile descriptions. If you have time, look at the historical descriptions. Then, use one of the following techniques to get in this altered state and choose your two favorite dogs.

Using Meditation or Reflection to Find Your Top Dog or Watch Dog

For this technique, first use the Dog Type Profiles you have reviewed or the list you have created. Place the profiles section or your list before you. Have some stick-on notes available to help you narrow down your choices.

Next, get in a very relaxed, reflective state by focusing on your breathing going in and out or staring ahead in an unfocused way for a minute or two.

Then, with the goal of looking for your "Top Dog" in mind, go back through the profiles or you list. Gaze one each profile in an unfocused way. You can also combine unfocused looking with putting your palm over that page or name on your list and feeling if you get a warm or cool sensation or feel a vibration. Then, listen to your inner voice tell you "Yes or No" or go by the sensation you feel – warm or a vibration for "Yes", cool or no vibration for "No". Mark the "Yeses" with a post-it note.

If you have more than one "Yes" selected, go through the process again with those "Yeses." This time, with your goal of seeking your "Top Dog" in mind, ask for an even stronger "Yes," warmer sensation, or stronger vibration. Once more eliminate any "Nos."

Continue this process until you end up with a single "Yes." That is your Top Dog.

To choose your Watch Dog, go back to your last selection of "Yeses." If there is just one other dog selected, that is your Watch Dog. If there is more than one, go through this process one last time to end up with a single "Yes." This is your Watch Dog — your second favorite choice.

Taking a Dog Walk to Find Your Top Dog or Watch Dog

This approach to finding your dog involves doing a visualization where you take a walk through a dog park to meet your Top Dog and then your Watch Dog. Be generally familiar with the different types of dogs or dog profiles before you start visualizing. Get relaxed and use the following visualization as a guide – or record it and play it back as you listen. Or in a group, one person can read this, while others have the experience.

Imagine that you are going into a dog park with a walking trail through a woods and meadow to a large lake. The dog park is a place where dogs can run free and off the leash. It is a bright, sunny day, as you drive into the parking lot, park, and walk into the dog park.

As you walk in, you see a large open area where many dogs are exercising and playing, while their owners are off to the side, watching. The dogs are running, jumping, cooling off in tubs of water, chasing through tunnels, and having a great time.

Watch the dogs for a while, feeling very comfortable and relaxed as you do. Then, you notice a trail off to the side of the park, and you head toward it, so you can meet the dog you like most or most identify with. This will be your Top Dog.

Now start walking on the trail. It winds around and goes into the woods. As you walk along through the trees, you notice some dogs appear on the side of the trail. They may be some dogs you saw playing before, or some new dogs. If they look at you, just smile at them and notice if any of them seem especially interested in you. Possibly your Top Dog may be among them, or maybe not. Continue to walk on to find your Top Dog.

Then, you come to an open meadow with a few scattered trees. You notice a number of dogs running around and playing there. They may be some of the dogs you saw playing before or some new dogs. Stop for a short time to observe. Notice if you seem to be especially drawn to or interested in some of these dogs and focus on observing them. If they look at you, smile at them and notice if any seem especially interested in you. Possibly your Top Dog may be among them, or maybe not.

Continue to walk on. Now you will come to a lake. This is where you will find your Top Dog. Go over to the lake and sit down on the bank and look into the water. Ask for the dog you like the most or feel the most identification with to appear. As you ask that question, your Top Dog will appear beside you to your right, and you'll see its face appear in the water. Should you see more than one dog there, notice which one you feel most drawn to and invite that dog to stay. Then, the others will leave and return to the meadow.

Now, turn to your Top Dog and take some time to get acquainted and make a connection with that dog. You can shake its paw, pet it. Then, talk to it. Ask it some questions about what it likes and doesn't like, and what activities it prefers. Notice the ways in which you are similar to that dog, such as in personality and appearance. Think about the things you especially like about that dog or why you feel the most identification with it. Consider the reasons you might feel the greatest connection with that dog; why you have chosen it to be your Top Dog – or maybe why it has chosen you.

Take a few minutes to reflect on these questions, and as you do, feel your connection with your Top Dog growing. Know that you can always turn to it for help, as well as any other dogs you might call on for assistance.

Then, with your Top Dog still seated beside you, look back into the water. Now ask for the dog you like next most or feel the next most identification with to appear there. As you ask that question, your Watch Dog will appear beside you on your left, and you'll see its face appear before you in the water. If your Watch Dog is the same breed as your Top Dog, that's fine. It just means you have an especially strong preference for or identification with that dog. Should you see more than one dog, notice which one you feel most drawn to and invite that dog to stay. Then, the others will leave and return to the meadow.

Now, turn to your Watch Dog and take some time to get acquainted and make a connection with that dog. Consider this dog your Top Dog's helper or companion. You can shake its paw, pet it. Then, talk to it. Ask it some questions about what it likes and doesn't like; and what activities it prefers. Notice the ways in which you are similar to that dog, such as in personality and appearance. Think about the things you especially like about that dog or why you feel the next most identification with that dog. Consider the reasons you have chosen it to be your Watch Dog – or maybe why it has chosen you.

Take a few minutes to reflect on these questions, and as you do, feel your connection with your Watch Dog growing. Know that you can always turn to it for help, as well as any other dogs you might call on for assistance.

Then, with these two dogs still beside you, feel their strength and power. Think of them as reflecting different aspects of yourself and as helpers that will teach you more about yourself, so you more clearly see who you are now and who you want to be. Also, know that you can always come back here to communicate with them – or you can always call on them when you want them to appear wherever you are so you can talk to them.

Now take a few minutes to say your "Goodbyes" and let them know you plan to contact them again. Then, turn and head back along the trail. Walk through the meadow and woods and then back into the dog park. Finally, walk back to your car to go home. As you walk, you feel very confident and secure now that you have found your Top Dog and Watch Dog, who you can turn to for more insights about yourself, as well as advice on what to do in different situations.

Working with Your Top Dog and Watch Dog

Now that you know your Top Dog and Watch Dog, you can work with this information to learn more about yourself, as well as think about what you might want to change and further develop in yourself. You can additionally work with these dogs as Inner Guide Dogs or Power Dogs, turning to them for advice or extra power in different areas of your life, as discussed in subsequent chapters.

When you change through this process, you may find yourself drawn to different Top Dogs and Watch Dogs. That's because the changes you make may lead you to prefer or identify with different dogs. So from time to time, check to see if you still have the same Top Dog and/or Watch Dog. If not, reflect on what this new Top Dog or Watch Dog has to tell you about yourself and where you might develop next.

Once you use this knowledge to learn more about yourself, you can apply this system to learn more about others and improve your relationships with them by determining or imagining their Top Dogs, Watch Dogs, and Underdogs, as will be described in a later chapter in more detail. For now, focus on learning to use the system for yourself.

Discovering Your Underdog

While your Top Dog and Watch Dog represent who you are or would like to be, your Underdog has qualities you don't have or don't want. Here's how to meet your Underdog. You use a first impression, guided meditation or journey, or both, much like you found your Top Dog and Watch Dog.

Using Meditation or Reflection to Find Your Underdog

For this technique, as in finding your Top Dog and Watch Dog, use the Dog Type Profiles or your list of dogs you have created. Place the chapter of the book with these profiles or your list before you, and eliminate from consideration your Top Dog and Watch Dog. Once more, get in a very relaxed, reflective state.

Now, with the goal of looking for your Underdog in mind — the dog you like the least or least identify with, go back through the profiles or your list. As you turn each page or look at each name, gaze at the profile or listing in an unfocused way. As before, notice if you get a warm or cool sensation or vibration from the listing of that dog and listen to your inner voice telling you "Yes" or "No," until you feel a strong "Yes" or "No" sensation. Once you end up with a single "Yes," that's your Underdog – the dog you least prefer or least identify with.

Going to the Dog Pound to Find Your Underdog

This approach involves using visualization to visit the dog pound to meet your Underdog. You should already be familiar with different types of dogs and their profiles, since you have used them to find your Top Dog and Watch Dog. The dog pound metaphor is used, since this is where you find many rejected dogs in cages, unlike going to a dog park to find your Top Dog and Watch Dog, because there you will find dogs off leash, exercising, and running free. So now get ready to find your Underdog at the pound.

Imagine that you are going to the dog pound located in the downtown or industrial area of your city. The pound is filled mostly with unwanted dogs that have been given away by their owners. Others have been lost or are strays. They're in separate cages, and most are bored, angry, or sad at being there.

You arrive at the pound, knowing that you are looking for your Underdog, the dog you like the least or feel the least connection with. Once you find it, you can release it from the pound, so you can meet with it for its help in learning more about yourself.

Once you arrive, park and go in. Inside, you see the pound director, who will take you on a walk through the pound. As you walk, notice the dogs in the cages on either side. They look at you with interest. Some jump up and down in their cages, eager to get out and join you. Others bark, wanting to show their anger at being in a cage.

Should you see any dogs that look like your Top Dog or Watch Dog, that's fine. Just pass them by, knowing they will not be your Underdog, too. They just happen to be in the pound.

Keep on walking. Make a complete circuit of the pound, so you see all of the dogs there. Then, go back to look for your Underdog, and as you walk around, notice which dog you like the least or feel the least connection with. You may notice that the dog senses this by withdrawing as you go by. Or maybe it will bark to let you know that you seem like an unwelcome stranger.

If so, this might be your Underdog, though keep walking around the pound to be sure. As you walk around, notice if there is another dog you don't like or feel little or no connection with. If so, go around again and choose the dog where you feel the least liking or connection. This is your Underdog.

Now that you know your Underdog, it's time to make some connection. So go back to that dog's cage and stand there trying to relate to it. Take some time to get acquainted. You may feel hesitant at first, but as you stand there, the dog feels more and more calm and comfortable with you. Then, you can shake its paw, pet it, and talk to it. Ask it some questions about what it likes and doesn't like; what activities it prefers. Notice the ways in which you are different from that dog, such as in personality and appearance. Think about the things you especially don't like about that dog or why you feel the least identification with that dog. Consider why you have chosen it to be your Underdog – or maybe why it has chosen you.

Take a few minutes to reflect on these questions. As you do, feel your connection with your Underdog growing, even though you still like it the least or feel little or no identification with it. For you have much you can learn from it.

To continue to learn from your Underdog, take that dog out of the pound. Take it with you on a leash or in your arms to your car. Next, take it with you to the dog park. As you release it, it is very happy in this new place and will be glad to meet with you again here or come to your house if you prefer. You can then turn to it for more information about yourself and for insights into the qualities you want to eliminate in yourself and how to do so.

Finally, see your Underdog run off, turn away and leave the dog park, knowing you can always call on your Underdog for more insights about yourself.

Working with Your Top Dog, Watch Dog, and Underdog

Now that you've discovered your Top Dog, Watch Dog, and Underdog, you're ready to work with them to learn more about yourself and the qualities you want to further develop, change, or eliminate. In the process, you'll want to get to know them, too, because as you know more about them, you'll learn more about you. Just check the dog's profile or what you know about the dog to do so.

To illustrate different ways of working with these dogs, the next chapter features a workshop with a group of people who experienced the process of finding their Top Dog, Watch Dog and Underdog.

CHAPTER 5: A WORKSHOP ON FINDING YOUR TOP DOG, WATCH DOG, AND UNDERDOG

In the previous chapters, I described how to find your Top Dog or favorite dog, Watch Dog or next favorite, and Underdog, the dog you like the least. Before discussing how to work with these choices to better understand yourself, here's an example from a small workshop I conducted with a dozen people. This illustration will also provide a guide for setting up your own small group.

With a larger group, after people pick their dogs, I recommend getting them into groups with similar choices to participate in various exercises and discussions together. In this case, everyone sat in one group, made their choice and later discussed their experience. I changed the identities and descriptions of the participants for confidentiality. Here's how I described the workshop.

The Workshop Setting

I used a relaxed, comfortable setting – a large room in my house with soft carpeting, large pillows, and low lighting. Everyone took off their shoes and sat around in a circle on the pillows.

I began with a brief introduction to the Dog Type system and what would happen tonight: they would meet their Top Dog, Watch Dog, and Underdog, and discover what they could learn from and about themselves. Holding up a picture of the Dog Star Chart to illustrate, I explained:

"This is the Dog Type system. If you're familiar with astrology, this is what the basic system looks like. It's divided into 4 sections that represent the major areas of personality — power, energy, social skills, and individual traits. Then these are further divided so there are 12 main dimensions. The different types of dogs can be profiled on these dimensions, which are like spokes on a wheel.

The basic underlying principle is that the kinds of dogs you are drawn to reflect your personality and lifestyle. The dogs you don't like reflect the characteristics you don't have or don't like in yourself, and you'd like to get rid of. I've combined the most important dogs into families of dogs, and dog profiles of the chosen dogs.

What we'll do tonight is look at how you connect to your Top Dog, which is your favorite dog or the dog you prefer or relate to the most. Then, we'll look at your second favorite dog, which is your Watch Dog. Finally, you'll meet the dog you like the least, and called appropriately the Underdog.

You'll see all of the dog profiles in this booklet of dog types. Look through it. Get a sense of the different types of dogs and those you feel a kinship with. Then, we'll do a visualization to find your Top Dog and Watch Dog. Then, we'll look at how you relate to your Top Dog and Watch Dog and discuss the qualities they have and the qualities you might like to develop."

Next, before starting the exercises, I asked the participants to describe a little about themselves and what they hoped to gain from the workshop. The participants also spent time talking about their dogs, since they were dog owners and their dogs were very important to them.

Among the participants were Andrew, a marketing sales rep; Flo, an elementary school teacher; Susan, an administrative assistant; Heddy, a retired secretary; Jim, a Web designer; and Paul, a supervisor at a manufacturing company. Here are some of their comments, to give a flavor of these introductions. Interestingly, the initial dog descriptions provided a context for the later discussions of how they felt a kinship with their chosen dogs

–sometimes the same as a dog they owned, but more generally a different type of dog.

Susan, emphasized the importance of giving her dog, an Arctic German Shepherd, instructions, and trusting him as a protector, qualities that led her to choose it as her Top Dog, too. As she described her dog:

> "I have an Arctic German Shepherd, and we are very bonded. I like her because she listens well and follows instructions. She knows if she's done something I don't like, even before I get to the area where she might have destroyed something. But mostly, she's a good dog and gets along well. If she's done something bad, she'll run to her bed and cover her head to let me know there's something wrong. She doesn't go outside much, because in my neighborhood, there are pit bulls, which are trained for fighting."

Flo, the teacher, emphasized the importance of her Rottweiler/German Shepherd Mix being both gentle with children and a good protector, noting that he won't let anybody come in the yard that he doesn't know."

Andrew spoke about his own Rottweiler being very aggressive, yet with a gentle disposition and easy to train. "He's like a big baby, and very intelligent. He listens to everything I tell him. I found him on the street and he's a good dog, very dependable, very protective. He likes to please you and is easily trainable." He also praised his second dog, a "very protective, really mellow" German Shepherd Mix. "Her name is Patience and she has a lot of patience, though she has a little evil side which comes out when she sees a dog on the street and begins barking and lunging. But basically she is a good dog and minds very well. I use treats and can train both my dogs to do anything." One reason he had for attending the workshop was that he hoped to learn why he was drawn to the big dogs, as well as learn more about the dogs he didn't like and why.

The others similarly described a little about themselves and what they hoped to learn. I handed out booklets with the dog profiles. Then I invited the participants to glance through the booklets to get familiar with the different types of dogs, since the dogs they chose as their favorites might not be the dog they owned, and they didn't need to own a dog. As I explained:

"What I'd like to do now is give you these Dog Profile Books, so you can look at the various types of dogs to help you choose your Top Dog, Watch Dog, and Underdog. Don't try to make your choice now. Just use the book to get familiar with these dogs, since the dog you choose could be the dog you own or it could be another dog you feel a kinship with."

While they looked at the pictures of dogs, I put on the What Kind of Dog Are You? theme song – a humorous song about why people choose the dogs they do to provide some lighthearted background music to keep the mood light and upbeat. In your own workshops, you can use whatever background music you like, or nothing at all.

Here's a copy of the What Kind of Dog Are You? song that was inspired by creating the Dog Type. You can download a copy of the song from the WhatsYourDogType.com website.

WHAT KIND OF DOG ARE YOU?[5]

CHORUS If someone asked you, what would you say?
What kind of dog are you?
Are you more like a toy,
A bundle of joy?
Or a rough tough mutt through and through?

---

[5]Copyright Gini Graham Scott 2003; Lyrics and Music by Gini Graham Scott

VERSE   Take Joe with a mastiff.
        He works as a bailiff.
        Tough guy in the courts and in life.
        Don't push him around,
        Or he'll run you aground.
        With the help of his bulldog-like wife.

VERSE   Now look at sweet Cherise.
        She chose a Pekingese.
        Loves to preen and show off in style.
        Has the same look-at-me walk.
        Same perked ears when she talks.
        Both seek love like the Queen of the Nile.

CHORUS 2 So if someone asked you, what would you say?
        What kind of dog are you?
        Are you more like a Chow,
        That's built like a cow?
        Are you more like a Hound,
        Your nose to the ground?
        Or a Whippet, like a bolt from the blue?

VERSE   And then there's old Pete,
        Found his dog on the street.
        A mutt from a long line of strays.
        Both lazy and laid back.
        Yet fight hard if attacked.
        Their pedigree: a great love of play.

BRIDGE So the answer seems clear.
        Your choice shows who you are.
        The dog you like the most
        Is like a sign up on a post.

FINAL   So what kind of dog are you?
CHORUS Yeah, what kind of dog are you?
                If someone asked you, what would you say?
                What kind of dog are you?

After the song ended, I explained that we would now do a guided fantasy meditation, so everyone should get comfortable, and I would lower the lights. Then, I explained the process of going to a dog park to find their Top Dog, Watch Dog and Underdog.

"You'll be taking a walk to find your Top Dog and Watch Dog. Then, we'll talk a little about that and next you'll find your Underdog. After that, we'll look at ways you can work with these dogs. We'll use this meditation where you go to the dog park to make your choice."

Now, with everyone relaxed and comfortable, I used the Dog Park guided experience, after about 30 seconds of introductory comments. I began by telling everyone, "Now concentrate on your breathing going in and out, in and out, feeling very calm and relaxed, yet alert and aware, so you hear the sound of my voice," to calm everyone and get them receptive to the experience. Then, I slowly read the guided experience.

The experience lasted for about 7 minutes, and was like going to a movie, which the participants created in their mind, as I led them along the trail in the Dog Park through a woods, to a meadow, and then to a lake, where they saw the reflection of their Top Dog, and then their Watch Dog, seated on either side of them.

Afterward, I used a short commentary to bring them back – "Now I'm going to count from 5 to 1, and as I do, you'll come back into the room:5, 4, you're becoming more awake and alert; 3, 2; More and more alert and awake; And 1, you're back in the room.

Once everyone was back, I asked them: "How did that feel? What did you experience?" Then everyone in turn described how they had met their Top Dog and Watch Dog. Afterward, I asked some follow-up probing questions about how the qualities of their Top Dog or Watch Dog reflected their own qualities.

For example, here's my exchange with Andrew, who reported that he was drawn to two big dogs – a Collie and a St. Bernard, though neither was the same as the Rottweiler and German Shepherd Mix he currently owned.

Andrew: "I was attracted to the Collie type of dog."

GGS: "What was it about the Collie that appealed to you?"

Andrew: "Because it seemed like a peaceful dog. Mellow."

GGS: "Are those qualities you feel you have or would like to develop more?"

Andrew: "I feel I have those peaceful qualities. I think I'm a little mellow."

GGS: "And what was your second dog?"

Andrew: "My second dog was a St. Bernard."

GGS: "What was it about the St. Bernard that appealed to you?"

Andrew: "The strongness and the bigness. He's big, but he doesn't have to use it. It's like his bigness gives him that assurance and confidence."

GS: "The St. Bernard is also known as a protective and loyal dog, and he's a well-known rescue dog. Would you say those kind of qualities describe you?"

Andrew: "Yes, loyal I think, because I really stay committed to other people I know and trust. And I think the rescue part fits me, because I'm always trying to help people."

Likewise, Flo felt a strong resemblance between the Golden Retriever she selected as her Top Dog and herself. She was especially impressed by the Golden Retriever's gentle, lovable qualities, combined with being an easy dog to train. Similarly, she had a very gentle, quiet, warm, friendly manner about her, coupled with an eagerness to do things that people asked of her most of the time. For her Watch Dog, she chose a German Shepherd, because of its qualities as a strong, trainable protector. Here are the highlights of my exchange with her.

GGS: "Flo, what was your experience?"

Flo: "I picked a Golden Retriever."

GGS: "What was it about the Golden Retriever that you especially liked?"

Flo: "They're gentle, though they can be aggressive, and they're very lovable. They're an easy dog to get along with and easy to train."

GGS: "Would you say those are qualities that you have, too?"

Flo: "Definitely."

GSS: "What about your second dog?"

Flo: "I would say a German Shepherd. I like those dogs because they are good watchdogs, good with children, easy to get along with, and very trainable. Once you train them, they'll be a real good housedog. And once you train them and tell them what to do, they just do it."

GGS: "Would you say that about yourself, that you're good at being trained, say by taking instructions when people instruct you?"

Flo: "Yeah, I'm good at doing things people ask me to do. Sometimes whether I want to do it or not, I just do it."

At this point, Flo's friend, Andrew, who had invited her to the workshop, also had his own insights about the good match between Flo and her Top Dog.

Andrew: "And Flo's real loyal. Definitely. When she says she's going to do something, she does it."

Flo: "Almost do or die."

GGS: "That's very true of German Shepherds. They're excellent at doing what their owner wants, and you associate that with them. They're police dogs and watchdogs, because they're really good about following orders. You train them not to bark, to be nice to people, and they do that, such as when the police use the dog to help them catch a criminal and then take it to school with them to meet and greet the kids."

Flo strongly agreed that shepherd dogs are so well behaved. "You can tell them: 'Lie down over there and stay there till I get back', and you get back, and they're still there. They're doing exactly what you asked them to do."

Then Susan explained why she chose an Arctic German Shepherd, the same dog she owned, because of the qualities of trust and dependability, though the dog sometimes acted as a surrogate for her in expressing her anger toward several neighbors, she described as "bad actors". Then, too, the dog had the same pugnacious, tenacious qualities, she had in going after what she wanted or felt was right. As Susan described her experience:

"Regardless of how I feel, if she wants something done, she'll keep walking back and forth, looking at me, until I eventually get up, which she wants.

"I like her because she's very trustworthy, she's dependable, I don't worry when I leave my house about somebody coming in that she doesn't know. I also like her because I live in an apartment, behind my garage, and she lets me know as soon as somebody pulls up if it's somebody she knows. Then she'll go "aaaah….aaaah" and run back and forth to let me know that. But if it's somebody she doesn't know, she'll bark and won't leave the door until I come to see who it is.

"And what I really like is her toughness, such as one night when my neighbor threw some charcoal in the backyard, when I was asleep. I kept hearing her bark, and she wouldn't lie down. Then, when I saw her running back and forth in the street, I realized something was wrong. So when I got up, the garage was on fire behind me, and she kept barking until she made sure I got up. So I know that I can count on her. She's trustworthy, she's lovable, and she's stubborn."

GGS: "Would you say those characteristics go for you, too?"

Susan: "Yeah. They are."

Then, Susan described her second choice, a Cocker Spaniel, again emphasizing the importance of trust and persistence. Plus she liked its sensitive nature and felt she had these same qualities, explaining:

"My second choice was the Cocker Spaniel, because they are so cute, and I believe they are trustworthy and loyal, which is very important to me.

"Plus if they like you they like you, and if they don't, they don't. And I'm like that, too. I either like people or I don't, and I show them just where they stand. If I like you, I'll open up my heart to you, and if not, I'm like, 'Get out of my face.'"

Then, Heddy described her choices, which were dogs she previously or currently owned. She was drawn to her first dog, a Cocker Spaniel, because she not only liked its playfulness – a quality she shared too, but she felt it was very protective, and realized that she was generally protective of other people. She liked the Rottweiler next, because it was a tough dog that helped her in putting up a stronger shield against other people she didn't want in her life. As she explained:

"I chose a Cocker Spaniel for my first dog, because I used to have a Cocker Spaniel and liked her very much. For one thing, I like to play with my dog, so she was perfect for me, because she was always very playful. Plus I liked that she was very protective, a good watchdog. I feel I am protective of other people, as well.

"And what I liked about the Rottweiler is he's protective about me outside. I'll go inside the house, and if he doesn't like somebody, he'll show that, which is good because of the neighborhood I'm in. Many people are phony or mean, such as the man next door. The man calls him "dirty dog", and he doesn't like that man either. And he shows how he really feels to my neighbor and his kids who come over and throw things at him. So he doesn't like these kids either. And he shows what I'd like to express myself. He shows what he thinks of him by going by his edge of the yard."

Nancy, who picked a Terrier, a dog she already owned, described how both she and her dog shared a similar memory for past slights and mistreatments, and never forgot. As she commented:

"When my dog was a little puppy, this friend of mine teased her, and to this day, she remembers that. For example, one day when he had to use my bathroom, he told me my dog was lying right in front of the door to block him from going in. My dog was there, because she never forgot what he did when she was younger. And like me, she's like that with anybody who ever mistreated her; she doesn't fool with them. She's very sensitive. Another example is I have a neighbor across the street who comes over to work in my garage. Once he hit her with a hammer, and now if he comes anywhere near her, my dog tries to bite him. So it shows that you cannot tease or mess with my dog and then expect to go anywhere near her.

"And I won't forget either. If somebody treats me badly, I don't want to be bothered with them anymore. I don't take it, just like my dog won't. For example, that happened once with my own boss, who tried to do me in. She first tried to keep me from getting another job. Then, she called the police and child protective services claiming I abused my son, who has some mental disabilities, but it wasn't true. And whenever my dog sees her, she just growls at her and threatens to attack. She knows she's no good."

Once everyone had explored their connection with their Top Dog and Watch Dog, the next step was for each person to go to the dog pound to meet their Underdog. I thought this was an appropriate place to find this dog, since the pound is a place for cast-off and unwanted dogs.

Using another guided fantasy meditation, I led them through a pound to choose their Underdog from the caged dogs there, using the Dog Pound exercise described in Chapter 4. Afterward, I asked everyone in turn what breed of dog they picked and why. Additionally, we discussed the contrasts between the dogs they picked as their two favorites and the dog they liked least.

Andrew began by explaining that he picked a Chihuahua for the dog he liked least.

Andrew: "They're so nervous. They're always anxious and shaking, not trusting. I feel like you try to reach out to them, and they don't trust you. They like to bite, and I don't like that. They're so fragile. It's like they're always afraid, saying 'Don't hurt me,' like a real scaredy cat."

GSS: "Your description sounds very different from the Collie and St. Bernard you described as very mellow and relaxed."

Andrew: "That's right. They're such anxious, little dogs. Usually you can't go to them and play with them, unless it's a puppy. Otherwise, they have this sense of 'Look at me, but don't touch me. I might bite you.' And I don't like that.

And I don't like people who are nervous and high strung either.

Additionally, Andrew had a second dog he didn't like – a Bulldog, though generally, people only select one Underdog and Andrew explained:

"I don't like Bulldogs, because they're ugly and they're mean. They look at you and want to growl all the time. Look at them too long, and they get defensive, such as with my neighbor's Bulldog. Look at him for a few seconds, and he starts growling. And some people think when you're looking at them, you're judging them, so they snap at you. They have this attitude of don't bother me, don't get in my face. And I don't like being around people like that, so that fits with my choosing a Bulldog as one of the dogs I least like."

Next, Flo, who previously chose a Golden Retriever and a German Shepherd as her two favorite dogs, described the Bloodhound as the dog she liked the least. The key reason was because she perceived the Bloodhound as a hard dog to control. As she commented:

"I don't like Bloodhounds because they're always chasing stuff and barking. There's a Bloodhound down the street who chases anything he sees – cats, chickens, buses, pigs. So his owner has to keep him locked up, and as soon as he gets out, he's out chasing things again – so I find Bloodhounds uncontrollable because they just chase everything. And they won't mind. They just take off on the chase."

GSS: "How about people that are like that?

Flo: "Yeah. There are some people you don't want to be bothered with, because they do what they want and don't listen to what you say. They don't care about cooperating with others. They either do what they want or want to be in charge, and I just want such people to leave me alone."

Then, Susan shared her Underdog choice, the English and Irish Setter because they didn't fit with her lifestyle. She liked staying close to home and participating in activities that didn't involve a lot of physical exercise or exertion, so she chose a pair of dogs who were very active as her Underdog. As she commented:

"With an English or Irish Setter, you have to be very active. You have to like physical activity, but that's not me. So I don't like outdoors animals. They want to go outside on walks, and if you like to run, that could be the dog for you. But for me, I don't want to be walking any miles trying to keep up with these dogs."

Heddy indicated that she didn't like the Chihuahua much like Andrew, because of its nervous, anxious nature. Plus she saw it as a dog that tended to withdraw from people, which didn't fit her style as a people person. As she noted:

"You can't get close to a Chihuahua. Like one day, I went to visit a friend who had one, and she had to chase him away from the door, because he blocked my way. He was just sitting there yapping, not wanting me to pass by, because he didn't want me to sit in a certain place. Then, I tried to pet him, but he began shaking, and each time I bent down to pet him, he went running to my friend. So I really can't stand this dog. He didn't want anybody to touch him or talk to him. He didn't want anybody to be there. So I didn't like him."

GGS: "Are there any people the Chihuahua reminds you of that you don't like?"

Heddy: Yeah. There are some people I know who are sneaky and some people from the neighborhood who come to my house bothering me. They don't say much, but just hang around, maybe smoking and drinking. They ask you if you mind, but if you tell them no, they ignore you."

Then, Susan, who had chosen the English or Irish Setter for her Underdog, based on not liking an active lifestyle, chimed in with reasons she didn't like the Chihuahua either. "It has a defensive, "small person's personality," which is characteristic of some people she didn't like a lot.

"The Chihuahua's personality is like a Napoleon or short-man's complex. They always try to take advantage of you by playing the victim role."

Then, the discussion turned to the way that dogs take on their owner's characteristics, whether or not the person picked that dog in the first place. As Susan pointed out:

"Sometimes you don't pick a dog, but then you bond with it and it'll take on your characteristics. That's what's amazing: your dog learns you. For example, I've always worked during the day, so Snowy (her Arctic German Shepherd) learned to sleep during the day. And now that I don't work during the day, she still keeps her same routine. She lies on her bed and goes to sleep. So once you train a dog, that's how they will react.

"And dogs pick up a lot of your personality, too. They can really sense what you are feeling and how you are relating to another person. For example, I can have a close friend over, and my dog is really cool with that. But, if we start to have an argument and the person starts to get too ugly, Snowy will come and stand by my side, like she's backing me up, and that'll make the other person back down or go."

Finally, Susan wondered what happens when people end up owning a dog they don't like –a dog they might choose as their Underdog? As Susan put it:

"Suppose dogs get with a person who has the wrong characteristics and personality? Would they change to be more like that person?"

I explained that such an outcome might not be the result. The relationship might be more like a dysfunctional union between people who don't fit well together. As I commented:

"If a dog and person don't make a good personality match, they might have trouble bonding, say when someone gets a dog that is unlike them. If you get a dog that's very outdoorsy, the dog will get very frustrated, because you're not going to take it out. Or say you get a Siberian Husky, which is a very independent, active dog. If you open the door, he'll run away.

"That's why it's important to choose a dog which makes a good fit with your own personality, and that's why there are all these personality tests to help people choose the kind of dog that feels right for them, and their lifestyle."

Finally, concluding the workshop, I explained how people might use the information they obtained about their two favorite and least favorite dogs to apply that in their personal life or in the workplace. For example, they might get insights on how to deal with problems with a boss, say to be stronger to keep a boss from taking advantage or holding back to avoid a confrontation.

Or they might use their Inner Dogs like spiritual helpers or teachers by imagining talking to them to get advice.

So, on that note, the workshop ended.

I have described this workshop at length to illustrate how you might work with your dogs by using a small group of friends or associates.

When you set up a workshop, keep in mind these general tips:

- Find a relaxed, comfortable, quiet place for the workshop.
- Choose a leader who has already selected his or her Top Dog, Watch Dog, and Underdog to lead the guided fantasy meditations, or prerecord the guided instructions on tape, speaking in a slow, quiet voice and leave a minute or two on the tapes for quiet reflection where indicated in the script. Still another possibility is for everyone to quietly reflect on the Dog Profiles and choose a Top Dog, Watch Dog, and Underdog that way.

- After participants select their Top Dog and Watch Dog, start a discussion in which each person describes the characteristics they associate with that dog (which may be those in the Dog Profiles or other qualities) and why they like or identify with that dog the most. Then, ask them to discuss how these characteristics describe themselves. Invite people to share stories about how they have expressed these qualities in different situations – and if people own dogs, invite them to talk about the traits they share with their dogs.
- After participants select their Underdog, have a discussion in which each person describes the characteristics they associate with that dog (which may be those in the Dog Profiles or other qualities) and why they don't like or least identify with that dog. Then, ask them to describe how they don't have these qualities or might want to get rid of them, and invite them to talk about any people with these characteristics they don't like. Invite people to share stories about how they have expressed these qualities in different situations.
- As much as possible, ask people to share in turn, although if people want to comment on what someone else has said or ask questions, invite them to do so.
- Keep the conversation focused on how the people have expressed the qualities of their chosen dogs. If the dog owners start to talk about experiences with their own dog or give tips on raising, caring for, and training dogs, gently guide the discussion back to focus on the traits of their favorite and least favorite dogs and how these traits are reflected in themselves and other people.
- Finally, have fun. Keep the mood fun and lighthearted, and feel free to do things to add to the mood (such as play the What Kind of Dog Are You song, make colored masks of dogs, have people draw pictures of their favorite and least favorite dogs. The idea is to both learn about yourself and others through this system, and have fun doing it.

CHAPTER 6: WORKING WITH YOUR DOG

Now that you know your Top Dog, Watch Dog, and Underdog, you can work with them to learn more about yourself and others. Then, use these insights to develop the characteristics you want, eliminate those you don't want, and work toward achieving your personal and professional goals. Use these techniques on your own, with a partner, or in a small group.

Consider them like your dog family, as long as they remain in these three positions, though as you change, you may welcome other dogs to your family.

If any are on your dog team of Guide Dogs or Power Dogs, you can call on them for that kind of help, too.

Learning More about Your Dog Family – and You!

A first step to working with your dog family is to learn more about them – and by extension, yourself. Work with your Top Dog and Watch Dog first; then meet your Underdog.

Getting to Know Your Top Dog and Watch Dog

Consider your Top Dog and Watch Dog as representing the qualities you have or would like to develop. Your Top Dog represents qualities that are strongest in you or that you most strongly want to acquire; your Watch Dog has those qualities, but not as strongly. This is like having a superior and inferior function or primary and secondary traits in the Myers-Briggs personality type system; or like having your birth sign and a rising sign in Astrology. Look at both aspects of yourself to promote a more rounded picture of you.

If you have chosen the same breed as your Top Dog and Watch Dog, that's like having the same birth sign and rising sign, like being a double Gemini or double Capricorn. You simply have those qualities or would like to develop them more strongly, though when you start the exercise for finding your Top Dog and Watch Dog, you may find a different Watch Dog.

Now, let's go. First move through this process with your Top Dog; then do the same with your Watch Dog.

Look at the Dog Profile corresponding to your Top Dog (and later your Watch Dog) and review the traits characterizing this type of dog. If you have other associations with this breed, add them. Get in a relaxed frame of mind and reflect on these different traits.

As you look at these traits, make a list in any order of all the traits you feel you have or want to acquire. You can use the chart on the following page to help you do this. For each trait, put down the number 1, 2, or 3, depending on how strongly you feel you have that trait or would like to acquire it. The higher the number, the more strongly you feel about that trait.

Do this yourself for both your Top Dog and Watch Dog, unless they're the same; then just do this once. This process will help you think about the qualities you have and those you want to develop. Later you will use this information in other exercises to gain more insight into yourself and how you see yourself in the future.

Traits of my Top Dog:
Type of Dog: _____

Traits	Traits I Have (use 1-3 to indicate their strength)	Traits I'd Like to Acquire or Further Develop (use 1-3 to indicate their strength)

Traits of my Watch Dog:

Type of Dog:_____

Traits	Traits I Have (use 1-3 to indicate their strength)	Traits I'd Like to Acquire or Further Develop (use 1-3 to indicate their strength)

Putting Yourself in the Picture

Now that you have consciously thought about how your Top Dog and Watch Dog represent your current traits and how you want to be in the future, reflect on this information using your intuition. To do so, get very relaxed and use any or all of the following exercises to gain more insight. The first is a reflective exercise in which you ask yourself questions; the next is a visualization in which you see yourself becoming one with your dog, so you feel the connection more closely; the third is a physical exercise.

1) Picture This!

Hold the profile sheet with the picture of your dog and the description of characteristic personality traits in front of you. Then, in a very relaxed, reflective state, ask yourself a series of questions. Don't try to guide the answers; just let them come to you, as self-talk in your mind, or imagine that your chosen dog is answering you. As the answers come to you, write them down or say them into a recorder, so you can remember and review them later.

Start with the following questions, and add any additional questions that deal with issues important to you.

- In what ways does this dog reflect me?
- What common personality traits or characteristics do we share?
- What traits stand out as especially characteristic of us?
- What kind of traits does this dog have that I would like to have or develop further?
- What kind of changes might I make in myself to develop these traits I would like to have or further develop?
- How can this dog help me make these changes?
- How would or does this dog fit into my current lifestyle?
- In what ways might I change my current lifestyle to better suit this dog?
- What do I need to do now to make these changes?
- How can this dog help me make these changes?

- What else does this dog have to tell me about who I would like to be?
- What other questions might I ask at this time? (Then listen to the questions that come to mind and ask them).

2) <u>Putting on the Dog Head</u>

In this technique, you seek to feel a closer connection with your chosen dog by imagining that you and your dog have become one. It's a technique you can use to connect better with people, too, so you can see the world from their point of view by walking in their shoes. Using this metaphor, you might imagine yourself walking with their dog paws to see the world and yourself in a whole new way.

To start the process, you can read the following visualization as a guide and then do it. Or read this into a recorder and play it back as you listen and visualize.

To begin, gaze at the picture of the dog you have chosen – or if you own a real dog of this type, gaze at that. Look deep into the dog's eyes, and imagine that you both are becoming one. Imagine that you are coming closer and closer to each other. Finally, you merge, and as you do, see yourself placing the dog's head on your own; see your own arms and legs become the feet and paws of the dog.

Then, feeling this sense of oneness or this sense that you have become this dog, look around the world as this dog. First look around your house. Since you now have a better sense of hearing and smell, pay more attention to what you hear and notice any smells around you.

Then, imagine you are going outside your house as this dog. In your mind's eye, go out your door and pay attention to what you see, hear, smell, or feel. Notice the path or soft dirt beneath your feet. Walk or run across the grass. Notice if there are people in the lawn or on the street, and trot by, weaving in and out of any people there. If someone reaches down to pet you, enjoy the sensation on your back and keep on going.

Should you see any cars, stop and let them pass by, and keep going. You feel curious, interested in exploring and observing what's out there, and you know you can always quickly run back home.

So take a few minutes, now experiencing the world around you as the dog you have chosen. If you meet any people or dogs along the way, know that they will be very friendly and helpful. And some will be very curious. They want to know a little about who you are. So if they ask, be ready to tell them. Tell them who you are and how you have gone out to explore. So just look around and see what you discover. You'll find you are drawn to things you are most interested in – such as people walking along, objects on the street, playground equipment with tunnels to crawl through, or other dogs.

Now as you move on, you come to a shiny mirror lying on the grass or on the side of the road. Go over to that mirror and look into it. You'll see your own face or your dog's face peering back at you – or maybe a combination of your two faces. As you look in this mirror, you can ask a series of questions about yourself. Start with these few questions and listen for the answers. Don't try to guide the answers. Just let them come to you. Then, you can add in additional questions and listen for those answers or you may see them appear in the mirror.

Here are a few first questions to ask; then add your own:
- *Who am I? How would I describe myself, if someone asked me this question?*
- *What are my strongest traits? My weakest?*
- *Is there anything about me I'd like to change? And how?*
- *Is there anything I should do differently?*
- *What should I do now?*

Now, ask your own questions. What else do you want to know about yourself?

When the questions and answers stop coming, turn away from the mirror and walk back the way you came through the grass or on the road. As you return to where you started, count slowly from 1 to 5, becoming more and conscious as you do…1….2….3….more and more awake….4…and 5 – you're back in the room.

Once you're back, take a few minutes to write down what you have learned on a sheet of paper or in your notebook, so you can remember and review this information later and put it into practice in your everyday life.

3) <u>Dancing Your Dog</u>

Another method to feel closer to your dog traces back to the dawn of human history – the technique of dancing an animal to feel a closer connection with it and draw on that quality for oneself. Sometimes the dancers put on masks representing the animal they are dancing, to feel the bond more firmly. The difference here is that you are going to "dance your dog".

This technique is also a fun way to experiment with what it's like to act like a dog –like putting on a mask and dog costume for Halloween or to go to a costume party.

Before dancing, you can create images of your dog to add to the sense of personal transformation into something else. For example, create a mask to put on or put a picture of your dog on your jacket and wear that. Or put a poster or statue of your dog on a table or counter, to focus on it as you dance. Or use a combination of any of these possibilities. You goal is to strengthen the sense of transformation through the physical experience with visual, auditory and other cues, so you are more completely immersed in the experience. You might even include the sounds of dogs barking in the background for additional realism.

To prepare for the experience, put on a rhythmic recording to listen to. Or use drums, rattles, or other instruments to make sounds and provide a recurring beat to help you feel the experience more intensely. (Or if you are working with a partner or in a group, you can take turns having one or two people play, while the others dance.)

Once you are ready, start the music, and let yourself go for 10-15 minutes, longer if you want to keep going. Just feel the sounds going through you, and as you do, imagine you are becoming one with your dog. Imagine the dog's head on yours, and you are dancing as this dog. For now, don't ask any questions. Just let yourself go, so you fully feel the sense of transformation. As you do, move as you imagine your dog walks. React to others who pass by as your dog might. Notice any sounds in the room besides the music. Become aware of any smells. And feel free to bark, howl, or otherwise make the sounds your dog might make.

When the music ends or you feel ready to stop, turn off the music, and quietly stand or sit (or get down on all fours) so you feel the sense of being your dog.

Then, holding onto that feeling, ask yourself the questions listed in the previous exercise. These are:

- *Who am I? How would I describe myself, if someone asked me this question?*
- *What are my strongest traits? My weakest?*
- *Is there anything about me I'd like to change? And how?*
- *Is there anything I should do differently?*
- *What should I do now?*

Add your own questions to ask what else you want to know about yourself.

Keep going until you feel you are running out of questions and answers. Then, write down what you have experienced, so you can remember and refer to this later.

Watching Out with Your Watch Dog

After you explore ways to better understand yourself and what to change or develop with your Top Dog, go through the same process with your Watch Dog. Then, take some time to compare and reflect on the different results.

Your insights from working with your Top Dog indicate your strengths or what you most want to develop, while the insights from your Watch Dog indicate additional areas of strength and development.

If you get the same insights from both, that's a double message underlining your strength in this area or emphasizing that this is an area to focus on developing.

If you get different insights, regard those as additional traits or strengths that you have or additional qualities to work on developing, to become even more well-rounded. Generally, focus on developing the qualities represented by your Top Dog first.

Celebrating Your Strengths

Once you have identified your top qualities and strengths, it's time to celebrate and affirm them to yourself. The next chapter will deal will making changes on the traits or qualities to develop. But first, focus on the great traits and strengths that make up you – the qualities you share with your Top Dog and Watch Dog.

So go back to the lists you have already made–The Traits of My Top Dog and The Traits of My Watch Dog – and create a list with your strongest traits first, then your next strongest, and finally your least strongest (which also may be traits you want to further develop). You can use "My Qualities and Strengths" chart page to do this.

Then, create a fun environment to celebrate yourself. For example, go to your favorite room in the house, put on some bouncy music, put out a small cake or plate of cookies with a candle. Perhaps hang up pictures of the breed of dogs you have chosen as your Top Dog and Watch Dog. Do whatever you want to create a festive setting. Plus include a glass of wine or juice to toast yourself. If you want, add some small blue ribbons or buttons to symbolize the awards you are giving to yourself – much like a judge at a dog show might give an award to an owner and their dog. Now, this is your award to you to remind yourself what a winner you are.

Then, as you look at the list, imagine your Top Dog and Watch Dog are with you in spirit, perhaps even sitting on either side of you, and think or say the following "I am great because…" affirmations. Fill in each of the traits you have listed as you do this. After you state each affirmation, pick up your glass of wine or juice and drink a toast to yourself. You might also pat yourself on the back, take a bow, or applaud to compliment yourself. Finally, if you have some ribbons or buttons, give one to yourself, as your "Blue Ribbon" award for being you and having the great qualities you do.

Following are some of the affirmations you might use. Just fill in the traits you have on the list:

"I am great because I am_____"
"I'm wonderful because I_____"
"People really like me because I_____"

After you finish celebrating each of these traits, give yourself a final round of applause, take a final bow, give yourself a large blue ribbon, and/or drink a final toast to yourself to recognize the many ways in which you are great. Then, say a final thank you to your Top Dog and Watch Dog for helping you recognize these qualities in yourself, and take a minute or two to savor how great you feel for honoring and celebrating yourself.

My Top Qualities and Strengths	
My Strongest Traits:	
My Next Strongest Traits:	
My Least Strongest Traits:	

Making Your Top Dog and Watch Dog Part of Your Everyday Life

Beyond getting insights from your Top Dog and Watch Dog, you can make an even closer connection with them and remind yourself about how great you are and how you are further developing yourself every day in two ways – you can find representations of your Top Dog and Watch Dog and post visible reminders to yourself.

Here are some things you can do:
- Find a small furry stuffed dog or ceramic statue of the same breed as your Top Dog and/or Watch Dog and put it in a prominent place in your house. Besides using stuffed dogs or statues for a decorative reminder, you can use it during exercises as a focus to represent your Top Dog or Watch Dog.
- Put up a poster featuring the same breed as your Top Dog and/or Watch Dog.
- Get greeting cards or postcards featuring the same breed as your Top Dog and/or Watch Dog.
- Put up "My Top Qualities and Strengths" list in a place where you will see it each day, such as in the bathroom, on your bedroom door, or on the side of the refrigerator.
- Get a small keychain-sized image of the breed of your Top Dog and/or Watch Dog and dangle it from your car mirror.
- Make a rubber stamp with the image of the breed of your Top Dog and/or Watch Dog, and use it on your letters.
- Put pictures of the breed of your Top Dog and/or Watch Dog on your Website or on your Weblog if you have one.

Additionally, you might imagine that your Top Dog and Watch Dog are accompanying you and lending their support as you go about your daily activities, along with any Guide Dogs or Power Dogs you are calling on for help. The process is much like what is done in many traditions, where people call on a spiritual guide, inner teacher, or helper. Now, you can call on your Top Dog and Watch Dog, too, as well as your Guide Dogs and Power Dogs.

How the Process Works

How well does this process work? Here are some examples of people gaining insights from the dogs they preferred or identified with in one of my workshops.

Nancy picked a Bassett Hound as her first choice and owns one. She felt a close identification with her choice and found they shared many of the same personality traits. And sometimes her dog's behavior served as a reminder to her of how to behave.

Why choose a Basset Hound? Because she felt drawn to it as a nurse and very warm person. She thought the Bassett Hound's similar warm, affectionate qualities made it a perfect companion to take to a senior center where she volunteered. As Nancy explained: "My dog Marci loves being with the elderly people. Marci's so gentle and loving, and she has the same care and compassion for others that I have. Also, she's got the same concern with behaving and doing what's right."

Nancy gave an example. "Sometimes I correct her, just like my mother used to correct me when I was a kid. I remember one time Marci got really excited when the mailman came, and she barked really ferociously – very unusual for her, because she is usually so calm and placid. But I quickly looked her in the eye and said "No", and she looked taken aback and guilty. She hung her head sheepishly and retreated to the living room. After that, when the mailman came, I saw her looking at me, as if to say, 'I know I shouldn't do that.' Then, she ran into the living room and didn't bark. Her behavior reminded me very much of me. I like to do what's right, and I very much like the approval that comes from knowing I've done the right thing."

By the same token, whether you own the dog or not, you might imagine your Top Dog or Watch Dog sitting beside you or walking with you giving you insights about yourself.

To take another example, in another workshop, one woman encountered a tiger and a panther who she thought represented two aspects of herself; an experience much like working with one's Top Dog and Watch Dog. As she thought about the qualities of the tiger and panther, she saw how they expressed her own qualities and suggested what she needed to do to develop herself – by seeking more balance in her life while she was going through a period of making choices.

Here's how she reported her experience and came to her insights, with the help of these two animals:

"When the journey started out, I came into a jungle, and the first animal that I met was a monkey, and he jumped on me. But I knew it wasn't my power animal. It was more like he was a greeter, just showing me the way.

Then I met a tiger and a black panther and they had very different qualities. The tiger reminded me of the tiger I had dreamt about twice the last two weeks. In both dreams, I slept with the tiger, and the tiger was very loving. We slept in each other's arms, like old friends. As for the panther, he reminded me of my sun sign, which is Scorpio. It's a very sharp, penetrating sign which represents my very deep, cutting edge that's harsh and slices through things.

So it felt like the tiger and the panther were my two sides. I felt like the tiger was the soft part, the panther the hard part, and now I felt drawn to that soft part. So instead of walking along with the tiger, I decided to go inside it, and it felt very good and powerful being in there.

Then, I switched back and forth, walking between those two cats and being inside the tiger. It was like I was experiencing the polarity of yin and yang, and finding that balance between them.

When I went inside the tiger, I felt very grounded. I felt a wonderful, strong, powerful feeling of being inside and being the cat, and I felt this wonderful feeling of soft power, which was helping me come to term with my female power by experiencing this warmth and nurturing, which I need right now. So it's like this tiger was my soft feminine aspect, while the panther was my cutting and aggressive masculine side.

I felt like having both of them walking side by side with me was showing me the two aspects of my power, which I'm trying to come to terms with, by getting more in touch with my feminine side."

As these examples illustrate, the process of finding your Top Dog or Watch Dog can be a powerful way of gaining personal insights, whether you own the dog or not, much like the taking a journey to connect with any animal representing you can provide deep insights about yourself and what to do next for your personal and professional development. Then you can later further your journey to learn even more.

Getting to Know Your Underdog

Now it's finally time to get to know your Underdog, that represents the qualities you don't have or least like in yourself and want to eliminate. You may not naturally want to look at these Underdog qualities but a key part of personal and professional development is getting rid of any traits you least like and replacing them with those you want.

You'll use the same kind of exercises as you used to better get to know your Top Dog and Watch Dog, but now your focus will be on getting rid of qualities, rather than embracing them.

First, pull out the Dog Profile corresponding to your Underdog. Now, look at this description and review the traits characterizing this type of dog. If you have other associations with this breed, add them. Then, in a relaxed frame of mind, reflect on these different traits and particularly on those you don't like.

Now, as you look at these traits, make a list of all the traits or characteristics you don't like about this dog, which is why this dog is your Underdog. Note any traits which you feel you now have but don't like about yourself; these are the traits you want to get rid of.

You can use the chart on the following page to help you make your list. List all the traits that come to mind in no particular order. Then, for each trait, put down the number 0, 1, 2, or 3, depending on how strongly you feel you have that trait. If you have put down a "0", great; time to celebrate because you don't have that trait. Then, in the next column, indicate how strongly you would like to get rid of those traits you don't like. (The higher the number, the more strongly you feel).

This process will help you think about the qualities you have and don't want in yourself.

Traits of my Underdog:		
Type of Dog:_____		
Traits	Traits I Have (use 0-3 to indicate their strength)	Traits I'd Like to Get Rid of (use 1-3 to indicate strength)

1) What's Wrong with This Picture?

Start by holding the profile sheet with the picture of your dog in front of you. Then, in a relaxed, reflective state, ask yourself a series of questions. Don't try to guide the answers, just let them come to you, either as self-talk in your mind, or imagine that the dog you have chosen is answering you. As the answers come to you, write them down or say them into a recorder to remember and review them later.

Start with the following questions. Add additional questions that deal with issues important to you.
- Why do I least like this particular dog?
- What traits does it have that I don't like?
- Which of these traits that I don't like do I also have?
- What traits would I like to get rid of in myself?
- What kind of changes might I make in myself to get rid of these traits? How can this dog help me make these changes?
- What else does this dog have to tell me about who I am or would like to be?
- What other questions might I ask at this time? (Listen to the questions that come to mind and ask them).

2) Putting Out the Dog

In this technique, you seek to experience an even stronger feeling of getting rid of those traits you don't want by imagining that you are putting out the dog. You can use this technique to mentally eliminate negative or difficult people from your life, too. See yourself opening the door and sending the dog away –to a backyard doghouse or further away than that.

As an alternative to doing this as a visualization, ask yourself: "What are the reasons I don't like this dog?" Then, think of any reasons that first pop into your mind and write them down. Review that list and notice what qualities you have yourself which you don't like. Choose one or two to focus on as qualities to work on eliminating from your life – and skip to the next section.

To start the visualization process, you can read the following guide and then do it. Or read this into a recorder and play it back as you listen and visualize.

> *To begin, gaze at the picture of the dog you have chosen. Look deep into its eyes, and as you do, think about the reasons that you don't like this dog. Notice the qualities that you don't like in this dog and that you don't want in yourself. Focus on the one or two qualities you most dislike and most want out of your life.*
>
> *Then, in your mind's eye, imagine that this dog is in your house. It might be in the kitchen begging for food; in the living room making noise; in the bedroom making a mess. Wherever it is, you don't want it there anymore, because it has those qualities you don't like in the dog and in yourself.*
>
> *Now call that dog to you, and if it doesn't want to come, since it may be badly behaved, snap on its leash and pull it to you. Then, lead your dog to your back door and open it.*
>
> *Now as you stand there, think about the reasons you want this dog out of your life. Think about the qualities it has that you don't want, to remind yourself why you are getting rid of this dog.*
>
> *Then, tell the dog to go out and go to its dog house – or just tell it to go. Explain why it has to go in various ways. You might say: "I don't want you anymore…It's time to go…You are not welcome here anymore."*
>
> *Even if the dog looks sad or doesn't want to go, keep repeating these words to reinforce your message. If your dog still sits waiting, hoping you'll let it back in, simply tap it on the back, push it out, and shut the door.*
>
> *As your Underdog leaves, watch it go, feeling that it is taking the trait or traits you don't want away with it.*

Later, you can use this experience as a reminder that you don't want this trait, that you are getting rid of it, that it is gone or going away.

Finally, as you see your Underdog disappear in the distance or go into its dog house, turn away from the door. Walk back into your living room, feeling very free and comfortable that your Underdog and the trait or traits you want to get rid of are gone and unlikely to reappear. Then, count slowly from 1 to 5, becoming more and conscious as you do…1….2….3….more and more awake….4…and 5 – you're back in present day reality.

Once you're back, take a few minutes to write down what you have experienced on a sheet of paper or in your notebook, and end with a positive affirmation about the trait or traits you have sent away with your dog. For example, note something like: "My anger is gone…I'm not angry anymore…I'll be calmer in the future." You might even put these comments on cards around your house as a reminder of the trait or traits you want out of your life.

3) Going, Going, Gone

To further emphasize that this quality you don't want is gone, physically sweep it away. Just like "Dancing the Dog" is an adaptation of the technique of dancing an animal that traces back to the dawn of human history this method is modeled after the technique of eliminating negative forces by sweeping them away. Such techniques have been traditionally used to get rid of illness or unfriendly spirits through various means – from brooms to brushes to bundles of leaves to cleanse a person. Here the technique is adapted to getting rid of qualities you don't want in yourself – like "making a clean sweep", where you sweep out the old, and open yourself up to the new.

You can visualize this process by imagining that you are using a broom, brush, or bundle of leaves – or better yet, hold a broom, brush, or leaf bundle in your hands, and physically do this cleansing and sweeping. Doing this physically makes this experience even more intense, so you feel this sense of ridding yourself of unwanted traits more clearly. You can use a broom or brush you find around the house, or create a bundle of leaves by gathering fallen leaves from your backyard or park, since these are already dead. To prepare for the experience, put on a rhythmic piece of music to listen to, particularly one with a strong forceful beat to underline your strength and power in taking action. Or use drums, rattles, or other instruments to make sounds and provide a recurring beat to feel the experience more intensely. If you are working with a partner or group, you can take turns having one or two people play, while the others dance.

Once you are ready, start the music, and let yourself go for 5-10 minutes, longer if you want to keep going. Just feel the sounds going through you and imagine that your Underdog is in a circle with you. Then, in your imagination – or in reality if you are holding a real broom, brush, or bundle of leaves – begin sweeping or brushing the trait or traits you don't want away. As you do, your Underdog backs off, moving further and further away, as you sweep or brush harder and harder. As it moves back, imagine that it is taking the trait or traits you don't want in yourself with it. So more and more you are casting off these qualities.

Finally, your Underdog turns and runs out of the room. As it does, imagine that these qualities are going away, too. Finally, when you can no longer see your Underdog, imagine these traits are gone for good and even say those words aloud to yourself. "They are gone…gone…gone."

When the music ends or you feel ready to stop, turn it off, and quietly stand or sit (or get down on all fours), so you feel the sense of satisfaction at sending away that trait or traits. So you feel a sense of cleansing and of being newly liberated and free.

Moving On

The exercises in this chapter have provided different ways for learning more about your chosen dogs and yourself. By knowing who you are and want to be, you can think about what to do to get there. Then with these insights, you can work with your Top Dog, Watch Dog, and Underdog to help you make these changes – or call on your Guide Dogs and Power Dogs, as well, so you have your whole Dog Team behind you, helping you change.

CHAPTER 7: FIND YOUR INNER GUIDE DOG – OR DOGS

Even before choosing your favorite dog or the one most like you, you can get help from your inner guide dog or a team of dogs that sometimes may be the same as your Top Dog or Watch Dog or could later attain this position.

Essentially, an inner guide dog is one you can call on for assistance in various circumstances – from setting goals to dealing with difficult situations. The process works much like calling on any inner help for guidance, strength, wisdom, and power with the assistance of a spiritual guide, helper, teacher, angel, or animal guide. It's an approach used in many traditions – from traditional religions to spiritual paths to New Age groups.

Now you can call on one of the many breeds of dogs for help. Just call on the guide that seems most suitable for you in a particular situation. It could be one you turn to regularly – or call on a different dog for different occasions, or as a comic might say, you simply turn to your "inner guide dog" by calling up images of that dog in your mind's eye. Then, you ask that dog to help in various ways.

Here's how the process works.

Which Guide Dog Is for You?

The great thing in calling on your inner guide dog is you can look for different dogs to help you in different situations. They can be dogs you are already familiar with, or use the Dog Profiles to become acquainted with other breeds and types of dogs.

You are simply calling on a type of dog that can give you the most help under the circumstances. Say you are struggling to lose weight and so far no diet has helped, and you just don't have the will-power to stay on it. That's where your guide dog comes in.

You pick a dog that might be especially good to help you strengthen your resolve, such as a Standard Poodle or Afghan Hound, who both are known for being thin, beautiful, and stylish.

Then, with the image of that dog in mind, call on it to give you advice and remind you to stay on target. You might also take steps to remind yourself to call on that dog, such putting up a poster with its picture on the bathroom wall, where you will see it several times a day. Or make or buy a sculpture of that dog.

Some people have regular conversations with their guide dogs, too. The process works much like self-talk, where you have a dialogue with yourself – or a group discussion between different parts of you. But instead, you talk to your inner guide dog like a helpful friend, advisor, or teacher, just like any spiritual guide or helper. Contacting your Guide Dog is a way of personifying a part of you. What makes this process especially helpful is turning an abstract voice in your head into a "real" being, so you gain more support, as you might from a real person offering to help.

Using Your Inner Guide Dog for Different Purposes

While some people may like calling on the same dog for different purposes, others may prefer finding dogs with different qualities to help them with issues that call for those qualities.

Take Mary, an administrative assistant, who has found it comfortable to call on a Collie to help in different situations. She was especially drawn to a Collie after doing an exercise to look for her Guide Dog, and she found calling in the dogs helped her feel more comfortable in a high-conflict work environment. When she heard some co-workers arguing down the hall and felt herself getting tense, she would lean back and call on the image of this warm, protective Collie to appear and tell her to relax. And, she would. Or if her critical boss berated her for something, she would imagine the Collie by her side, telling her: "Be cool. Be cool." So she was able to keep her cool – and her job, rather than telling off the boss in the heat of the moment.

Subsequently, she called on the Collie to help with other tasks, reasoning that if he helped her in these circumstances, he would be a worthy helper in other situations. Then, as she thought this, the Collie would give her the help she needed because you give the dogs you call on the power to help by calling them into reality.

But often, people call on different breeds of dogs in different situations, based on the qualities they associate with that dog. For example, if you feel too tense much of the time and want to become more relaxed, maybe call on the Beagle or Bassett Hound, because these are two very laid-back dogs. They are often found parked on the family couch or cozy armchair, and like to hang out. By calling up the image of either dog, you similarly cause yourself to become more relaxed.

Or suppose you want more "Power", because you were left behind at work after a round of promotions. You think you aren't being recognized for your true worth, because you don't have enough power and you feel a need to be more assertive, aggressive, and thick-skinned to get the recognition from others to get ahead. In this case, a likely candidate for your inner guide dog might be the Great Dane, Mastiff, or Bull Mastiff. These are strong, powerful, big dogs – and an infusion of this image might be just what you need to help you take on your co-workers and boss. For instance, as you focus on that image at home, you can see the power you want pouring into you. Then, you can go to work with that sense of the Great Dane or Mastiff within you.

Some Exercises to Connect and Communicate with Your Inner Guide Dog

If you are already familiar with different breeds of dogs, start with the exercises right away. If not, take some time to review the Dog Type Profiles or list of dogs to become familiar with them and feel you really know them.

Then, you can use various exercises to connect with your Inner Guide Dog just to get acquainted or for help with a particular issue. Use the exercises that feel most comfortable for you.

As an alternative to doing a visualization, ask yourself the question: "Which dog would I like to be my Guide Dog?" and listen to the first impression or thought that comes to mind. Then, repeat the question to pick additional Guide Dogs. While these visualization exercises are fun and help you access your intuition and powers of creativity, you can tap into your these abilities in other ways.

To do any of the visualization exercises, first get into a comfortable, relaxed state. To help you relax, you can use repetitive drumming, listen to relaxing soothing music, or focus on your breathing as you count backward slowly from 10 to 1. Then, use one of the following exercises. Use the descriptions below as a general guide or recite the exercises into a recorder, play it back, relax, and enjoy your journey to meet your dog.

Before you begin, decide if you want to connect with a Dog Guide generally or for help with a particular issue or problem. In the latter case, keep that issue or problem in mind as you go on your journey.

Pet Store

In the following guided journey, you'll imagine going to a pet store where you see many different kinds of dogs and choose one.

Now imagine that you are going into a very large pet store either to find a dog guide to help you generally or to help with a particular problem or issue. You arrive in the parking lot, park, and walk into the store.

As you walk in, you see a large ring where many dogs are exercising. Then you see several long rows with dogs of different breeds sitting in small cubicles or cages.

As you walk along through the rooms, some of the dogs move forward to greet you. Nod or smile at them as you pass. You may find that one dog is particularly eager to greet you, or you feel particularly drawn to that dog.

Stop and take some time to make a connection with that dog. You can shake its paw, perhaps imagine that you have become that dog's owner. Then, talk to it. Ask it some questions about what it likes and doesn't, what activities it prefers, and most importantly how it can help you. Don't try to control the answers to your questions; just let them come to you.

If you feel comfortable with that dog and would like it to become your helper, take it home with you. Lead it out or pick it up and take it to your car.

Then, with the dog on the seat beside or behind you, drive home slowly, feeling very confident and secure that you have found your Inner Dog guide to help you generally or with a particular problem.

Dog Director

In this case, you imagine yourself as a director of a movie which deals with the area where you want help. Start by consciously deciding on the issues you want help with – or if you're not sure, let that come to you. The following guided journey will help you become this director and find your "cast" of "top dogs" to help you with this "movie".

Imagine that you are a director for a movie that deals with an issue where you need help in your life. If you haven't already decided what the movie will be about, decide now. Think about what problems or concerns are most important to you and see that scene in your life playing out on the movie screen in your mind. Notice what particularly bothers you, what is especially difficult, and where you would like some help.

Now imagine that you are putting out a casting call for help. After you do, you see a number of dogs come in through the door and head over to a bench by the wall. They sit down side by side in a long row.

Now you go over to talk to them one by one, or you call them in turn to come over to you. Conduct your interview to ask each dog how he or she can help. Look for ways a particular dog might be likely to help. For example, say you are having a problem being assertive and powerful; maybe a large powerful dog would be especially helpful. Or suppose the issue involves relationships and teamwork. Maybe a dog that is especially friendly and good with people would help. Don't try to direct the answers; just let them come to you.

Should other dogs suddenly appear for an interview, that's fine. Just invite them in. Or if you feel you would like more dogs to talk to, imagine you are extending your casting call.

Now take some time to talk to each of the dogs. As you do, ask questions, such as: "How can you help me?" "What would you do in this situation?" or "What would you like to see happen in this film?"

Then, invite the dog or dogs you feel would be most helpful to join you on the set. As you see the movie play out before you, ask that dog to help you direct the outcome. You can either ask for advice or invite the dog to go into the movie. For instance, say you want to stand up to someone; that dog might go in front of that person and bark. Say you want a warmer relationship with someone. You might imagine the dog bounding on the set to be affectionate with that person.

Now, take some time to ask your guide dog (or dogs) for help and let them give you that help.

Finally, when you feel ready to wrap up your movie for the day, thank your guide dog (or dogs) for the help you have received, knowing you can always call on that dog for guidance and help in the future.

Dog Team Leader

Another technique for finding your Guide Dogs is viewing yourself as a "Dog Team Leader", assembling your team to help you get to a goal or resolve a problem. This time, instead of using a visualization, you'll create a list of major issues or areas to improve and the type of Dog Guide who might most help in that area.

These areas correspond to the 12 dimensions or "Dog Houses" on the Dog Star. You may find some of the same guides can help in different areas – or different dogs may be most helpful in each area.

Just go down the list and think of the first dog that comes to mind to help you with this area. Later, you can always go back and come up with other helpers to replace or add to those you have selected. It helps to develop an ongoing relationship with your guides over time, just as you might get more help by cultivating a continuing relationship with a friend, teacher, or counselor. Then, you can always seek-out extra help from other sources, or you can even bring in experts when you need more specialized help. So, why not with your Guide Dogs? They are there to help you – so seek out the guides who offer the most help under the current circumstances.

Digging Deep to Find Your Guide Dogs

In the following technique, you journey deep into the earth to meet your Guide Dogs. This technique draws on the shamanic journeying approach that has become increasingly popular as the subject of many workshops and seminars on "Shamanism" today, although it is an ancient tradition that goes back to the dawn of human society. You can use this technique to meet any power animals or teachers, although I adapted one of the exercises to focus on meeting your Guide Dogs.

So now, get your dog sled, so to speak, and be ready to travel on it to another world. Use the following guided journey as a general instruction by reading it beforehand, or read it into a recorder and play it back as you relax and take your journey.

Start by getting relaxed, and in a few minutes, you'll be going on a journey into the lower world. First, focus on your breathing to get in this relaxed state. Notice your breath going in and out, in and out. You find yourself getting relaxed, but you are also staying alert and awake. Let your breathing go in and out; in and out; feeling very peaceful and relaxed, yet very aware as well.

Be aware of your purpose in going on this journey below the earth. You are going to meet a power animal – in this case, one of your inner Guide Dogs. But don't try to meet that dog yet or decide what kind of dog you want to meet. Just let that happen when you go down there.

Find an opening to go down to this lower world. This opening could be someplace in the country, or city, someplace you're familiar with, or someplace new. It's some kind of opening going down to the ground.

See yourself going to the opening. As you go in, you find yourself in a tunnel or tube, and you feel very comfortable and very safe. There's plenty of room to move around. See or experience yourself moving through this tunnel. You are going down, down. Then, as you come to the bottom or end of this tunnel, it opens up into this lower world.

Now look around. Notice what you see, hear, feel. Notice your surroundings. It could be a little like a cave, or it could open up on a landscape. Experience yourself moving and looking around in this lower world, noticing what you see, feel. Experience whatever happens.

Now start going around to look for your Guide Dog. As you look, you may see different animals and different kinds of dogs wandering around. One of these dogs will stand out for you, come to you, or seem drawn to you. Or if you don't see that dog at once, keep going and pass by other places, other animals, until you feel drawn to one of these dogs or notice one that seems drawn to you. Then, go over to that dog or have it come to you.

Now meet it; get acquainted. Simply talk to it, and make friends with it. As you talk to or experience that dog, you may feel that this dog represents a little part of you, too. So, notice the qualities that dog has, and as you do, you might notice how these represent qualities of yourself.

You might also ask that dog if it has anything to tell you about itself, such as where it has been, what it does in the lower world, what it likes to do, or other questions. Then, listen to its response.

Now, as you get to know this dog, feel this dog is ready to be helpful. You can come back and visit this dog again and call on it for the help or advice you need in the future. The more you get to know this dog, the more help it will give you, and the more it will be a source of information and power for you.

If you want, follow this dog around and let it take you on a short journey, so you can explore a little bit more of this lower world and notice what's there. There's a path there you can follow. It could be straight or it might wander around. As you travel along it, you feel very safe taking this path, for your Guide Dog is with you. And you know this is just the beginning of exploring this world. Later, when you come back, you can meet this Guide Dog again, or you can meet other Guide Dogs and explore further. But for now, keep walking around with your Guide Dog. As you do, you might be aware of the heat, or coolness. You might be aware of the sounds around you. You might notice if there are any smells. Just get a real sense of this total environment as you explore.

Now, you are ready to go back. So you turn around, and your Guide Dog is starting to lead you back to where you first met it. On the way, your Guide Dog tells you that he will be there waiting for you the next time you come to see him. If you find this Guide Dog continues to be helpful, you can continue to visit it. But feel free to go back to meet other Guide Dogs, that can be helpful to you later.

Now you are back where you first met. So say good-bye to your Guide Dog as you would to any friend.

Then, travel back along the same path, and go back to the tunnel again. Now you are traveling through the tunnel back to the opening.

At the opening, step back out to where you began, and start counting backward from five to one. As you do, you will feel more and more awake and alert, and come back into the room. Five, four, more and more awake. Three, two, just about back. One, and you are back in the room.

Now that you have met your Guide Dog, as in other exercises to meet these dogs, think about what this experience means and how your Guide Dog can help you.

A Chart to Keep Track of Your Guide Dogs and How They Can Help

Use this chart to list your Guide Dogs. As you complete your list, feel free to repeat the breeds of dogs to call on for help. You can select more than one type of Guide Dog for each category, and later select one as your primary Guide Dog or work with those you have selected as a team. You can give each Guide Dog a name, or wait until you call on that dog for help.

LIST OF GUIDE DOGS		
Type of Issue	Breed of Guide Dog to be Asked for Help	Name of Helper
Becoming stronger and more powerful		
Exercising leadership		
Becoming more assertive		
Having more energy		
Working faster and smarter		
Achieving more balance in my activities and life		
Become a better people person		
Increasing my ability to influence others		
Becoming a better team player		
Improving my ability to think and remember		
Improving my style and appearance		
Developing selected personality traits		
Other:		
Other:		

Getting the Help You Need

However you have chosen your Guide Dogs, you can turn to them at any time – just as you might with any kind of inner guide or inner voice– from using spiritual helpers and teachers to self-talk.

Initially, it helps to use some quiet time to develop the relationship. By taking time to know each of your Guide Dogs as friends and companions, this will help you open up communication channels and feel comfortable turning to them, so later, they will be there when you want their help.

Getting Acquainted

To get acquainted, spend about 15-20 minutes a day having a mental dialogue with one or more of your Guide Dogs. A good way to do so is by getting relaxed in a quiet room in your house. An ideal time is just before you go to bed.

If you keep a journal, you can write down your conversations and thoughts there. Or use automatic writing to record the advice you get by writing in a very relaxed state, where you become a channel for whatever thoughts or words come to you. Then, you write them down without consciously thinking about what you are writing. In effect, your unconscious is speaking to you – through the communication you get from your Guide Dogs.

Asking for Help

When you are ready and receptive, start the conversation or dialogue as you might with any real person and listen for the answer. Let it come from you without your trying to consciously direct it – and respond. Some questions to ask might be something like:

"How are you doing?"
"How was your day? What did you do?"

In many cases, you might get the kind of answers you would expect from a dog, such as: "Oh, I hung out in the backyard," or "I had fun running around in the woods and catching balls." But in other cases, your Guide Dog might give you the kind of answers a person would, such as: "Oh, I went to your office, and I hung around the water cooler listening to what people were saying. "Accept whatever comes as part of getting acquainted.

After you break the ice, ask about whatever issue is important for you now. Ask for suggestions or images that will help you deal with whatever the situation is. For example, ask something like:

"I don't know what to do about my conflict at work with my boss. Can you give me some advice?

"I'm trying to make a hard decision now. What decision do you think I should make and why? Or can you give me a sign to know what to do?"

You can also ask your Dog Guide for specific steps to take, such as what to do next and then what to do after that to reach your goal.

Whatever your questions, whatever help you are seeking, as you get your message, write it down. You can use that input later in the real situation you have asked about. Writing it down will help you remember what to do and be more thoughtful about the suggestions you have been given. Then you can further assess how and when to use this advice, or determine if you need further information to best put this input into practice.

Getting Help on a Dog Walk

Another way to gain insights is by going on a Dog Walk with one or more of your Guide Dogs. This approach is like going on a journey to get help from a wise teacher, counselor, animal helper, or other being with knowledge. But here you are, getting insights from one of your Guide Dogs. They are like "Seeing Eye Dogs" helping you see things in new ways.

To do this Dog Walk technique, imagine yourself on local park trail walking with your Guide Dog (or team of guide dogs) to a place where you will gain new insights. You can either go with your dog or send your dog ahead to get this information and bring it back to you.

Use the following guided journey to help you on this walk. Read it first and play it back as you listen in a comfortable, relaxed state.

Get relaxed and imagine you are in a park or wooded area, about to walk along a trail to get an answer to a problem or issue in your life. It is a nice warm, comfortable, sunny day. You have brought along one of your Guide Dogs who you think can best help you with this issue. Or take along two or three Guide Dogs for extra help.

Now, start walking along the path, the dogs by your side or walking a little in front of you. Let them go ahead if they want to explore or lead the way for you.

As you walk on, think about the issue or problem you want to deal with. See it in on the horizon ahead in your mind's eye.

Now you come to a meadow with a tall tree and a large pool of water. Go over to that tree and sit down under it, with your Guide Dog or Dogs beside you.

Now reflect on your issue even more. As you do, tell your Guide Dog or Dogs about the problem. Explain what is especially difficult or upsetting about the situation. As you explain, your Guide Dog or Dogs listen quietly, eager to understand and show their support. Take some time now to tell them your thoughts and feelings about the problem.

When you feel complete about what you have shared, get up with your dog or dogs and walk over to the pool of water. Then, look in the water and ask what you should do now.

Observe what happens. You may see the answer appear in the water as an image or an object. You may hear a voice with the answer. You may see a person or animal come out of the water with information to give you.

Ask your Guide Dog or Dogs to help you get that information. For example, send your Guide Dog out to retrieve an object floating on the water. Ask it to accompany you to meet that person or animal.

Then, pay attention to whatever answer you get and ask your Guide Dog or Dogs for help in putting that answer into practice. For instance, ask your Guide Dog: "What should I do now?" and listen to the answer. Later, you can ask your Guide Dog more questions or for ongoing support as you put this advice into practice.

Putting the Advice You Get Into Action

Once you have gotten insights into what to do, the next step is to put that advice into action.

In some cases, this may involve working out a plan for what to do, and you can always turn to one of your Guide Dogs to help your planning. For example, say you realize you need to be more open and communicative with a partner. You might have a mental conversation with your Guide Dog about what to do; then write down your Guide Dog's suggestions.

Or if you already have a clear vision of what to do, you might look to your Guide Dog for support, much as you might ask a friend or spiritual helper to be with you. Say your insight is that you need to quit your job and strike out on your own by creating your own business. You might ask your Guide Dog to be with you as you take these steps. Or suppose you have called on a Bull Dog for his strength, courage, and tenacity in confronting a boss with whom you have had a difficult relationship. You might imagine the Bulldog with you as you go into your boss's office, giving you the courage to say what you really want to say, along with the thick skin to not feel upset regardless of your boss's response. Then, when you go to that meeting in reality, imagine that the Bulldog is coming with you, giving you that support, strength, and courage you need to confront your boss.

Using the Qualities of Your Guide Dog to Help

Another way to get help is to call on the Guide Dogs with the qualities you need for a particular situation.

For example, in the problem boss situation, suppose you are suddenly confronted by that boss who is angry about some problem and you have to react. If you feel a strong response is appropriate, say because your boss is unfairly accusing you of something, you might imagine that you have a tough, large, aggressive Guide Dog, giving you the strength and power to respond in a tough, firm way. Or say you feel it would be more political to take the abuse without getting personally upset, because you know your boss has a low boiling point but the problem will soon blow over if you don't react to make it worse. Then you might draw on the help of a Guide Dog who has a quality of stoic forbearance, such as a German Shepherd. In this case, you might imagine this dog there beside you, giving you the quiet strength to listen and stay calm, without getting angry.

You can also call on your Guide Dogs for help with a more personal relationship. Say you want to be more open and affectionate in your relationships, since you feel your reserve is holding you back from obtaining greater depth and intimacy. You might call on a Guide Dog with these qualities, such as a very affectionate Pomeranian or cuddly Pug, that is beside you coaching you on how to be more warm and cuddly yourself. Or perhaps imagine yourself as this Pomeranian or Pug to help you act warm and affectionate.

In short, you can call on your Guide Dog not only for advice but to help you express the qualities of this type of dog.

Some Examples of Working with Guide Dogs for Help

Here are some examples of how people have worked with Guide Dogs, drawn from workshops I conducted on working with power animals. In this program, the participants found different kinds of dogs to help them, using varied techniques.

One expressive, outgoing woman met a very playful little dog that reflected a warm, playful quality. As she described it:

"I ended up in a place where there was a small pond with trees next to it. I entered by going into the water and went through the tunnel. When I got to the end, I stepped into this place with the pond and the trees...

The animal I met was a little dog with a really long nose. It was like a cartoon character. It seemed to be always smiling, but very wise. It was running around and leaping up and down, and I felt I could really relate to it, because I could feel the excitement, too. It had this spontaneous energy. And it was very curious, eager to find out what's coming next, and very attentive. It seemed to be very independent, too...

I guess you could say those traits characterize me, too. Anyway, I liked this friendly little cartoon dog."

In this case, the woman was only trying to learn about herself by meeting her Guide Dogs, but you can also use these contacts to get information on how to deal with a particular situation in your life, as the following woman did. As her experience indicates, information may not always come to you directly, but may be in the form of symbols or signs you must interpret. At times, the information may give you guidance about some specific action to take; but at other times, the visualization or journey may be a way to release your feelings about something, so you feel a sense of completion or resolution; then there is nothing more to do.

That's what happened for one woman who had been feeling very angry about some damage she believed her neighbor did to her property. She went on a journey in which her animal helped to symbolically heal her property and take symbolic revenge on her neighbor. Afterward she felt better because she had released her negative feelings toward her neighbor.

When such negative or destructive images appear in a visualization or journey, that doesn't mean you should act on them. Rather, this experience acts as a psychological healing, which released back feelings of anger and hostility. Later, should such feelings continue to surface, you can engage in similar exercises to do more releasing.

Here's how she used a journey to express and release her long-standing anger. In this workshop, where people were invited to call on any animal for help, she imagined a gorilla coming to her aid. But if she had been calling on her Guide Dogs, she could have easily asked any of the more powerful dogs for help – such as a Great Dane. So instead of the gorilla, I have used a Great Dane in telling her story of how calling on a power animal helped.

"I went down into the tunnel, and immediately I saw this huge Great Dane, and I went up to him and asked him my question: 'How can I get revenge on my enemy?' and he said: 'Who is your enemy?' Then, I explained it was my neighbor who mutilated my oak tree while I was on vacation.

So he just beckoned to me, and I followed him, and he went up this long, long tunnel. Then we went out and across the street. I showed him the neighbor, and I could see him through his kitchen window. Then, I showed him my mutilated oak tree.

So he climbed up in the oak tree, and I realized then why I picked a Great Dane as my animal, because he was so strong, powerful, and protective. Then, he started patting the tree, as if encouraging the tree to grow.

After that, he came down and went into the neighbor's yard. Then he climbed up the neighbor's tree, and whack. He took off the top of his tree. At this point the neighbor came out, and the Great Dane took the neighbor and bashed his head open on the step, which gave me great satisfaction. Then, he went loping off up the street, waving goodbye. And he left me on my doorstep feeling gratified."

After such a journey, the next step is to interpret it. In some cases, the experience might suggest a plan of action, though here, the experience recalled a fantasy scenario of what you would like to do if you could, although realistically, you know you can't. (After all, you can't bash in the head of your neighbor, no matter how much he or she annoys you). In this case, the visualization or journey becomes a way to symbolically act out what you can't do in real life, so you can release your pent up feelings associated with the situation and move on.

The process is akin to writing an angry letter to someone, but not mailing it. The writing process gets out the anger; but you realize mailing the letter would only create worse problems, so you tear it up, and feel better for having written it.

You decide what's appropriate when you review your experience, determine what it means, and choose whether to act on it or just view it as source of insight and release. That's what the woman who got help from the Great Dane did. As she explained: "I've been puzzling and puzzling and trying to figure out what to do about my neighbor, and that's why I asked the Great Dane." But when she considered her options – from secretly going to her neighbor's property and cutting down his tree or sending in lawyers to do battle in court, she decided that it was more appropriate to consider the journey as a way of symbolically getting the revenge she had wanted to get.

Getting this symbolic revenge worked well for her because she reported that she felt better, and more satisfied seeing him and his tree injured symbolically, so she had been able to release some of her anger.

"Then, if I still feel angry in the future," she commented, "maybe I might go on a similar journey again to release more anger, and keep doing this until the anger is gone."

As she recognized, any direct real world actions against the neighbor might only inflame and escalate an already bad situation, thus using the journey in a symbolic way made the most sense, though in other cases, a journey might suggest real world options.

If you're not sure after reviewing a visualization or journey whether to take action or use it symbolically, you can always go on another journey to get clarification. To do so, simply begin your journey with the question: "Should I take some action based on my previous journey? Or should I use my journey symbolically?" Then, go to meet one of your inner Guide Dogs to learn what to do.

In other cases, your experience may suggest this isn't a question or problem to deal with now, because you can do nothing or need to wait before taking action. Sometimes your Guide Dog will tell you this directly, or if you get a jumble of confusing images or blanks, this can indicate that you should wait to act because you need to get a clearer picture of what to do.

This was the experience of a woman who turned to a Pomeranian to learn what to do about her love life. She chose a Pomeranian for help because it is a very warm, friendly, loving, affectionate dog. So what better dog to ask about love?

Unfortunately, when she asked her question and went on a journey to find the answers, she kept getting blanks and a lot of disconnected images which she didn't understand. As she reported:

"My journey didn't make any sense to me. I went back into the lower world, and when I got there, my little dog was very happy to see me. And I said: 'Here I am. I want to know about my love life and what should I do about it?'

But then, I just saw blanks for the longest time. So I thought about this one guy that I know now, and his image gradually faded away. So I began thinking that might mean I should do nothing about my love life now.

Then, I saw a street light, and I felt it was night and I thought I'll just stand on a street corner. But after I did, I wasn't getting anything. I was just standing there, and when I looked around, I saw a lot of blanks and a series of images that faded in and out. Everything seemed so disconnected.

Then, I felt it's time to go and felt unsatisfied, because I really didn't see anything. But then I said to myself, "Well, there's nothing out there, because there's nothing really you can or need to do right now.

So I guess that's what my little dog was trying to tell me. Don't do anything now. Just wait and relax. Let things happen when they will."

As these examples illustrate, when you call on your Guide Dogs in a visualization or journey, you may sometimes get direct statements advising you what to do. Or your Guide Dog may show you an image or experience, which you need to interpret, if you are not sure what this image refers to. In some cases, the advice or experience may lead you to take a particular action; in other cases it may suggest not to do anything now; and in still others it may offer a symbolic action to take in order to release your negative feelings, so you don't need to do anything more.

CHAPTER 8: PUTTING ON THE POWER DOG

Once you choose your Guide Dogs or Top Dog, you are ready to discover even more ways to work with these dogs: to unleash your creativity (pun intended!), express yourself more fully, increase your energy, relax, or just have fun. An ideal is to become more powerful by calling on or drawing on the power of a dog you consider very strong or powerful – your Power Dog for short.

While you can call on your Top Dog, Watch Dog, or Guide Dog to become a Power Dog, you can pick any dog you want to work with. Just pick on any dog that you associate with the kind of power you want at the time, whether it's the power to better perform a skill, express yourself more fully, or acquire more power in a relationship or negotiation.

While you can work with any of these techniques and exercises on your own, they are great to do with a friend, small group, or in a workshop setting. And besides being great for raising power, they're also fun.

Why These Exercises Work

These exercises are effective for several reasons.

First, from a historical perspective, they have roots deep in human culture at a time when people had a much closer kinship with animals of all types, including dogs. In many traditions around the world, dating back to the beginnings of human society and still used today, shamans have turned to animals for help and power. These techniques have their parallels with these old time techniques – though here the animal helpers are different types of dogs.

Or, for a more contemporary analogy, you might think of these exercises as much like raising excitement like a cheerleader at a football game. Or think of these exercises like raising energy at a party or celebration. As everyone gets in the spirit of the occasion, you can experience the mounting energy of the crowd and yourself surging through you. So you feel more and more power, like a charging battery.

Then, too, when you associate yourself with images and symbols of power, you draw on that power for yourself. People use everything from objects to costumes and masks to identify with and express their power. For instance, if you hold a rock or sword, put on a costume of a military leader, or put on a mask of a powerful warrior, you can feel the power of these objects transferred into you, so you experience more power. In much the same way, when you call on the help of a power animal that power surges into you.

Powering Up with Power Animals

For more information on the power of power animals, here's a historical interlude. Or skip ahead to work with these various power exercises.

When you use these different power techniques, the dogs you work with are like power animals or animal allies. Some early examples of how this works comes from ancient rock art, such as from the cave of Les Trois Frères in France, dating back to 30,000-10,000 B.C. There is the image of a half-man, half-animal creature, with a man's face and legs and a stag's antlers and tail. Sometimes it is called "the dancing sorcerer" or "le sorciere". A later image from Siberia from about 3000 B.C. shows a shaman wearing the head of a bird, and nearby a drum has two fish-like images on the canvas. Presumably, scholars believe, the shaman put on the animal mask or became the animal in a ritual in order to acquire that animal's powers.[6]

Many more recent examples show shamans, as well as others in the community, taking on the powers of different animals or transforming into these animals for a brief time in ritual. In the upper Amazon, shamans commonly turn into jaguars through singing or putting on the skin or teeth of the jaguar. In the Pacific Northwest, the Kwakiutl and other Indian groups put on the masks and skin of wolves, bears, foxes, and other powerful animals to become those animals as they dance.

In some cultures, shamans have used power animals to transport them into another spiritual world to gain insights and power from the beings or forces encountered there. For instance, the Siberian shamans ride horses or reindeer, and use drumming – or "windhorses" as they call their drums — to take them there. Other shamans use a bird to transport them into the sky or a fish to help them swim and dive in the water.[7]

The images of these animals can also be a source of power – whether during a special ritual or in everyday life. In Alaska, the Eskimo shamans carved wood or ivory animal figures as power objects; and many shamans use these objects like power charms with healing energy to help their patients.[8]

Likewise, you can use similar techniques to create a powerful working connection with any dogs you have chosen or later choose to work with. You can use these techniques on your own or incorporate them into fun group events, where you call on or become your dog with others. You are in effect putting on the dog – or more precisely, the Power Dog — to draw on that power, creativity, and spirit of self-expression for whatever you want.

---

[6] Stephen Larsen, *The Shaman's Doorway: Opening the Mythic Imagination in Contemporary Consciousness:* New York: Harper and Row, 1976, p. 6.
[7] Piers Vitebsky, *Shamanism*, University of Oklahoma Press, 201, 70.
[8] Ibid., p. 83.

A Collection of Power Exercises

Following are a series of exercises for increasing your power by working with your Power Dog. Choose whichever exercises feel most comfortable – and powerful – for you.

Dancing the Dog

This is a great exercise for raising your energy and feeling closer and more attuned with the dog you have chosen for this exercise. This also is a great technique for just exercising or having fun. While you are choosing one type of dog, if you feel so inspired, you can dance any other kind of animal. (In fact, that might be a fun experiment – try dancing a dog, a cat, or other animals and notice the difference). And if you want to do your dancing in a group, the more the merrier.

To prepare for this exercise, find a room where you can move around comfortably and listen to music.

Once the room is set up, pick a particular dog to dance. (Or in a group, each person picks their own dog). You can choose one of your dogs, your Top Dog, or whatever dog you want. The key is to choose a dog whose power you most want to access now. For example, to be more outgoing, choose a friendly, outgoing dog like a Pomeranian; to be more powerful, choose a large, powerful dog like a Great Dane.

Next, turn on some rhythmic music or play the sound of drumming in the background. (Or in a group, someone could drum or play this music).

As you listen to the music, imagine you are putting on the head or becoming the dog you are dancing. Should you have anything that represents that dog, such as a mask, fur jacket, or charm on a chain, put that on. (A fun activity that contributes to putting on your Power Dog is making these masks, jackets, or charms). If you are doing this in a group, spread out, so everyone has plenty of room for dancing their dog.

Now, as you listen to the music or drumming, feel yourself becoming more and more the dog you have chosen. Move like that dog. Imagine yourself looking at the world through that dog's eyes. Imagine your sense of smell is stronger than usual and notice any smells in the room. Notice that your hearing is keener too, so focus on all of the things you can now hear as you turn your head slowly around as you dance. Then, as your energy builds, feel free to bark or howl like that dog. Just let yourself go into the experience.

Should there be others dancing at the same time, move around and interact with one another as the dog you are each dancing. For example, move around and sniff at each other as dogs do. Hold out your hand like a paw to shake paws. Or circle each other and playfully dart forward and back, much like many dogs do when meeting at a park. Then, after a period of playful engagement, draw back and move on.

Apart from using this exercise to raise your energy generally, use it to access the type of power you associate with your chosen dog. Feel that power infusing through you and shaping the way you dance. For example, imagine you are sucking or breathing in the strength of the Great Dane, the aggressiveness of the Mastiff, the outgoing bubbly nature of the Pomeranian. Then, feel that power surge through you as something you not only feel now, but a power you can tap into when you need it, such as when you want to be more outgoing at that upcoming social event, instead of shyly hanging back as usual.

Keep dancing for 10-20 minutes, so you really feel this power and make it part of you. When you feel ready, stop dancing and turn off the music.

Afterward, take some time to relax and reflect on the experience. If you participated on your own, this is a good time to write in your journal or share your thoughts with a recorder. Or if you are experiencing this in a group, take some time to share your reactions and feelings with your partner, in a small group, or with the group as a whole.

This is a good exercise to repeat from time to time, so you continue building your connection and ability to tap into that power. Also, you can call on that animal you danced with at times when you need help. You will feel an even closer connection and feel the stronger power you need coming from that animal, because you have focused your energy on promoting a strong connection through the dance.

Relax, Relax

Say you feel jittery, nervous, or anxious about something or are wound up and want to calm down. This fun technique will help you relax – and before doing this physically, you can use the image as a reminder to calm down every day.

To prepare, find a place that's very quiet or where you can listen to soft calming music, such as environmental sounds or sitar music. Then, sit down on a comfortable chair or lie down on a couch, a bed, or pillows on the floor.

As you listen, imagine you are a dog you associate with being relaxed and lazy, such as a Beagle, Bassett Hound, or Chow Chow. Or pick a family or friend's dog that lazes around on a favorite chair, living room couch, or front porch. Then, with this relaxed dog image in mind, see yourself becoming that dog as you relax in the quiet or listen to soft music. Breathe in this dog with each breath, becoming more and more relaxed, more and more calm. Perhaps even say these words over and over to yourself as you see yourself as this dog: "I am getting more and more relaxed…I am getting more and more calm."

Continue to do this for a few minutes, until you feel completely calm and relaxed.

Later, in a tense or stressful situation, you can call on this image of yours as the dog being very relaxed to help you calm down.

One time may be enough to give you this image to use at other times. Or do this in reality several times to reinforce the experience, and later it will be a stronger image you can use. The process works like classical conditioning – you are essentially building an association between seeing the image of this laid back dog, relaxing yourself, and later using that associated image when needed to calm down.

To Unleash Your Creativity

Here's a way to have fun and become more creative by unleashing your inner dog. The process is like taking a dog off the leash in a park and letting it run free and explore. Likewise, in taking the leash off your "inner dog", you can tap into its power to try out new forms of expression in different media.

You can use any type of dog for this process, whether a Guide Dog, the dog you most like, identify with, or even a playful cartoon dog. Essentially, you imagine yourself as this dog, take off the leash, and imagine running about and exploring as this dog. You can see this in your mind's eye or on your mental screen or hold onto this image as you take part in various activities, such as running, dancing, or creating art.

Generally, it's best to imagine you are a young, playful active dog. Choose whatever breed you like, as long as you view it as having lots of energy, enthusiasm, and playfulness.

Start the process by seeing yourself as this dog in any number of ways:
- Visualize in silence or with rhythmic music that you are becoming this dog or it is becoming part of you. Perhaps imagine that you are putting on the head of this dog as part of this transformation.
- Dance as you hold this image of this dog in your head, so you dance the dog into yourself;
- Play on drums, as you imagine this dog coming toward you and stepping into you, so you become one;
- Combine any of the above activities with putting on any objects you associate with the dog you want to become – such as wearing a mask, furry jacket, or jewelry with a picture of that dog.

Once you feel you have become one with this dog, try new ways of playing with this experience. For example:
- Take a walk through your neighborhood or hike to a nearby park or beach, and look around as if you are this dog. You might sniff the flowers, jump around, and just let yourself go and enjoy. (If you are doing this with a group or are in a safe enclosed space, such as a meadow or a beach where no one else is around, try getting down on all fours or rolling around). Just think of yourself as a dog having fun and experience the enthusiasm and excitement of being that dog. (You might even try this exercise with a real dog and you become a new dog companion for your dog).
- Incorporate your experience and image of yourself as a dog in a creative project. For example, start painting or mold clay while you feel imbued with this dog spirit, and let that energy guide the process. Engage in some free form dance by yourself or with a partner as you imagine yourself as this dog. If you're with a partner, your partner can similarly imagine him or herself as a dog. Again, let this image guide you as you move in tune with the music.
- Engage in a sports activity as you imagine yourself as this dog and notice how this affects your play. For example, you are likely to have more energy, move more quickly, and be more responsive. You may experience more strength and power.

After you have imagined being a dog and expressed this feeling in any activity, reflect on your experience – on your own, with a partner, or in a group. As you reflect or share, consider how putting on the dog affected your creative process. Was there anything different about what you did, and if you did, what? Was there anything different or unique in the outcome of this creative activity, such as in your drawing or painting or in the way you danced with a partner?

Later, you can try this exercise again with the same dog or a different dog. If you do use a different dog, reflect on any differences between how you engaged in the creative process or the results.

Express Yourself More Fully

Another way to work with your inner dog is to let go to fully express yourself. Using the image of a dog for this purpose works well, because dogs are such emotion-driven creatures. They can respond with excitement or can be very laid back, because they react on a more feeling, emotional level. Since, their bodies and facial expressions reflect that emotion, you can usually quickly tell what a dog is feeling – from the happy, open mouth, and licking tongue that denote an eager, friendly dog to the bared teeth and grimace that reflect anger.

In this exercise, you'll use the image of a dog – a Guide Dog, your favorite dog, or any other dog – to help you release your feelings. Do this just for fun to express different emotions more intensely. Or if you have a particular situation where you want to express your emotions more freely – say a partner feels you are too reserved in expressing love and affection. You feel uncomfortable expressing your anger to others and want to be more assertive – you can use this exercise to deal with that issue.

To begin, pick a dog you associate with the feelings you want to express. For instance, choose a Pomeranian or Pug to express love and affection; a Great Dane to express calm authority and confidence; a Pit Bull to express aggression; a Siberian Husky to show independence and spontaneity.

Then, use one of the above techniques to identify with that dog, such as visualizing yourself putting on the dog's head of or dancing that dog. Then, by yourself or with a partner, act like that dog would in expressing feelings you want to express.

For example, say you are working on expressing love and affection as a Pomeranian. As this Pomeranian, start doing what these dogs do to show that. Hug someone, or hug an object representing that person, or visualize yourself doing this (though the more actively you can express these feelings in a physical setting the better).

Lick someone's cheek, use a round object to represent this, or visualize yourself licking someone. Bark eagerly to show how happy you are to see someone or visualize yourself doing this or come up with other things Pomeranians do. Whatever you decide to do, do it with lots of energy, excitement, and passion, just like Pomeranians.

Or say you want to be more comfortable expressing your anger rather than holding it in and are using a German Shepherd to express this. Imagine yourself as German Shepherd in a situation where you might normally express your anger, such as a police dog confronting a criminal in a large warehouse filled with boxes. A common scenario might be that you have been chasing the criminal all over the warehouse and have finally trapped him behind some large boxes, and boy, are you angry. As this German Shepherd, act or imagine yourself confronting this criminal. You could bark loudly and furiously. Bare your teeth. Snarl. Paw the ground. Arch and stiffen your back. Glare at the man with a penetrating mean gaze. In short, express all the ways you imagine a German Shepherd might express his anger. You'll find it feels good and energizing to do this. And later, when you are in a situation where you feel angry, but feel uncomfortable expressing it, think of how you did so as a German Shepherd. You'll generally feel much more assertive and able to express how you feel, if it's appropriate to do so in this situation.

If you want to experiment with experiencing a range of emotions, pick out different dogs you associate with these emotions. Then, imagine yourself putting on each of these dogs and express that emotion in various situations –physically or in your imagination, on your own, with a partner, or in a small group. If you have a particular emotion and issue to work with, pick a dog you associate with that emotion.

Increasing Your Energy

Just as you can use the image of a laid back or lazy dog to help you relax, so can you use the image of a high-energy, excited dog to help you build up your energy for whatever you are doing. You can select the same dog to increase your energy whenever you use this exercise, or use different high-energy dogs. Or imagine yourself as part of a team of high-energy, excited dogs, upping your energy and excitement even more.

First pick a dog you think of as a high-energy dog and use a technique to identify with that dog. Then, as you imagine yourself as that dog, act to release that energy –by yourself, with a partner or in a small group. Since you are dealing with energy, act rather than try to visualize doing the exercise, though you can later use a visualization of your experience to increase your energy in everyday activities.

In deciding how to act to release that energy, let your imagination be your guide. Imagine all the things the dog you selected would do – and do them, or experience yourself as this dog in whatever activities you do. For instance:

- Run as fast as you can.
- Jump repeatedly as high as you can.
- Hop up and down on different legs.
- Chase after a stick, grab it in your teeth, and bring it back (or imagine you are grabbing it) as quickly as you can.
- As you toss balls or Frisbees back and forth, imagine you are this dog as you excitedly run to catch the ball or Frisbees.
- Find something you can climb up or over and start jumping.
- Roll around excitedly on the carpet or in the grass.
- Set up some cones or boxes in a line and run in and out of the line, just as dogs do in agility trials, going as fast as you can.

- Crawl through a doorway, under a tree in the backyard, or under a table, like a dog going through a tunnel.
- And so on.

Just think of all the things this dog might do when excited and full of energy, and do them. You'll find this technique is a real energy booster for whatever you want to do next. Also, if you're in a situation where you need energy – say a long or dull meeting – visualize your experience of raising energy. You'll immediately feel a charge of energy no matter what you are doing.

Summing Up

In sum, you can use these Power Dog techniques for various purposes – from increasing your creative abilities to better expressing your emotions to just having fun. The key techniques are the following:

- Dance the dog to feel a closer identification with the dog you have chosen to work with.
- Relax, so you become more calm, rested, and less anxious.
- Unleash your creativity by letting your inner dog run free, so you can apply it to various creative endeavors.
- Express yourself more fully, by letting your emotions run free like a dog off its leash.

PART IV: GETTING EVEN MORE HELP FROM YOUR DOGS

INTRODUCTION TO PART IV

The first two books in the Dog Type series were devoted to learning about the profiles of different types of dogs and about the five most common types of helper dogs.

As previously described in *Discovering Your Dog Type?*, there are about three dozen categories of dogs, classified by working, herding, sporting, non-sporting, terriers, hounds, and toys. You can use the dogs you like best and least or associate with others to better understand yourself and others. This knowledge will contribute to better communication and relationships.

As described in *Getting Help from Your Dogs,* the five types of dogs include your Top Dog, Watch Dog, Underdog, Guide Dog, and Power Dog. You can call on their help in various ways. For example, look to your Top Dog for general support, your Watch dog to help you stay safe, and your Underdog to show you where you are weak or lack skills so you can build yourself up. Your Guide Dogs are useful for advice, and your Power Dogs help you feel more powerful and exercise your power wisely. A series of exercises were introduced to help you contact and get to know these helper dogs and call on them to help you solve and resolve everyday problems and issues.

Getting Even More Help from Your Dogs is designed to provide you with additional ways to work with your dogs, along with another helper, a Rescue Dog, who can step in when you need more help.

The following chapters discuss a variety of techniques for being more successful in whatever you want to do, including having better relationships with others. The first chapter deals with ways to make changes in yourself and in your life by calling on different dogs to help. The process is like having several assistants on staff to call on for their help with different types of problems.

The next chapter focuses on better understanding others by using the dog types, such as when you get a first impression or want to gain more insights into that person. The chapter also discusses how you can increase your power in relating to others.

Finally, the last chapter describes a workshop I did to help others apply these methods to improving their own lives.

CHAPTER 9: MAKING CHANGES: "TEACHING AN OLD DOG NEW TRICKS"

Once you know who you want to be, the next step is deciding what to do to get there, with the help of whichever members of your team – your Top Dog, Watch Dog, Underdog, Guide Dogs, or Power Dogs – you want to use under the circumstances. Consider these options like having a team of corporate advisors and employees from all levels of the organization. You select the team you want for a particular project.

This chapter draws on techniques for changing yourself, which I discussed in several books dealing with creativity and visualization. These include: *Mind Power: Picture Your Way to Success; The Empowered Mind: How to Harness the Creative Force Within You,* and *Want It, See It, Get It!* Here the techniques are applied to help you in gaining additional help with the assistance of your Dog Team.

The Need to Be Flexible

Being able to make changes in your personality or style is especially important in today's rapidly changing global world, so you can play different roles in different situations with different people. For example, you may be Bulldog tough with some people, soft and gentle like a Poodle with others. You may be all business like a stern German Shepherd with associates and in some situations; wild and crazy like an eager Pomeranian with friends when it comes time to party. Whatever your primary traits, reflected in your Top Dog or Watch Dog choices, you can adopt other traits as needed by imagining you are with or supported by the type of dog you would like to be. For example, visualize yourself having the power of the Bullmastiff as you go into a tense meeting, or the style and confidence of an Afghan Hound at an art gallery opening.

As you think about your own situation, you'll find many times when it helps to change your personal style to meet new role requirements with different people and in unfamiliar situations. So you can call on the dogs to help. Just decide what kind of person you want to be in the situation; then ask the appropriate dog to assist. You can use the Chart "Determining What Personality Trait to Change and How".

Some typical situations might be:

- You are asked to take charge and aren't sure what to do.
- You have to make a career change, and the culture of the new field is different from the one you are leaving.
- You are working with a new group of people with different values and expectations and want to get along.
- You want to advance to a new position with different tasks and roles.

All such changes mean learning to act in a new way, perhaps change your image, and bring out a hidden side of you. That's where understanding yourself based on your Top Dog, Watch Dog, and Underdog preferences can help you clarify your strongest qualities and how you want to change.

This first category of change reflects "positive" or "pull" changes — things you want to move toward. Alternatively, the things you want to stop doing represent "negative" or "push" changes – things you want to reject. For example:

- You are too shy and unassertive to get what you want or get ahead.
- You are often difficult to work with, since you are too sensitive and irritable.
- You are too pushy and aggressive, so people you would like to work with are often afraid of you or try to avoid you.

In short, for whatever reason, you can make changes to better fit in, get along, or otherwise get what you want. And you can and will. As the popular expression goes, you are "teaching the old dog new tricks."

An Example of One Man's Self-Transformation

Here's an example of how you might use the process, based on how one man made changes. He used his Dog Team to help facilitate the process.

In this case, Sam was a fairly shy and bookish guy, when he worked as a systems engineer in the high-tech field. People looked up to him for his knowledge, and his boss praised him for his quiet persistence and conscientiousness. Outwardly, there was a good fit between Sam's work and how he behaved. Perhaps he was like a quiet, well-behaved Pekingese.

However, Sam was unsure of himself with people, and often he didn't feel at ease going to parties and making small talk. On his job this lack of social skills didn't matter, because his employers were more interested in his technical designs than how he interacted with others.

For several years, nothing changed. Sam imagined it would be nice to be more outgoing and comfortable in social settings, but he did nothing about it, since he had created a comfortable niche for himself –like a dog having a cozy warm box in the basement.

Then, due to company cutbacks, Sam suddenly found himself out of work in a super-tight jobs market. So he *had* to change, not because he wanted to be different, but for economic survival.

After reviewing his strengths and weaknesses, he felt a good combo might be combining his technical skills with the social skills he wanted to develop, so he could market high tech products. But he was starting off with no sales and people skills. So he had to make himself over to step into this new role.

At first, Sam was very nervous about approaching people to sell them anything. But he began imagining himself in this role and practicing at home in front of his mirror – a good time to call on his Dog Team for extra help. He envisioned himself taking on the qualities of a warm, friendly, social, yet powerful dog – a Great Dane – to see himself in this leadership role. He imagined the dog beside him, supporting him as he practiced, and visualized himself becoming that dog to feel those qualities.

Such practice was just what Sam needed, and finally he mustered up enough courage to start interviewing. As a result, he landed a job in telemarketing. Later, as he gained more confidence through his work on the phone and continued visualization and mirror practice at home, he got a job as an outside rep. Gradually, he moved from *playing* the role of the enthusiastic high-tech marketing rep to <u>being</u> in the role. At the same time, his more outgoing personality at work carried over into his personal life, and he was more comfortable in social situations. He gradually left his shyness behind as he became accustomed to working with people every day. Thus, after a while, he was no longer the shy bookish systems engineer but had become the knowledgeable, friendly high-tech marketing rep, and that felt good.

How You Can Change Your Basic Personality Traits

Sam's dramatic change — from normally shy introvert to outgoing extrovert— illustrates that you can change your most basic personality traits when necessary. Although we develop certain traits due to our experience dating back to childhood — and certain traits may feel more comfortable, so we think that's "our nature", in fact, we are very plastic. As a result, we can adapt in many ways. Even a 180-degree transformation may come to seem very natural after a while – such as switching from being like an affable, relaxed Pug to being more like a proud, self-assured Irish Wolfhound. Alternatively, say you're an overly aggressive, impulsive Bull Terrier type, which has worked well for you as a self-staring entrepreneur. But now you're taking on a corporate job. Perhaps becoming more like a placid, determined Blood Hound might better suit the work culture in a conservative corporate setting.

Whatever the changes you might cultivate, a good reason for developing this other side of yourself is that you can then shift back and forth, choosing whichever style is more appropriate in a particular situation. Or in other cases, the new style is best suited for replacing the way you were, and you have made a permanent alteration in your life.

The key to making this personal transformation successfully is to determine the personality traits that no longer work in your new setting and figure out the qualities you need to adopt to be successful in these changed circumstances. That's where your Dog Team can help – helping you zero in on the qualities you want and don't want and supporting your efforts to change. Then, with a little help from your Dog Friends, you can work on practicing such traits. For example, if, like Sam, you have to learn to be more outgoing and comfortable with people, you would do things like:

- Put yourself in social situations, like cocktail parties and professional mixers, and force yourself to meet and talk to people. (Imagining an especially friendly member of your Dog Team beside you can help you push yourself to be more outgoing in this anxiety-producing situation).
- Volunteer to do things in a social organization that forces you to relate to people, such as helping to set up programs and introduce speakers, hosting at meetings, and doing publicity for the group. (Seeing yourself as a dog with a reputation for assisting, like a St. Bernard, can help).

Alternatively, to become more introspective and thoughtful, you would put yourself in situations such as:

- Go for a weekend retreat at a calm, peaceful location.(And to calm down even more, imagine yourself as normally laid back, calm dog like a Labrador);
- Volunteer to do Internet research for an organization. (And for support in your research role, imagine you are closing in on your quarry like one of the scent hounds; like a Blood Hound).

You can use the chart on the following page to help you identify traits that no longer work in your new situation, determine the traits you need to adopt, and consider what to do to become more comfortable with this new style of relating.

DETERMINING WHAT PERSONALITY TRAITS TO CHANGE AND HOW				
New Situation Requiring Change	Differences in New Situation	Personality Traits That Aren't Working – and the Dog Breed Associated with Those Traits	Personality Traits I Need to Develop – and the Dog Breed Associated with Those Traits	What Can I Do to Develop These Traits – And How My Dog Team Can Help Me

Creating a Better Balance in Your Personality Traits or Expressing Them

Another way to change yourself is to create a better balance in the traits you have or become more aware of when you express different traits, to use them more appropriately. You need to be able to use one trait in certain contexts and a different trait in others, so you can better respond to the wide range of circumstances in your daily life. The process is like learning to not only become an actor, but to be a great one. In the process, you become better at calling on and controlling your Dog Team, like guiding a team of sled dogs through the frozen arctic. You choose the best dogs to be on your sled to help you win the race.

This is what Paul had to do. He was the coordinator of a large volunteer organization, and the members loved him because he was so compassionate and caring. They also liked his casual spontaneity that put people immediately at ease. He was like a warm, loving Collie or Shetland Sheepdog.

Yet, too much of a good thing created problems in managing the group, because he was often too nice, spontaneous, and disorganized. Since he wanted so much to help people and be liked, he sometimes lacked the necessary discipline to control some members. At one point he even tried an ill-fated experiment in democracy that led some people in the group to rebel against his authority and try to run the program themselves. Also, at times, he was so playful at meetings – like a cuddly, eager puppy — that instead of creating a warm rapport between people he became annoying and disruptive. In addition, his disorganization sometimes led him to lose important documents or fail to follow-up on important leads.

Paul's need was not to stop being nice, caring, and spontaneous, but to better control these traits and balance them with a greater assertiveness, firmness, and order. In effect, he needed to combine his warm, friendly Collie or Shetland Sheepdog with some infusion of Mastiff and Great Dane.

Thus, realizing what he needed to do, Paul began to alter his personality. He still kept the warm, friendly, playful traits that endeared him to people and motivated members to remain involved. But he toned them down, so they were more controlled, and he became more direct and forceful with staffers when necessary. As a result, he reestablished his authority and undercut a growing "lct's take over the organization" movement that would have undermined the group. Additionally, realizing he needed help in getting more organized, he got some people who were detail oriented to help organize his office, and he set up a system to track his papers and the tasks he needed to do. He learned to control his tendency to be funny and playful at inappropriate times. And he made changes in his thinking and attitude by visualizing himself acting differently.

Once you make the changes you need to reinforce and correct those changes, they stick. To reinforce his changed way of thinking, Paul could use an image of the dog linked to the desired trait as a trigger to act that way. For instance, to release his warm, friendly side, Paul could think to himself, "Now I'm a Collie" or "I'm putting on my Shetland Sheepdog." Or to step into the tough, more forceful role, he could say to himself: "Now I'm a Mastiff" or "I'm putting on my Great Dane." Or perhaps Paul could use a physical visual image as a reminder, such as putting on a hat with the picture of a Collie to bring out his softer, playful side, versus using a picture of a Great Dane to show his tougher, no-nonsense side. Or instead of a picture, he could use a ceramic sculpture, postcard, poster, or other form of reminder. Then, over time, like a conditioned response, just seeing the image could become an automatic trigger for him to act in a certain way. In short, you internalize the role and soon act that way without thinking about it – thanks to your Reminder Dog.

Here's How It Works

Here are two examples to illustrate how to "call on your dogs" when you need help in changing yourself. One is based on a personal experience; the other from a job situation.

Example #1: A Conflict with a Family Member

Say you are having a conflict with a family member – let's call him Jack. Whenever you see each other, you both tend to rub each other the wrong way. You say something, Jack responds, you make some insulting comment, and soon the argument is on, disrupting the family gathering and almost leading to blows before people pull you apart. Yet, you can't avoid seeing each other, because there will always be that family gathering. Here's how calling on the dogs might help.

First, suppose looking at your profile, you see that your Top Dog is a Jack Russell Terrier and your Watch Dog is a Norwich Terrier; both fairly feisty dogs. By contrast, your underdog is a

Bassett Hound, which you consider a sad-eyed, slow-moving dog. Well, maybe you need to work on taming your Top Dog and Watch Dog so you can and bring out more of your usually repressed Bassett Hound qualities. Then, you might be less likely to react so quickly.

Yet, suppose you still aren't sure what to do, so you call on one of your helpful Guide Dogs, a wise old Yellow Labrador. He sits quietly and listens, as you use self-talk –having a conversation with yourself, though you imagine you're talking to your Yellow Lab.

Then, you listen to some of his suggestions. "Whatever you do, don't engage…You don't have to respond… Don't try to one-up Jack. You'll only increase his anger…You don't have to get angry no matter what he says…When you feel insulted by Jack, don't think you have to respond to save face…Just smile to acknowledge the comment…Say something like: 'Sure, you're welcome to your opinion…Then walk away…" and so on.

In such a conversation with your Guide Dog, you may get a string of different suggestions of what to do, how to feel, and how to respond. As you hear them, write them down, to remember them, and later you can choose among them. You can use the previous Chart "Determining What Personality Traits to Change and How" to help you go through this process.

Then, when you check about what to do when you meet Jack again, your Power Dog might help by being with you in the situation. Or possibly you may experience yourself becoming or putting on that Power Dog to help you deal with that situation, such as helping you work out a plan for how to respond or not respond. You might even try some role plays to practice what you will do in the future.

So now you are in the situation, where Jack is making his usual insulting remarks and putting you down in his usual sly way and boy are you mad. You know you shouldn't respond; you've told yourself to walk away, and that you need to be more like a laid-back Bassett Hound, rather than your usual Jack Russell Terrier self. But for you that's hard. You know you should go, but you really want to stay and fight.

Then it's your Power Dog, a big husky St. Bernard, to the rescue. Just as you are ready to stab with a sharp zinger comment, you gradually withdraw, and finally pull back. Whew! Another family fight averted. A little later, as you grab a drink at the buffet table, you imagine your St. Bernard giving you that well-deserved drink as a reward for staying out of the fray. Later still, whenever you see Jack at a family get-together and feel ready to go over to resume the combat, you think of your St. Bernard just behind you, pulling you back, so you resist the urge, and this time there's no heated family fight.

Example #2: A Problem with a Co-Worker

Say your problem at work is a co-worker, Judy, who gets all the glory. She is more outgoing and knows what to say to get on the best side of your boss. Yet, you have been doing much of the work and giving Judy advice on how to do her job, so she looks even better. But you don't know how to get more recognition that might lead to more money and a promotion for yourself without coming across as a complainer, and worse, jeopardize your position, because your boss thinks so highly of your co-worker.

What to do? You start by looking at your profile, which shows your Top Dog is a soft, cuddly Pug; your Watch Dog is a lively, affectionate Pomeranian, who loves to be loved, and your Underdog is a Pit Bull, because you think of it as a vicious attack dog. That profile is a good clue for what's not working for you at work – you are too eager to be helpful and loved and don't stick up enough for yourself. You are letting yourself be a pushover because of your need to belong, be accepted, and be thought good. You have essentially chosen to be a "lap dog" which is fine when you make a great companion for someone who reciprocates your friendship and affection. But you can easily be taken advantage of, as in this situation, and that's when you need to be more of a Pit Bull and unleash the qualities you may not like, but need to apply now.

Once you have made this assessment, the next step is to figure out what to do, and that's when you can get help from your Guide Dogs. In this case, you take some time at home to reflect on what's happening at the office and what to do and ask your two

Guide Dogs for advice. One is a Siberian Husky, known for being independent, willful, very intelligent, and a good team player; the other is a strong, solid Chow Chow. As you reflect on what to do, you get different insights by asking questions and hearing different suggestions; like listening to a conversation in your head. For example, some of the suggestions are: "Be firm…You need to get credit for what you have done…Don't let Judy take advantage of you…Find a way to get credit without complaining…Continue to help but ask for credit when you do."

Eventually, as a result of this reflection, you come up with a plan for the next time Judy asks for some assistance. You will be glad to help, even take extra time to do a really good job. But in return, you want to be included at the meetings with the boss to discuss the project. This way, you can tell Judy you will know firsthand what needs to be done (and though you don't say this, by being at the meeting, your boss will know that you are contributing, and if you ask good questions and make good suggestions about what to do, your boss will recognize your valuable contribution.) And if Judy doesn't want you there, be prepared to say no to helping her. In other words, if she wants your help, you need to get the credit for what you are doing. If not, no help.

Then, once you have decided what to do, you might practice how you will act in a future encounter with Judy.

After that, your Power Dog can help. Though you've got your plan in mind, when you talk to Judy, you want some extra support, so call on your Power Dog to come with you. In this case, it's a big strong Alaskan Malamute, a dog that wants to be helpful and is a great team player, but it won't take any flak from anyone. In other words, if Judy wants your help in pulling the sled, she has to make you a co-captain. You're not going to help and stand behind the sled anymore, watching it race away after you've help to load it.

The Four Steps to Change

Now that you've got the general idea of how this change process works, here's how to change yourself to take on the personality or play the role you want. The four steps to change are:

1. <u>Determine how you want to change; what or who you want to become</u>.
To do this, think about the traits of your Top Dog, Watch Dog, and Underdog. That process will help to highlight those qualities you want and those you don't; then the qualities of your Underdog may be just what you need to develop to help you act differently to achieve your goals.

2. <u>Decide how to act in a particular situation in the future to express these changes</u>.
Now, use self-talk to have a conversation with yourself about your options, and what you might best do in a particular situation. As you do, call on your Guide Dogs for their input and advice. Also, you can imagine yourself enacting your plan and create a mental script to see yourself in this new role. Then, see yourself doing whatever you ideally would like to do in the future. Also, you can envision other likely outcomes and see yourself respond in varying circumstances. In short, plan what to do in varying scenarios, so you are better able to respond and guide the process in reality.

3. <u>Practice what to do in the future.</u>
Now, besides imagining what might be likely to happen and what to do in your imagination, practice in reality. Practice exercising self-control and politely walking away when a jerky relative starts to engage you in an argument; rehearse how to confront that co-worker who is using your work without giving you credit.

Through the rehearsal process, you not only act out a new way of responding, but you reinforce this new desired image you want of yourself – and this new image of you will carry over into other situations.

In some case, you may not have time to use this step, since you have to quickly turn your plan into action. But ideally, take time to try out this new way of being and acting, since this will give you greater confidence when you actually play out the role – much like an actor feels more self-assured after practicing rather than trusting to a quick read and spontaneous action to produce a good performance.

4. Play out your plan or mental script in actual practice.
Now it's time for action. You have thought through what you need to change, have developed your plan or mental script, and if possible, have rehearsed. Now, lights, camera, action – you're ready to perform. And this is where your Power Dog can help by cheering you on, so you confidently act in this new way.

Initially, when you act in this different way, it may feel like an act, and that's fine. Then, as you continue to act– possibly with the continued help of your Power Dog reminding you to play this new role and supporting this effort, you will increasingly find this new way of action familiar and comfortable. In time, you will internalize this new way of being as part of you, so you not only act the part, but feel the part. When this happens, you may find you have a new Top Dog, Watch Dog, and Underdog, because you have really changed, and as a result, your chosen dogs may change as well.

Determining How You Want to Change

Besides changing in response to particular situations, you can make more general changes, again with some help from your Dog Team. Start by asking yourself: "How would I like to change? What or who do I want to become?"

Think about what aspects of your personality you don't like and imagine their opposite. Say, if you feel you are too quiet and retiring, like a Bassett Hound; think about what it would be like to be more assertive and outgoing, like a Bullmastiff. If you feel you are too standoffish and reserved, imagine yourself participating more, like a warm and friendly Golden Retriever or being cheery and comical like a Chinese Shorthaired Crested. If you lack confidence, see yourself as an assured, confident Dalmatian, regally seated on a fire truck as it passes through town.

In short, change the picture of yourself with the qualities you don't want to a picture of yourself possessing the qualities you hope to have. Use the dog you associate with that image, such as one of your Power Dogs, as a reminder of the qualities you want to acquire.

Exercise: Changing the Qualities You Don't Want to Those You Do

One approach to making changes is with the Transforming Unwanted into Wanted Qualities Chart, if you like doing things in a more logical, organized way. In column one, list those qualities you would like to change, then the qualities you don't want to have. List them as they occur to you; don't try to edit or analyze them. Then, go down column two and for each one, list an opposite or different quality – the ones you would like to have to replace the qualities listed in column one. Write down the first quality that comes to mind so you keep your responses spontaneous.

Finally, for each pair, create a picture in which you see yourself in a scene with the original quality. Again, let the picture come to you spontaneously. Then, imagine that this picture is suddenly being torn up, and see yourself with the opposite or a different quality. Experience yourself possessing this quality for about a minute. Repeat the visualizations of yourself with these new qualities over the next few days, and try putting each one into practice. As you go through this exercise, your dogs can help in various ways:

- When you are listing the qualities you have that you want to change, think of your Top Dog, Watch Dog, and Underdog and ask yourself: "What qualities do I most associate with each of them?" "How do I like those qualities in myself?" "Is there anything I want to get rid of or change?" These questions will help because you may overlook or not want to look at certain qualities in yourself. But looking at these three dogs will help you identify these otherwise overlooked or avoided qualities.

- When you imagine yourself with the quality you want to develop, using the image of a dog you associate with that quality can help you focus more clearly on that quality and feel it more intensely. This focus is especially helpful in the case of qualities you want to develop, and thinking of the dog identified with that quality can serve as a trigger reminding you to express that quality. In effect, you are "Putting on the Dog" and choosing the particular dog to put on.

As you use the Transforming Unwanted into Wanted Qualities Chart, call on your dogs to help, think about the qualities you currently have but don't want and those you want to acquire.

TRANSFORMING UNWANTED INTO WANTED QUALITIES

Qualities I Don't Want to Have	Opposite or Different Qualities I Want to Have
1.	1.
2.	2.
3.	3.
4.	4.
5.	5.
6.	6.
7.	7.
8.	8.
9.	9.
10.	10.
11.	11.
12.	12.

Recognizing What or Who You Want to Become

Another way of changing your personality traits is through an intuitive holistic approach, where you use a process of mental scripting.

Say you have trouble being authoritative and feel uncomfortable being in charge, because you aren't sure people will follow your directions. Visualize yourself being more powerful and authoritative, and show more leadership in your position.

Or say you have difficulty controlling your temper with certain people or in certain situations, because you are overly sensitive and become angry when you feel disrespected or slighted. Imagine yourself controlling your anger and becoming a team player.

In the course of doing these visualizations, you can incorporate your chosen dogs, Guide Dogs, or Power Dogs to provide you with insights, advice, and support. For example, imagine one of your Power Dogs by your side as you give out directions and people follow you. Or see one of your Power Dogs jump in front of you to block the way to keep you from acting out your anger.

The following exercise will help you identify those characteristics you want to eliminate and those you want to adopt. After the exercise, you can use the Influencing the Personality Traits I Want to Change Chart to record your results.

Exercise: Identifying the Personality Traits You Want to Change

As you hold a copy of the Identifying the Personality Traits I Want to Change Chart before you, relax and close your eyes. Imagine one of your Guide Dogs is there to give you advice, and ask him or her: "What personality traits do I want to eliminate?" Be receptive and see what comes to you. As ideas or images come to mind, write them down on the chart in the first column. Don't try to judge whether you can get rid of that trait or not. Keep going until you have listed at least five traits or have started to slow down.

Then, ask your Guide Dog the question: "What difficult situations have I encountered in the past few weeks?" Again, be receptive and see what comes. As each scene appears in your mind, notice how you are acting and whether anything you are doing has been making this situation difficult for you. If so, this is probably a personality trait that you want to change. Write down this personality trait, too, in the first column. Keep going until you start to slow down.

Next, ask your Guide Dog the question: "What traits do I want to acquire?" In some cases, these traits may be the reverse of the traits you want to eliminate; in other cases, these may be different ones. Whatever comes to you is fine. Just list whatever comes up in the third column. Don't try to critique or evaluate the trait. And don't try to judge whether or not you can realistically acquire that trait. Again, keep going until you have listed at least five traits or have started to slow down.

Finally, ask you Guide Dog: "What new situations would I like to be in, where I am different than I am now?" Again be receptive and see what comes. As each scene appears, notice what personality traits you have that are making the situation feel very comfortable and natural. These may be personality qualities you want to acquire but don't have now. Write down in the third column any of these qualities that come up for you. Keep going until you start to slow down.

When you feel finished, you are ready to prioritize which traits you want to eliminate or develop first. To do so, look down the list of traits you want to eliminate; for each one, come up with the complementary or opposite trait you would like to acquire and list it in the second column (if you haven't already listed that trait in the third column). Ask your Guide Dog for advice on what should be most important or in your best interest if you aren't sure. Then, after you have listed this complementary trait or found it is *already in the third column, cross out the trait you want to eliminate from the first column.*

Now, look down the list of all the traits in columns two and three and prioritize them. To do so, rate each trait from 0 (low priority) to 3 (high priority), again asking your Guide Dog for advice to help you in making these ratings. Finally, look at the traits you have marked with the highest priority. Should you have more than one or two traits marked in this category, go through this list again and rank them again, until you have selected one or two traits that are the most important for you to work on. If there are two, note which is most important to you.

You have now established your priorities, so you can work on developing the quality that is most important to you. Should you have the time and energy, you can work on acquiring two qualities, but it's best not to work on more than two at a time. Once you feel solid about having made a particular trait or traits a part of your personality, you can go on to the next traits on your list in order of priority. Then, when you feel you have completed this process by incorporating these traits into your personality, you can make a new priority list for further changes.

IDENTIFYING THE PERSONALITY TRAITS I WANT TO CHANGE

Column 1	Column 2	Column 3	Column 4
Personality Traits I Want to Eliminate	Complementary Traits I Want to Acquire	Personality Traits I Want to Acquire	Priority Rating

Changing Your Overall Personality Orientation and Specific Traits

After you have identified the personality traits you want to change, you can work on changing your overall personality or your ability to change it under certain circumstances, or both, but don't try to change more than 2 or 3 things about yourself at a time. Remember, your overall personality traits, those associated with your Top Dog and Watch Dog, reflect your more general approach to relating to others and the world and reflect how you perceive information or make decisions. But you may express other personality traits and behavioral patterns, in response to a particular situation – the difference between the core you and your acting a role.

Using Mental Scripting to See Yourself As You Want to Be

Now that you have identified the personality traits to eliminate or acquire, you have a good baseline for thinking about what you want to change and who to become. You know the qualities to develop or eliminate and the specific traits to acquire. Now you can work on eliminating or acquiring these traits.

A good way to do this is through mental scripting to create new patterns and approaches in your mind that you can play out in everyday life.

How Mental Scripting Works

Mental scripting to develop or eliminate personality traits is much like the mental rehearsal technique to practice a particular skill or ability. However, in mental scripting, you create a more detailed scenario in which you mentally play out a desired role again and again until you create a habit pattern of action. As you repeatedly experience the action mentally, you reinforce the pattern in your

mind. This process makes you feel increasingly certain you can play the role, and that confidence carries over into playing the scene in everyday life. You are like a movie director creating a scene for your own movie; you create the setting in which to play out your imagined script, where you possess the personality traits you desire.
Meanwhile, your Guide Dogs or Power Dogs act as a team lending their support and cheering you on. It's like they are sitting beside the director's chair, and as you complete each phase of action, you can hear them bark and slap their paws on the ground to show that.

Perhaps you want to be more assertive and authoritative at work to advance your career. Picture yourself as more assertive and authoritative in your present position and see others respond to you in a more cooperative, agreeable way, acknowledging your desired leadership ability. You might see yourself giving instructions clearly and firmly, imagine others listening to you more seriously, and experience employees coming to you for advice. You might also project yourself into the future and see yourself expressing the desired leadership qualities in your new position as you sit in your new office, feeling very comfortable. Or imagine yourself doing the tasks you want to do, such as giving instructions to your staff, attending a board meeting, and flying to see an important client. In response, people defer to you and respect you in your new role. Meanwhile, as you do this visualization, you might imagine your Power Dogs are beside you giving you their support and power, so you feel even more calm, powerful, and self-assured.

The following exercise will help you create a mental script.

Exercise: Create a Mental Script to Be Who You Want to Be

Decide which trait you want to work on changing or acquiring. As before, get relaxed and close your eyes. Take a minute or two to focus on your breathing to get very calm and relaxed. Notice that one or more of your Power Dogs are beside you, lending you their strength and support for whatever you want to do.

Then, with that trait you want to change or acquire in mind, imagine a setting where you want to express that trait — at work, at home, with friends, anywhere. Tell yourself that you now have the trait you want to have, and see yourself expressing that trait in that setting. You are in the situation in which you have been, but now you are acting in this new way. See yourself vividly doing so. Notice the environment around you. Notice the colors, the people around you, the smells, the objects. Experience yourself interacting, talking with others. As you do, remind yourself that you have this quality you want to have, and you feel very comfortable, very natural, very confident, acting this new way. Meanwhile, your Power Dog is on the sidelines cheering you on. Experience this for a few minutes.

Now, project yourself into a future situation where you have this trait. It might be a move, a promotion, a new relationship. Whatever it is, tell yourself that you have this trait you want to have, and see yourself expressing it in this future setting. You see this future scene very clearly and vividly, as if it is happening now. Notice the environment around you. Notice the colors, the people around you, the smells, the objects. Experience yourself interacting, talking with others. As you do, remind yourself that you have this quality you want, and you feel very comfortable, very natural, very confident, acting this new way. Meanwhile, your Power Dog is on the sidelines cheering you on. Again, experience this for a few minutes.

When you feel ready, let go of the scene and let it fade. As it does, you feel very good, very confident, ready to put this new trait into practice in everyday life. Also, know that whenever you want to re-experience these feelings, this sense of assurance and confidence, you can think of your Power Dog, who has been here supporting you, and you will experience those feelings of assurance and confidence again.

Then, holding in your mind that feeling and enthusiasm to go out and act the way you want to be, return to the room. Count backward from 5 to 1, and as you do, you will come back. Five, four, becoming more and more alert. Three, two, almost back. And one. You are back in the room.

Practicing Your Mental Script

Once you have created a mental script you like, practice applying it in the real world. Practice a few minutes a day, until you really feel that new trait has become a part of you. Include the image of your Power Dog in the script, so when you call up that Power Dog association, you will feel that way, such as being more authoritative in the office, as noted before.

You may additionally want to replay a scene from your script, where you see yourself in this desired role. Then, should an appropriate situation arise when you want to be assertive, assert yourself and be firm. As you do, remember the feeling of confidence you felt as you asserted yourself in your mental script. And think of your Power Dog by your side, continuing to cheer you on and give you added support.

Similarly, if you imagined yourself being a more cooperative team player, go to work with this firm intention. Remind yourself that you are determined to be warmer, and friendly, and perhaps replay a scene from your script seeing yourself this way. Also see your Power Dog encouraging this warm, friendly behavior. Then, when at work, look for ways to express this intention, such as being friendlier than usual when you greet people. Or if you start to feel angry about something, think of the image of your friendly Power Dog and remind yourself that you are going to be cooperative and express yourself in a more gentle, accommodating way.

Turning Your Mental Script into Everyday Reality

Initially, when first working with mental scripts, you may have to pay extra attention to your script and repeatedly remind yourself that you are seeking to change by substituting a new way of feeling and acting. You may need to replay parts of your script from time to time and pay careful attention to what you say and do to break old patterns and replace them with new ways to act. You may also need to more consciously remind yourself that your Power Dog is ready to help you.

Eventually, though, as you keep inserting your new scripting into the way you act, it will become a habit, and after a while, you don't need to use the script anymore. The new trait and your behavior reflecting this trait will have become a part of you.

CHAPTER 10: TECHNIQUES TO UNDERSTAND AND IMPROVE YOUR RELATIONSHIPS

To better understand and improve your relationships with others, keep the basic personality, behavioral, and ethical styles in mind as you think about the people you know, want to know, or want to know better. Additionally, be familiar with the different types of dogs, which are organized in this book into 40 types or families of similar dogs. The more familiar you are with them, the more insights you can gain.

Maybe someone seems like a gentle, placid Collie, and you are very familiar with Collies, because someone down the block owns one. But as you learn more about the different dog types, you realize the person is more like the less familiar Chow Chow, because of his steadfast, quiet, reserved nature.

The following techniques illustrate how to use various visualization and reflection techniques to learn more about and improve your relationships. Since these exercises are designed to open up your ability to tap into your intuition, feel free to substitute quick "top-of-mind" impressions if you already get such insights. You'll also find that as you work with these techniques, you will increasingly get strong quick impressions, too.

Getting a Quick First Impression About the People You Meet

You can get a quick insight into someone when you first meet in two key ways:
- Through your immediate auditory or visual impressions when you first approach the person;
- Through your first impressions when you physically touch the person with a handshake or hug.

In both cases, you gain this insight by listening to your inner voice or noticing any spontaneous images that appear when you meet. This will give you clues about the person. While you can use any kinds of images to gain insights, using the different dog types, along with any other images, can help you develop an even clearer picture of that person. That's because you have already built up a series of associations with different dogs, so when that image appears, you immediately draw on those associations you already have. Any associations you have with other images are valuable clues; then the dog that comes to mind gives you another layer of associations and insight.

Suppose when you are introduced to a new business associate, you hear your inner voice say the word "tiger"; or suppose you see a tiger image briefly flash by in your mind's eye. Then, you see the image of a Great Dane, or hear your inner voice saying: "Great Dane." Those brief insights are significant. First, they suggest the person may have the characteristics you associate with a tiger, such as being wily, aggressive, and tenacious. Second, they suggest that the person has the characteristics associated with a Great Dane, such as being strong, powerful, and exercising leadership. So this is a person who likes to be dominant and in command, along with being crafty and clever. In dealing with this person, you can take these qualities into account.

Or suppose you only get a single image of a dog when you meet someone. That's fine, too. Just use your associations with that image, though you can seek additional images by saying to yourself: "What else do I think of when I see this person?" Then, let whatever image or images this question triggers come to mind, and think of your associations with that image or images.

This process of looking for images and associations may sound like a long process, and when you first start doing this, you generally need to consciously remind yourself to think of these dog and other images. But after a while, the process will become second nature, so these images will quickly come to mind when you first meet someone without you consciously directing the process.

Then, too, you can use the process to confirm or deepen your initial impressions on subsequent meetings. Say you picture the tiger and Great Dane at your first job interview. Then, the person calls you back for another interview. Notice if these same images come to mind or if you get other images. If so, these additional images can help you refine or add to your original image, or even correct your first impression. To illustrate, perhaps besides the tiger and Great Dane, you get an image of a small cat and a Collie. This might suggest that initially the person comes on as a strong, dominant, powerful person who wants to show leadership. However, he or she also has a warm, gentle, affectionate side when you get to know each other. In other words, the outer person is more like the tiger and Great Dane; the inner self is more like the cat and Collie. Another way to think of these contrasting personality images and personality traits is that the Great Dane is like the person's Top Dog, the Collie like their Watch Dog. This distinction is comparable to what the Myers-Brigg's system refers to as the Superior and Inferior Functions, or the birth sign and the rising sign in astrology.

The following exercises will help you become more aware of your first impressions and your accuracy, so you can feel more confident of your abilities. Over time, your sensitivity to others will increase as you practice paying more attention to your initial responses.

In doing these exercises, carry a small pad or notebook to jot down your impressions when you first observe or meet someone, though, make these notes discreetly. If you're in a class or meeting, where you can take notes on the spot, fine. If not, find a place to make your notes unobserved as soon as possible after your observations.

When you get to know the person better or learn about him or her from others, compare your initial impressions with what you learn later. You'll find you are quite accurate and that your accuracy increases with practice.

There are three types of initial impressions to observe: (1) when you first see someone; (2) when you first meet someone; and

(3) when you make an initial physical contact by shaking hands. The following exercises illustrate how to do this.

Getting First Impressions

- <u>Get Impressions When You First See Someone</u>. *This technique is ideal for when you go to an event and see someone you expect to talk to or meet later. Or use it at a meeting when you first arrive. Look in turn at each person you want to know about, and think of the first word or picture that comes to mind along with the first dog you think of. Write these images down as soon as you can and think what that word or picture and dog mean to you. That will give you a general impression of the person. After you meet the person, review your comments to see how accurate you were — and watch your accuracy increase as you continue to do this.*
- <u>Get Impressions When You First Meet Someone</u>. *This technique is ideal for a gathering where you can meet someone or observe that person meeting and talking with others. As you walk up to meet the person, be aware of the type of dog and any other words or images that pop up when the person speaks to a group or meets another person. Write down these words and images as soon as you can and think about what they mean. Later, as you get to know this person or see him or her in action, review your comments to check your level of accuracy.*
- <u>Get Impressions When You Make Initial Physical Contact by Shaking Hands</u>. *This technique is ideal whenever you shake hands with someone you meet and expect to engage in further conversation. While you shake hands, focus your awareness on that handshake, and notice what dog and any other words or images appear in your mind's eye. Ask yourself what they mean to you, and if you continue to converse, check your accuracy. How much did this first impression tell you about the person? And how consistent is this impression with what you sense or learn from the*

person as you talk? Again, you'll find your accuracy goes up with practice.

Getting Advance Impressions of Someone Before You Meet

When you are about to meet someone you don't know for whatever reason, some advance insight about this person's personality type can help you act so the meeting goes more smoothly.

The personality types and behavioral styles described earlier will give you the framework for organizing the insights you receive. It is helpful to review any preliminary information you have about the person, including name, nickname, occupational title, photograph, or organizations the person belongs to.

Once you have this information in mind, you are ready to perform this technique.

Get relaxed, close your eyes, and call up an image or the name of the person you are going to meet in your mind's eye. Concentrate on making this image or name expand and contract for about one minute. Next, see the image form into a white ball of energy, and watch that energy swirl around and form into a computer screen. On that screen, you first see the image of a dog appear. Next a word appears that describes the person as a take-charge personality, an analyzer/explorer, a people person, or a conscientious planner. Should you see two dogs or two or more names appear simultaneously, the person is a combination of these primary types.

Then, with an image of that dog and that word in mind, think of the traits you associate with that image and word. Now with this image, word, and associated traits in mind, see yourself meeting this person for the first time. As you do, notice what you say and how you act.

Later, when you meet the person, this mental rehearsal will help you make a good impression and relate to the person from his or her perspective.

Gaining In-Depth Insight into Others

After you have met someone and have an ongoing relationship, these in-depth techniques can help you gain additional insights about the person or further your relationship. At work, these methods can help to promote smoother relationships with co-workers, manage a work team more effectively, or influence an employer to regard you more favorably. In a personal relationship, these can help you have a closer, more loving relationship with a partner and get along better with friends and family.

These techniques work by focusing your intuitive abilities on reading the individual's personality in more depth than an initial impression. As such, they are much like the techniques used by professionals who do a personality reading on someone desiring spiritual or psychic counseling. But everyone has these intuitive abilities. The more you practice with them, the more accurate and detailed information you will get.

The basic approach is to use an object, imagery or new way of seeing to perceive information about someone. You gain this information intuitively by calling up images of the person's past, body, thoughts, or surrounding energy field and the dog you associate with that person. The person can be physically present or not. If he or she isn't present, just visualize him or her in front of you.

Besides using the images of dogs, you can use any other images and even create your own symbol system. Any imagery system will work if you get used to using it. To become more accurate, try reading some people you don't know well; then ask for feedback to check your accuracy. If you're off at first, don't worry. Your accuracy will improve with practice, along with your confidence.

Get relaxed for all of these techniques, and except for the aura reading technique, close your eyes. Preferably, sit upright in a receptive position.

Using Objects to Learn About Others

Using objects to gain information about others is a technique, often called "Psychometry," that involves getting associations from an object a person owns. You hold the object and think about the images and associations that come to you. Sometimes people do this technique by just looking at a portion of an object. Here's a guide you can use for this technique.

To begin, ask someone for a small object. Then, with the person present or at a later time, hold this object in your hand and meditate on it. See it in your mind's eye. Try touching it to your forehead. Notice what dog and what other words, images, or impressions appear, and think about the associations you have with that dog and the other words, images, or impressions you experience.

Say your thoughts aloud if the person is present, such as in a workshop or one-on-one exchange. Write them down if you like. And if the person isn't present, record what you experience.

These impressions can provide clues to the person's personality, interests, relationships, and life style. If possible, share your impressions with your subject and get feedback. Alternatively, pay attention to how this person interacts with you and others to see how well you have done in assessing what this person is like.

As with other techniques, your accuracy will improve over time as you continue to work with this technique and become increasingly familiar with the dog types and the characteristics associated with each type.

Learning About a Person from His or Her Energy Centers

This energy center technique draws on the principles of many holistic health and spiritual traditions, which state that each person has a series of energy concentrations or centers in the body, located from the base of the spine to the top of the head. These centers, sometimes called "chakras" (a term borrowed from the Hindus and Buddhists), can provide a window into a person's inner self, because the personality is reflected by the flow of energy through the body.

There are seven primary centers, each linked with a different personal quality. These are:

1. The base of the spine – survival
2. The reproductive area – sexual energy
3. The stomach or solar plexus – identity, will
4. The heart – warmth and emotions
5. The throat – communication
6. The center of the forehead (third eye) – perception
7. The top of the head (crown charka) - spirituality

To read someone's energy centers, call on the help of a Guide Dog or Top Dog who will act as your counselor and advisor. To begin, sit in front of the person you will be reading or visualize him or her before you. After you relax and close your eyes, visualize as follows:

First, call on your Guide Dog or Top Dog to help you. See this dog sitting beside you, giving you support and advice.

In this process, you'll imagine a rose in front of each energy center in turn, and you'll also see what dog comes to mind at each of these centers.

First, see the petals or the whole rose and stem. Then, notice that your Guide Dog or Top Dog is especially interested in this rose. He looks at it closely, and perhaps goes to sniff it, to really feel a close connection with this rose.

Now starting at the base of the spine, place an image of the rose in front of this energy center. Observe what happens to the rose. Ask your Guide Dog or Top Dog to give you advice as you observe and ask a series of questions. These are: What type of dog is next to the rose? Does the rose change color or shape? Does it begin to move? Does it assume the shape of an animal or person? Does anything else happen to it? Let the impressions come spontaneously, and don't try to analyze. Say them aloud or write them down, as you wish.

Once these images stop coming, ask yourself what they mean in light of the characteristics associated with the first lower energy center. Notice what impressions or explanations spontaneously come, and jot them down.

Now go up to the next energy center and observe what type of dog is next to rose. Again, notice what happens to the rose and ask what this means.

Keep doing this process until you conclude with the energy center at the top of the head.

In performing this exercise, be aware there is no fixed meaning for any image, although there are some general associations with each type of dog. What's most important is what the images or symbols mean to you, as every person is different and has a different symbol system. Also, an image means different things depending on which energy center it is associated with.

For example, say you are focusing on the lowest energy center at the base of the spine, which is associated with survival. Suddenly, the image of a Pit Bull appears, and then a rose opens up and becomes very bright. These images suggest that the person is very ambitious, because he or she is acting strongly in the area of survival (suggested by the bright open rose), and is willing to aggressively go after what he wants (suggested by the Pit Bull). In fact, more than being just aggressive, the person may be willing to fight with great tenacity, much like a Pit Bull trained to fight.

By contrast, if these same images appear in front of the heart center, it may suggest the person is very warm and emotional (the rose), and even impulsive and quick to respond (the Pit Bull), as his or her heart opens up.

Learning about a Person's Past or Future

You can read someone's present and past, whether that person is with you or not. You simply see this person before you in your mind's eye and, you call on your Guide Dog or Top Dog to act as your counselor or advisor. In either case, use the following scenario as a guide.

Now, on your mental screen, see yourself going into a large library with your Guide Dog or Top Dog.

A large marble stairway is before you. You go up the stairs, your dog beside you. At the top you see a door with a sign that says, "Reference". You go in with your dog and enter a large room, which has many long tables and files.

You walk toward a series of large file drawers in the center of the room. There are some letters on each file, and you look for the drawer with the letter corresponding to the name of your subject. When you find it, pull out this drawer and flip through the cards. Invite your Guide Dog or Top Dog to help you look, perhaps by sniffing as you flip through the files for the scent of the person you are seeking information about.

Finally, you come to that person's name, pull out his or her card, and noticed a date on the top right hand corner. Look at it. It designates a period in this person's life in the past, present, or future. To learn what happened or will happen, look at the center of the card. A biography is written there. Read it and learn what you want to know.

After you read the card, put it back. If you wish, pull out another card and read it, too.

When you are ready, leave the library with your Guide Dog or Top Dog. Go down the same marble stairs, and when you return to the street, return to normal consciousness.

As a variation on this technique, enter the library with a time period in mind and find a card with that date. Visualize the cards arranged in a time sequence, and flip through the cards until you find the right date.

After you complete the reading, record your impressions to better remember them. Later, get feedback when you can to test your perception. If you can't ask your subject directly, say because you don't feel comfortable telling your boss, "I've been trying to learn about you intuitively", try to bring up the topic in the course of conversation. You'll find your accuracy improves over time, and even if some specific details are wrong, you'll find your overall impression is correct. (For instance, you get an image of a friend as a boxing champ as a teen, whereas he fought to protect himself from neighborhood gangs.)

You can use these insights to help you build a better relationship with this person. For instance, some insights might suggest topics of conversation to improve your rapport. (Say you sense the person has been a scrappy fighter since childhood; you might comment on a recent newspaper article about a whistle blower or someone who foiled an attempted robbery).

These insights might also give you guidance in how to better relate to that person. Say you get an image of the person as an adventurous traveler and outdoors person. If that person is a friend, that might suggest not only talking about travel and outdoors activities, but going on a trip with this person. Or if you are that person's employer, that might suggest giving the person additional challenges to solve, since this is someone eager to face down hard challenges.

Increasing Understanding Through Identification

Another way to gain information about someone to improve your relationship is by using visualization to identify with that person and by using a guide, such as your Guide Dog or Top Dog to ask questions of yourself as this person. One approach, featured in the following exercise, is to imagine yourself putting on another person's head and responding as he or she would, as your Guide Dog or Top Dog asks questions and gives advice. Use the following guide to experience this.

> *To begin, close your eyes and get relaxed. See your Guide Dog or Top Dog seated beside you, ready to help you ask questions and give you advice.*
>
> *Now visualize the person you want to know more about standing in front of you. Observe his or her face carefully. Notice the eyes, lips, and facial features. Look at how he or she smiles. Next, stretch out your arms and lift his head from his body and place it on yours. As you do, your Guide Dog or Top Dog sits beside you watching.*
>
> *Now look around and experience how the world looks through this other person's eyes. What do you see? Hear? Feel?*
>
> *Now invite your Guide Dog or Top Dog to ask you questions about your new self or ask some questions yourself. Ask about whatever you want to know. Depending on who's asking, ask the question as "You" or "I" questions. For instance, your Guide Dog might ask: "What do you like to do?" "Where did you live as a child?" "What kind of work do you do?" Or you might ask: "What do I like to do?" and so on.*
>
> *Don't try to answer consciously. Just let the answers pop into your mind. Then, say your answers aloud or write them down.*
>
> *Now, start asking your questions for a minute or two.*
>
> *After you finish your questions, take the head off and put it back on the person's body. Then, thank your Guide Dog or Top Dog for his or her help, return to normal consciousness, and open your eyes.*

Later, if you can, get feedback directly or during an ordinary conversation from this person to check your accuracy. With practice, your ability will improve.

Taking a Visual Visit

Another way to gain information is to project your consciousness outside your body and imagine visiting a person's house. While you can visit on your own, you can get additional insights by taking your Guide Dog or Top Dog with you, to get their opinions and advice. The way the house looks in your imagination, whether accurate or not, and your associations with that house, will tell you something about what that person is like.

To begin, imagine your Guide Dog or Top Dig is beside you, eager to help and give you information. Now visualize the person you want to visit. It can be someone you know or not.

Then, see yourself leaving your body in a rush of energy, which rises from the base of your spine, spirals up, and goes out through your head. This energy continues to rise, lifting your inner self with it, until you come up to a soft, white cloud floating by. You get off onto the cloud, and for a few minutes, you float, feeling completely peaceful, calm, and free.

Then, as you relax on this cloud, your Guide Dog or Top Dog comes over to you to act as your advisor and counselor.

Now it is time to descend for your visit. Float down off your cloud with your Guide Dog or Top Dog beside you. Below you, see this person's house. Note what it looks like. Observe the surroundings. Ask your Guide Dog or Top Dog what he or she thinks about the house and the type of person who might live there.

Then, float in through the door with your Guide Dog or Top Dog following right behind you. If anyone is there, do not talk to him. Just observe. What is the interior like? How many rooms? How large? What shape? How about the furnishings? Are there any animals or plants? Who else lives here besides this person? Notice, too, what type of dog comes to mind when you characterize this person or any other people living there.

Then ask yourself or your Guide Dog or Top Dog what each image tells you about this person.

When you finish reviewing the images, return to your cloud with your Guide Dog or Top Dog and float back to where you first got off. Then, spiral down, and let your energy and consciousness return to your head.

After your experience, record any details. Later, if possible, get feedback from the person you visited to check your accuracy. How accurately did you perceive his or her house? More importantly, how accurate were you in describing the characteristics of this person from your observations?

Using Energy Fields to Learn More About People

Another source of information is the electro-magnetic energy field around each person, which is often called the "aura". Some research has suggested this is a real physical field, because Kirlian photography has been used to photograph the radiant heat surrounding the physical body. If you prefer, think of it as a radiating energy capsule surrounding the body.

Depending on a person's state of mind, mood, and personality and your perceptions of the person, you will see this field expand, contract, or change color. As you gaze steadily ahead, your eyes out of focus, you will normally be able to see or sense this aura, and obtain information about the person from it. While you can use this technique on its own, as described in *Mind Power*, you can gain additional information with the help of your Guide Dogs or Top Dog and by noticing any dog images that appear in this energy field.

A Quick Introduction to the Aura

If you aren't already familiar with energy fields or auras, here are a few general characteristics, so you will understand what you see. An aura usually looks like a light filmy after-image surrounding each person. It tends to expand when a person is positive, healthy, active, assertive, or thinks of power; and to contract when one is negative, ill, passive, withdrawn, or thinks of weakness. It frequently appears with colors — usually light, fuzzy, pastel tones — and these colors express a person's personality traits.

One observer may perceive these images of the aura differently from another, since each person is different, and the observer-subject interaction differs in each case. However, certain color associations are common, though the associations may vary in different countries and cultures. The common associations in the West are:

- Red - energy power, courage, strength, love, warmth
- Yellow – intellect, thought
- Orange – sexuality, activity, job
- Green – health, healing, spiritual growth
- Blue – peace, calm, spirituality, coolness
- Purple – royalty, mysticism, spiritual truth
- White – purity, spiritual attainment
- Gray, Black – sadness, depression, illness

In addition to colors, you may notice that the image of one or more dogs appear in the person's energy field in various forms, such as standing close to the person or superimposed on the persons' head. When you do, add your associations with the dog or dogs to your interpretation of the person's energy field.

Observing the Aura

Now, use the following guide to help direct your attention, start observing the aura and interpreting what you see.

To see the aura, look at the person in an unfocused way, as if you're staring into the distance. Then, keep looking. The aura will emerge as a frame of light and color around the person. Usually it will appear around his or her head first as a white shimmer of energy, then it may encircle the whole body. At first, you may see only white. But as you practice, colors should appear, usually with a fuzzy, pastel quality.

In time, you can see auras under any condition. Just look, and they will appear. You may even be able to see them by just imagining that the person is in front of you. As you concentrate on the person in your imagination, you will gradually see an aura emerge, just as you would if the person is there. This ability takes a little longer to develop, but many people can do this.

To facilitate seeing these auras initially, practice under optimal conditions: in a quiet place with dim lighting. Ideally, have your subject (perhaps a friend you are practicing with] sit against a large white or softly colored wall. Imagine that your Guide Dog or Top Dog is with you as a counselor and advisor.

Then, stare at the center of the person's forehead for a few minutes. Watch for a fuzzy whiteness to appear around *the head. This is the aura. Gradually it may grow larger and brighter. It may vary in size and intensity around different parts of the body. Soft colors may emerge, too.*

As you continue looking, you may see the image of a dog beside the person, or you may see its head imposed on the person. Notice what breed or type of dog this is. Later you can interpret the meaning of the colors and the type of dog you have seen.

Once the aura and any dog image emerge, shift your eyes to observe the aura around different parts of the body. But keep your awareness unfocused. Should the aura begin to fade, look back at the subject's forehead, until you see the aura's strength return.

After several minutes of looking, ask your Guide Dog or Top Dog what these colors and images mean and listen for the answers. Don't try to direct these responses – just be receptive and listen.

Next share your observations and initial interpretations with your subject, and add any additional interpretations of what you have seen. Again, seek feedback about your accuracy to help you improve.

Two Aura Exercises to Develop Your Ability to See Auras

To further develop your ability to see auras, try these aura exercises with a friend. One of you should meditate on some idea or image to affect your aura, while the other observes. Then, the observer compares his or her perceptions with what the mediator was doing. While you can look at auras on your own, you can gain additional insights by imagining your Guide Dog or Top Dog is sitting beside you as a counselor and advisor, who asks questions or gives suggestions about what you are seeing. You'll be amazed at your accuracy. Three experiments to try are:

- One person concentrates on an image of power or weakness to expand or contract the aura, while the other observes.
- One person concentrates on sending his or her energy to the left or right, while the other observes.
- One person concentrates on imagining different types of dogs on either side, or imagines putting their heads over his or her head, while the other observes.

How to Apply Insights Gained from the Aura

Once you are sensitive to perceiving the aura and understanding what it tells you about the person, you can apply this information on an ongoing basis to build a better relationship.

Improving a relationship can be especially useful in a business setting to better build rapport with those you work with or for better relating to clients and customers. Or use the insights of aura reading with friends and family members to gain a greater closeness and better get along on a day to day basis.

Gaining a better relationship from aura reading can occur because reading a person's aura can make you more sensitive to everyday mood swings, so you can react appropriately. For instance, say you approach your boss to ask for a raise and you notice a great deal of red and gray in his aura, along with the image of a Jack Russell Terrier. The colors suggest a mixture of anger and sadness, while the Terrier suggests a willingness to fight if provoked, although outwardly your boss appears calm and impassive as usual. This insight tells you that may not be the best time to seek a raise; rather you may do better if you wait until you sense that his aura has more positive colors, such as red, along with yellow, orange, or green, suggesting power, warmth, happiness, and health.

Similarly, if you are negotiating with someone, you might pick up information from the aura about the person's relative strength or willingness to give in or compromise. For instance, if you see lots of reds in the aura along with the image of a Bulldog, that suggests that the person is not only feeling strong and powerful, but may be determined to stick to whatever position he first embraces. Thus, you know you must strengthen your own position to prevail and you may have to be especially forceful and convincing. But if you see yellows and the image of a different, more docile dog – say a Labrador Retriever, this suggests the person is becoming more thoughtful and may be ready to compromise. Should you see blues or dark colors or the image of a small, usually yielding dog – say a Chinese Crested, the person may be willing to concede, and it's time to press toward a close.

In short, you can use information from an aura reading to supplement the other more visible cues a person is giving off through body language, gestures, facial cues, words, and eye movements.

Using Visualization and Dog Profiling Techniques to Improve Your Relationships

Besides gaining insights and information, you can use visualization techniques to directly affect your relationships. One way is to make people feel better about the relationship by chasing away any negative, angry feelings or by emphasizing warm, supportive, loving feelings. Another way is reinforcing your feelings of power and making others more aware you have this power.

The basic process involves setting your goal for the relationship. Then, focus your mental energy on this other person as you visualize your goal and mentally send a message about this to the person. You can gain even more strength in the process by calling on your Power Dogs or Top Dog to contribute their support and strength.

This process works on two levels. First, it helps you change your attitude toward the person, so when you see each other again, you will interact in light of your desired goal, which will influence the other person to respond accordingly.

Secondly, since thoughts have energy, as shown by some research in which monkeys have directed a computer cursor with their thoughts, the person to whom you direct this thought transmission will receive it on an inner neural, psychic, or mental level. Consciously he or she may not be aware of your message. But your mental communication may inspire or remind him or her to relate to you in this desired way.

One common use of this visualization approach is smoothing the way for a future meeting with someone. Also, some people use this method to send their thoughts to encourage someone to get in touch with them.

The following exercises will help you to improve your relationships with these techniques in various ways.

Creating a Warmer Relationship

To overcome angry feelings, resentments, misunderstandings, or make someone feel warm, friendly and positive toward you, send a little love someone's way. You can call on one of your Power Dogs or Top Dog to help send it.

Sending love will help eliminate any negative feelings and make you feel good. This process can be especially helpful after an argument with someone, since your positive thoughts can reduce or eliminate any remaining hard feelings, so when you see each other again, the conflict may be gone. Sending love can also make someone who is distant from you in reality or is just reserved become closer. For instance, if someone is in another country, this technique is ideal for giving a supportive energy boost.

The first exercise involves sending love to prepare the way for a better meeting. The second is designed to send love and persuade someone to contact you.

- **Sending Love**

    Put up a picture of the person to whom you're sending love before you and imagine a glowing ball of love radiating out from your heart to this person. At the same time, imagine that your Power Dog or Top Dog is seated beside you sending these warm vibrations of love and concern, too.

    As you send out this beam of energy, say the word "love" over and over to yourself, and send these words along this beam. Notice that your Power Dog or Top Dog is sending out this love energy, too, perhaps barking happily and enthusiastically or just radiating this warm light.

    As this beam arrives, notice that the person begins to glow and radiates love back. You may even see the person's Top Dog beside him, basking in the warmth of this beam of love you are sending.

Continue to focus on this image for several minutes. Notice how it becomes more and more brilliant as you continue sending love.

Now visualize the next meeting you expect to have with this person. See the setting as vividly as possible. Notice whatever is around you, imagine what the person is wearing and doing. As you approach, with your Power Dog or Top Dog still beside you, continue to feel these warm, friendly feelings, and notice that the other person responds the same way. If you have felt any anger or resentments toward each other, that is gone.

After this initial meeting, you can continue your conversation with this person and notice that you now have a better rapport. When you conclude the conversation, you feel satisfied that you have achieved your goal of a warmer, more comfortable relationship together.

Later, when you see this person in reality, notice that you feel more open and warmer when you meet, which will contribute to creating better rapport with each other.

- **Promoting Communication**

To get someone to contact you or be more receptive to a call from you, visualize sending this person a message. Use your Power Dog or Top Dog to put even more energy into sending out this message.

If you feel there has been any problem in the relationship to overcome (such as an argument or feelings of resentment), or if you want to make the relationship warmer, start by sending love as in the previous exercise. Then, use the following mind to mind communication technique to promote the desired contact.

Take a few minutes about the same time each day to get relaxed in a quiet place. Then, visualize your Power

Dog or Top Dog beside you, and see the person you want to communicate with in your mind's eye. Now mentally ask him or her to contact you or be receptive to your call by imagining a cable of pure white energy radiating from your mind to this person with your message. Also, see the energy of your Power Dog or Top Dog going into this message, making it even stronger. Imagine that this beam of energy continues to transmit your request with all this energy invested in it for about 2-3 minutes. Then, see this person contacting you by phone, letter, e-mail, or in person — however you wish to receive the message, or being receptive to you when you initiate contact.

Do this visualization regularly for several days, and frequently, you'll find the person will call. Or if the person hasn't, feel confident you have paved the way for a successful call when you call yourself. Then, get ready to make your call, feeling infused by all the energy you and your Power Dog or Top Dog have sent out to prepare the way.

- **<u>Promoting a Closer Relationship</u>**

Another way to promote a closer relationship or to get someone to contact you is by using an object representing you and the other person, such as a candle, to help you focus and reinforce your message. This technique has frequently been used to impress a love relationship, but you can also use it to promote friendships and closer understandings with the people you work with. In addition, to increase the energy you are sending out, imagine your Power Dog or Top Dog beside you, sending out energy, too.

As in the previous exercise for Promoting Communication, take a few minutes each day for several days to go through this process until your message starts having its effect. The following example uses candles as the object, but you can use whatever you feel most comfortable with, such as small figurines, statues, or even chess and other game pieces, to represent you and the other person.

To prepare, get two candles, one representing you and the other the person you want to hear from. (For example, pink and blue candles might be used for a woman and man respectively, although any colors with personal meaning are fine.) The first day you do this technique, set the candles about twelve inches apart. On each successive day, begin by placing the candles two inches closer together, until on the seventh day, they touch. Thereafter, leave the candles touching.

Now light the candles and turn off any lights. Imagine your Power Dog or Top Dog is by your side as you do this, sending you even more energy and power.

Look back and forth from one candle to another for about one minute. Then, close your eyes and see the candles burning in your mind's eye. Next see the two flames draw together, until they become a single flame. Observe the bright yellow beam that radiates from this flame.

Now put one hand around the base of each candle, as you imagine your Power Dog or Top Dog seated beside you, sending you its energy. Continue to hold your hands there, while you visualize this beam traveling across space and time to the person you want to contact you. Continue to hold these candles and concentrate on this image for 2-3 minutes. Then, gently, push each candle about an inch toward the other (or once they are together, press them together tightly). As you do this, think to yourself: "We are drawing closer and closer together. We are drawing closer and closer together. May he (she) contact me. (Or be receptive to my call.)" Or express these sentiments in your own words.

When you feel the message has been sent, let go of the candles, return to normal consciousness, and open your eyes.

After you finish the exercise, leave the candles in position, if you plan to do this technique again.

Do this exercise regularly for about a week, and expect your call. Quite frequently, the person will have called you by then. If not, feel confident your call will be successful and contact the person yourself. When you do, feel infused by the positive energy you have generated with the help of your Power Dog or Top Dog to prepare the way.

Increasing Your Power in a Relationship

To increase your power balance in a relationship, use the same principle as in the techniques to create warmer feelings. Here you'll visualize a mental scenario in which you experience yourself being powerful, and you call on your Power Dog or other dog you think of as very powerful to make you feel more powerful. Then, you imagine yourself in a likely scene with this person, in which you express this newly felt sense of power.

The following is a sample scenario you can use to increase your feelings of power.

Put up a picture of the person with whom you want to experience your greater power, and see the image of your Power Dog or any other dog you consider very powerful before you. Additionally, call on other images of power to surround you, such as a powerful animal like a lion, a powerful vehicle like a rocket ship, a powerful person like a weight lifter or body builder.

Concentrate on seeing these images of power vividly in from of and around you, and feel the power that radiates from these images.

Then, direct a beam of your energy from your power center in your stomach area to this person. Feel the energy from your Power Dog and other dogs infusing you with their power, like recharging a battery. At the same time, say the word "power" over and over to yourself, and send these words along this beam. Notice that you are feeling more and more powerful as you do, and notice that the person you want to impress is also aware of this. Continue to focus on this beam of powerful energy surging from you for several moments, and notice that it becomes stronger and stronger as you continue to beam your power into this image.

Now visualize the next meeting you expect to have with this person. See the setting as vividly as possible. Notice whatever is around you. Imagine what the person is wearing and doing. As you approach, continue to feel these strong, powerful feelings, and notice that the other person responds accordingly. He or she regards you with increased respect, is more deferential, is more willing to listen to you. Notice, too, that any feelings of uncertainty you may have felt are completely gone, and you feel confident and sure of yourself.

Once you meet, continue your conversation, and continue to relate to this person from your power place. When you conclude the conversation, you feel satisfied that you have achieved your goal of having and exuding more power when you interact with this person in the future.

Later, when you see this person in reality, notice that you feel much more confident and powerful, which will contribute to the person treating you with more seriousness and respect.

Influencing Your Relationships in Other Ways

You'll find that using these visualization techniques with the help of your Guide Dogs, Power Dogs, and Top Dog will improve your relationships, either by changing the way you relate or by modifying how others perceive and respond to you.

While many people are especially interested in improving the emotional tone or power balance in a relationship, you can create other techniques to influence your relationships in other ways. To do so, create a visualization that expresses your goal in a relationship. Then, call on your Guide Dogs for advice or insights or call on your Power Dogs to increase your power. Call on your Top Dog for either kind of help.

For instance, say you want to take more initiative or responsibility in the relationship, and you want the other person to give you more space or trust, so you can do this (as might be the case when an employee wants to expand his job responsibilities or when a partner in a relationship wants to become more assertive). To gain this increased initiative or responsibility, create a visualization with an image of doing something when you take initiative or responsibility. You can use the image of a dog you associate with these qualities, such as a St. Bernard or Bernese Mountain Dog, or choose another animal with those characteristics, such as a fox. Then, direct your beam of energy into that image, and see yourself interacting with the person in this way.

Or say you want more freedom and independence (perhaps to set your own hours and schedule). Create an image that suggests freedom or independence to you (such as visualizing a dog like a Siberian Husky or a free-ranging animal like a bird or tiger).Then, beam yourself into that and imagine you are interacting with the person, while holding that image in mind.

In short, make these exercises your own by using symbols with meaning for you, as well as calling on the dogs that feel most supportive. You'll find that your relationships change dramatically in the direction you want. One reason is that these exercises will help change you, as you clarify what you want and focus your energy toward achieving your goal. At the same time, the energy you send may contribute to changing the other person, for the same reason that the thoughts of a monkey can impact the movements of a cursor on a computer. As researchers are finding, there is something very real about these mental energies, so by visualizing what you want and pouring your energy into that, you have a real impact on others.

So whether you want more warmth, rapport, or power in your relationships, or want to influence your relationships in other ways, use visualization to help you shape what you want. At the same time, call on your Guide Dogs, Power Dogs, or Top Dog to help guide your visualizations and provide you with even more energy and power to shape what you want.

CHAPTER 11: A WORKSHOP ON WORKING WITH YOUR GUIDE DOG

Discovering Your Dog Type included a workshop in which people discovered and contacted their Top Dog, Watch Dog, and Underdog to show how people could gain insights about themselves for personal and professional development.

You can similarly hold a workshop to show how the Dog Type system can be used to better understand others, improve relationships, and deal with everyday issues and problems. Here are highlights from a workshop I conducted on working with your Guide Dog.

The Workshop Setting

After a brief introduction to the Dog Type system and the Top Dog, Watch Dog, Underdog, Guide Dogs, and Power Dogs, I invited participants to say a little about themselves and what they hoped to gain from the workshop. This time the participants included Andrea, a financial adviser; David, an interviewer for a marketing company; Ellen, a city clerk; Paul, a salesman; Frank, an investment broker; and Sharon, a social service agency supervisor.

Andrea, who owned a Rottweiler, was particularly interested in knowing how people with the traits of different dogs interacted with others. Plus, she was curious in mingling with other dog owners and about the odd disparity that sometimes occurred between the personality of a dog owner and their dog, though their personalities matched.

Why? I explained it's a little like choosing a mate:
"You are often drawn to a dog that is similar to you in personality, but at times you may be drawn to one that has traits that complement your own or has traits that

you'd like to develop yourself. That's much like how people choose mates – either they have similar characteristics that echo them or they have complementary qualities they don't have. For instance, an energetic person may be drawn to a laid back person, because one is relaxed by the other, while the other person gets energized. Or somebody who's very quiet and introverted may be drawn to somebody who's very outgoing, so they balance each other."

Then, David wondered why he chose mixed breeds as did most of the people he knew.

"Then, if you feel one breed doesn't quite fit you, your Top Dog might be a mixture of two types of dogs." I explained.

For Ellen, the big question was personality differences that led to clashes between people and between dogs. "What if you get a dog that's different from you in personality? Does the dog adapt to you, or do you adapt to the dog?" And what if you have a relationship with someone and you're different as night and day, too? What do you do? How do you work things out?"

"There could be a compromise, or if you recognize you are in a dysfunctional relationship, you might think about how you might change it to create a more successful relationship. Or if that isn't possible, you might leave it and move on. Consider the possibilities and decide what works best for you," I told her.

Meeting One's Guide Dog (or Dogs)

While it is possible to achieve these insights directly by thinking of the first association that comes to mind when you meet someone, I used the guided visualization described in Chapter 4 in which people go to a pet store and see many dogs from which they choose their Guide Dog. I also provided a brief introduction to set the stage for this exercise:

"I'd like to begin by having you meet your inner Guide Dog. You can have one or more of these. Your

Guide Dog can be the same as your Top Dog or Watch Dog or a totally different dog. It plays the role of a teacher, helper, or wise person. You might compare Guide Dogs to spiritual teachers, guides, angels, or other helpers that people call on for help on a visual plane.

In this exercise, you'll imagine you are going to a Pet Store, where you will find your Guide Dog."

After the exercise, I asked everyone to talk about what type of dog they chose and why. Some of the key reasons were seeing a dog as a protector; intelligent, confident, wise teacher, or just a fun companion. In some cases, the participants drew on an experience where their own dogs had acted as helpers and guides in various situations, such as protecting them from danger or steering them away from unpleasant people.

Andrea said she chose a German Shepherd because "He's very sensitive. I saw him as very strong and protective, and I feel I need that now."

Ellen explained that she chose a Collie, because she found him playful as well as protective.

"I'm at a time in my life, when I want to relax and enjoy whatever I'm doing, since I feel I've been working too hard, and I live in a fairly tough neighborhood, where there's a lot of crime and drug dealers. So a Collie seemed just perfect for me. I can play with it and be protected by it."

David chose two dogs and he used his real-life knowledge of different dogs to decide to call on as a personal Guide Dog. As he explained:

"I ended up with two very different dogs. One was an Alaskan Sled dog, a huge, dog, who's very confident and in control. The other one was a Border Collie, which is like a cattle dog, very intelligent. For example, when I've seen them play with other dogs, I've seen them run in circles around them and gather them into a group, like they are herding the other dogs. Now that's pretty smart, I think."

When David wondered why he had chosen two very different dogs, I explained he could use them for very different kinds of advice. "Consider them like a team of dogs. You can always add more Guide Dogs to the team that you can call on for different purposes."

Getting Help from One's Guide Dogs

After the participants selected their Guide Dogs, who they could ask for advice, I took them on a "Dog Walk", using the exercise described in Chapter 4.

After the exercise, we discussed what people experienced and how they had gotten help from their Guide Dog. Here are some highlights of what people experienced.

Frank found he had three Guide Dogs who helped him, explaining:

"I had three dogs that joined me – one was my dog in reality, and two other dogs who came to help him. I found my dog really helpful and wise, since he always seems to know the way. For instance, he guides me through the urban forests when I take him on a walk, and it's like following a trail in the woods. He starts to smell which way to go, and I've had a lot of dreams in which he has guided me through problems. So, he was there by my side with these two other dogs."

For Sharon, her Guide Dog provided some reassurance that everything would turn out all right. She felt she especially needed such support now, since she had recently lost her job due to the economic downturn and city budget cuts, and she was unsure whether to stay in the social service field or seek other types of training and jobs. As Sharon explained:

"My Guide Dog comforted and protected me by assuring me that everything would be all right. I like to feel protected and I especially need that now, and I feel the dog I choose – a St. Bernard – helped to give me that protection. I feel like I'm going into unknown territory, not really sure what I'll do next. But I had that assurance that I was supported whatever happens. So I feel a little more comfortable facing uncertainty."

In Ellen's case, she didn't have a problem now, so she just spent time enjoying being with her Guide Dog and getting to know him better, so she could call on him in the future when needed. As Ellen described it:

"I felt like it was a fun day, and we were there to have fun, play around, and enjoy the weather, because it was nice. So I had a good time throwing balls around, and then my Guide Dog, a big floppy English Sheepdog named Harry, brought them back to me. After that we just lazed around in the sun, and that felt very good. So I didn't have any problem to deal with, but I feel like Harry will be there later when I need some help."

Finally, Paul pointed out that he got some tips from his Guide Dog on how to deal with feelings of stress or anxiety in the future – by doing something to unwind and take his mind off his tension, so it would gradually disappear. As he explained:

"I experienced being stressed out, and when my Guide Dog saw me doing that, he took a tennis ball, came over to me, and shoved it in my hand. Though I wasn't feeling up to it, I got the sense that my Guide Dog, an Irish Setter, was telling me: "I know this is going to be good for you. So throw the tennis ball." Then I did, and I experienced the feelings of stress flowing out of me, and I felt much calmer. So that led me to think that in the future, that's what I need to do: find some activity to release my feelings of tension, even if it's not something I feel like doing at first. But if I do it, that's what's good for me to do. And maybe my Guide Dog will be there to advise me to do it."

Gaining Insights about Another Person

Now the workshop turned to getting insights about another person. While participants could ask their Guide Dog to help, such as by making suggestions on what to think, the goal of the next exercise was to think of some of the people they each knew and think of what dog came to mind and why. "You want to think about, "How well that dog fits each person and what that tells you about them. So now think of somebody in your life, what sort of dog you associate with them, and why."

After everyone shared their reactions, I asked them to reflect on how this information could help them to better deal with that person. As an example, here's my exchange with Andrea, who described her sister as being like a nervous Chihuahua:

Andrea: "I have a sister I associate with a Chihuahua, because she's really nervous and antsy. It's never peaceful being around her. She's always worrying and dealing with some crisis or another. So I guess I picked a Chihuahua to describe her, because they're so scared of something all the time, and they have to continually be reassured that you're their friend and you're not going to hurt them. I think my sister is like that, because she is so nervous, and then she's always trying to suck you into her world, like a Chihuahua."

GSS: "Is there anything about the way you deal with a Chihuahua that would help you deal with your sister?"

Andrea: "Yeah, since Chihuahuas always get so frightened of things, they need to be reassured. You have to make them feel safe and comfortable, such as talking quietly to them a lot, encouraging them to do something, not making quick sudden movements, and not acting like you're going to hurt them, because they're so fragile. My sister's the same way. As I found, you've got to talk to her a lot and not to do anything very quickly before she is agreeable to go along with you on something. She wants to know everything and is really inquisitive, so you have to tell her things and reassure her that everything's going to be okay. And that works with her. Talking to her and reassuring her helps to calm her down."

In David's case, he associated a Dachshund with his ex-wife, feeling the Dachshund's scrappy, snappish behavior fit his wife's personality to a T. Plus, he found the techniques he used to control a Dachshund –isolating it and calming it down, were methods he had used with his ex-wife in the past and would again. Here's how he explained the process:

David: "I thought immediately about my ex-wife and her Dachshund. My wife and I would walk down the street with my other dog and the Dachshund between us, and the Dachshund would walk along with great confidence, always barking and ready to snap at everyone. It was like it was saying: 'Don't mess with me, or I'll sic these other people and their big dog on you.' And my ex-wife is so much like that. She raised that dog from a puppy, and that helped to make the traits common to a Dachshund – being fairly aggressive and snappish – even more common. So it became like a Dachshund with all the unmitigated bad traits of this kind of dog. It's like this Dachshund became scared of everyone. So it barks a lot and bites first, and then tries to make friends. And my ex-wife was very much like that, too."

GGS: "What would be an example of when your ex-wife aced like this?"

David: "Walking through bad neighborhoods, she was like that. She would snap at everyone. For instance, when a bunch of teenagers walked by, she would glare at them with that steely gaze that said: 'Just shut up and walk, don't start anything. Nothing's happening now, so don't let anything happen, or else.'"

So how did David deal with his ex-wife when she became snappish toward him?

David thought one approach was especially applicable, in this and in future relationships:

"With the Dachshund, I took it for a lot of walks, and the way I dealt with its aggressive, snappish behavior, like dealing with my ex-wife, was to create a very controlled environment. For instance, I would take the dog on a fire trail in the park, knowing

I'm not liable to run into anyone. So she wouldn't be able to bite and bark at anyone, and in this more controlled setting, she would be more likely to listen to me."

David sometimes used a controlled environment with his ex-wife, as he explained:

David: "With my ex-wife, a controlled environment was not going out. I'd say I'm not going to take you out if you're not going to be nice. Or I would tell her I was too tired. It's too much to do now. Let's rent a movie."

In turn, such suggestions seemed to placate his ex-wife, making her more comfortable and protected in this more isolated setting. David noted:

"I think she sometimes felt like crawling into her shell in fear, but she was more aggressive and extroverted about it. It's like she was putting up her protective barriers by being aggressive in turn to say: 'I feel like something bad is going to happen, but 'm not going let it happen. So don't bother me.'"

Given this insight, David indicated that he planned to be careful about his relationships in the future and avoid getting involved with overly aggressive women.

Sharon, too, felt she had gained some insights about how to be more cautious with people who were very controlling, people who reminded her of some bigger more powerful dogs, like the Mastiff. As she explained:

"I thought of several people I know who are really controlling. They want to control your emotions, personality, and everything about you. They remind me of a very big dominant type of dog, who is really scary to be around. In the future, I need to be more cautious about being sucked in by such people. So if someone makes me think of such a big tough dog in the future, like a Mastiff or Presa Canario, that's a sign I need to be more careful and not get caught up in such a relationship.

Getting First Impressions

Then, the focus of the workshop shifted to first impressions. The question was: What associations with different dogs come to mind when you first meet someone and how might that help you relate to that person? Here are some highlights of these discussions.

Andrea, a dog owner, used these associations to help her decide whether to get to know a person better. As she described it:

"When I met a friendly person, an outgoing person, I think of a dog that is like very outgoing and happy, like a Pomeranian, Labrador, or Irish Setter. They seem happy and can fit in with anything. When you meet people like that, you get a good rapport with them, like they're someone you want to be around. Or when you meet people that are lovable and you just want to hug them, the dog that comes to mind is a St. Bernard. They're so warm and lovable."

David described how he was particularly drawn to people who reminded him of mixed breeds, and commonly these people owned mixed breeds, too.

"When I meet anyone, I correlate them with dogs. So I'm drawn to someone I think of as a mixed breed person, which means to me someone who is different, unique. They can't be put in a box, so I think of them as more adaptable and creative. And some can be very warm and friendly. For example, I was thinking of my friend's mixed breed dog, Rug. He lays on the floor a lot, and the kids love to play with him. It's like they're all part of the pack, so there's no real barrier between the dog and the kids. When I think of people as mixed breeds, that's the feeling I get – that they'll fit in and want to connect with many different types of people. They're not just tied to one breed."

Apart from getting their own impressions on meeting people, the participants thought asking the question: "What kind of dog do you like or like most?" would be a great opener. It would be a way to better understand the person right away, and it could get them to open up more about themselves.

In fact, Andrea had already asked this question when she met people in learning if they were dog owners. As she explained: "Sometimes people have approached me on the street when I'm walking my dog to ask about her. Then, it'll come up in conversation, when I ask them: Do you have a dog? I'll also ask them, 'What kind of dog do you like, and then they'll tell me.'"

Then by asking them questions, she found people more open. "When you ask a person that question that seems to open them up. They start thinking about the qualities they like in a dog and why, so you have some insights about what they would be like. You don't even have to ask them why they like that dog. They'll explain it themselves, and you can see their emotions by the expressions in their face. You can also tell if they're a dog owner. Or if they don't have a dog, you can tell what kind they would like to get if they do."

In Ellen's view, asking a question would help her in forming first impressions. As Ellen described:

"I think an answer would help you gain an immediate insight about who that person is and how to relate to them. Later, you can always check out those impressions once you get to know someone. And usually they will be correct, because when people tell you what dog they like the most, that will express how they feel, and what they are really like, without them thinking about the question or trying to impress you. They'll come right out and let you know, because it's easy to state a preference for a kind of dog. Then, as you get to know them, you can see them act out those feelings. So just by the little a person tells you about what dog they like, you'll have a more real picture of who they are, and so you can be more trusting of them."

Apart from gaining insights into others, the participants also thought asking the question could be a great conversation starter and then a good way for people to get to know each other.

An Exercise on Getting First Impressions

Our next exercise focused on getting first impressions throughout the day. While it can be good practice to do this in reality – say you come up with quick reactions as you pass people on the street, this technique involved visualizing a series of encounters from morning to night and coming up with an association for each person they met. As I explained the process:

"In this next exercise, you'll go through your day to day activities, where you'll visualize the people you meet and notice what kind of dog comes to mind. This exercise is something which you could do in reality whatever you do that day.

For example, say you go into a supermarket. When you check out with the supermarket clerk, notice what image of a dog comes to mind.

We'll do this as a visualization in which I'll lead you to different places where you will participate in various activities throughout the day Along the way, you'll visualize the people you meet and the different dogs you associate with them."

After everyone was ready to do the exercise, I began as follows:

Just get very calm and relaxed. Now imagine you are in your house getting up, ready to start your day.

Now you're dressed, ready to go out, and you're going to take a walk around the neighborhood. So go outside, and as you walk, notice who you meet. As you meet or pass by each person, just imagine what kind of dog they are. See the image of the dog come to mind and notice the personality of the dog and the person. And think what about the person suggests that type of dog.

So take that walk now, and I'll be quiet for about a minute while you do…

Now I'd like you to imagine that it's lunchtime, and you're going into a local restaurant. As you do, the waitress or waiter comes over or you see the person behind the counter, and you get an impression of them as a dog. What kind of dog would that be?

Now you have a friend who's meeting you there. You see your friend come in, and he or she sits down with you. As you greet your friend and talk, imagine what kind of dog that friend would be. Then, notice the qualities you associate with that dog and that person...

Now you're finishing lunch, and you're going to take the afternoon off to do a fun thing you like to do — like going to the park, to the zoo, or for a boat ride. As you do whatever you want, you meet people along the way. And you associate different kinds of dogs with these people. See what comes to mind, and how the characteristics of the dog or person you meet fit with that person...

Now you're returning from what you were doing in the afternoon, and you're going to go to an after-hours cocktail party. It could be at a friend's house, at a business club, at a local night club. You go in and meet some people there. These may be the bartender, some people you socialize with. Again notice who these people are and what kinds of dogs you associate with them. Then, notice the personality characteristics that come to mind...

Now before you go home, you're going to relax in a movie theater. As you watch any movie you'd like to see, and see the actors and actresses on the screen, you see the image of a dog associated with actors or actresses. Again, just notice what personality characteristics they have which you associate with the dog...

Now you see yourself leaving the movie theater going home. You're feeling very relaxed, very good, having had a very nice, interesting day. You go into your house and sink into an easy chair or couch. And you're feeling really good, as you return to everyday reality.

A Day of Seeing Dogs

Once everyone was back from the visualization, I asked people to share their experiences. Here are the highlights of their comments.

David: "The experience made me more aware about the breeds of dogs, and especially their body language, since one breed can look like the other, but their personalities are very different. That's what happened when I went through my day.

"I was doing field interview work for the marketing company I worked for, and I met a range of people with different personality types – much like I do at work. For instance, when I came up to some of the houses, some of the people had a watch dog, and it was going: "raahh, raaah, raaah."But after the owner introduced the watch dog to me, all of sudden, I was part of the family, and the dog stopped barking at me and tried to be friendly."

GSS: "Did you see any associations of the dogs and personality types as you met different people through the day?

David: "Yeah, I noticed that the mannerisms and temperaments of the different people I met went along with certain types of dogs. For instance, the tough guy in the underwear who answered the door had a Boston Terrier, and a teenage girl in a short mini shirt had a small yapping Yorkie. So definitely, yes, there was a strong connection though I also noticed, with dogs, as with people, after they feel okay with you, say you're doing research, not trying to sell them anything, they get more relaxed and friendly. So I experienced a lot of personality change, as I went from house to house.

Then, David reported briefly on his other experiences.

"In the lunch room, I saw a woman sitting at a booth in the back, who was like a Great Dane, sitting there in a confident and friendly way.

"And at a cocktail party, the people reminded me of dogs sniffing at each other, or they milled around sniffing at each other, trying to decide who to go home with for the night. You've got basically 30 seconds to convince someone you're a great person, so the other person will want to keep you around, or they're on to meet someone else. This quaint interchange is a lot like what dogs do. If they don't like the smell of another dog, that's too bad. They take off and they're gone.

"And then I met a waitress at a nightclub, who was a real Bassett-Hound type, which means that she was a really good waitress, loyal and devoted just like a friendly Bassett.

"Then at the movies I visualized Clint Eastwood as a Coon Hound, and Robert Redford, like a Springer Spaniel or English Setter. Why? I think I saw Eastwood like this dog because he seems like a hunter, a guy that's strong, confident, always on the prowl, and he's good at sniffing out dishonesty and anger. And Redford? Well, he's got that friendly, outdoorsy, family quality about him, and I think of these dogs as being like that."

Here's what Andrea had to say about the matches she found with women in the street, a writer, and a friend bartender.

"I started out going to the bank, and I met this woman who was walking down the street. I saw her earlier today and tonight I visualized her even more clearly. She really stood out, because this is a blue collar neighborhood, but she was dressed elegantly and was very confident. Then, I noticed that she had this dog, like a Yorkie Terrier, which she carried under her arm like a purse, and this dog looked very confident like her. It seemed to be proud to be there, like it knew it was on display and really fit there. It looked like she picked that dog, because it looked good with her, like an accessory.

"So as she walked along, she seemed very proud and arrogant and didn't look at anybody, and just like I sensed earlier, she didn't want to talk to anyone, which was like a confirmation that I was right to not say anything to compliment her earlier that day. It's like both in reality and in my visualization, when I looked at her, she looked away, like she didn't want me or anyone else to intrude on her space. And her dog looked away, too, just like her. So it was a perfect match.

"Then at the restaurant, when a waiter wearing a tie came over to me, a boxer came to mind, because boxers are such slick, neat dogs, and I've seen pictures of boxers wearing ties. Then when my friend sat down at the table, I pictured a Labrador…I guess because Labradors are a very relaxed and friendly, and that's what my friend is like.

"Later, at the park, I saw dogs and people running around, everyone having a good time. And the dogs I envisioned there were like Setters and mixed breed dogs, because when I think of those dogs, I think of everyone enjoying the outdoors and having fun.

"Next, at the club I saw a bartender who reminded me of a Doberman, because they're both tough. Or maybe, I thought, he might be more like a Rottweiler, because he seemed really controlled as he looked around, checking what everyone else was doing, to see that customers were being treated properly and everything was going smoothly.

"Then, as I looked around the club, I thought of Poodles and Collies for the women there, because they were dressed up and showing off. After that, in the movie, as I watched a comedy, I thought of mixed breeds for some of the comedians. I imagined a shaggy dog, because the comedians were dressed like that. Finally, when I was relaxing at home, I imagined a Shepherd or Collie was there with me, because I live in a tough neighborhood, and a Shepherd or Collie could be my protector. "

And so, as each person went through their day, they experienced multiple images of dogs associated with many different types of people, and it almost always was a good match.

So now, as I explained, they could apply this technique in everyday life. "Here's how you can apply the method every day.

As you go around during the day, notice what associations you have with the different people in your life. Or when you see people on the street, think of the first dog that comes to mind. Later, if you can, check out your perceptions with the people for whom you make these associations. You'll find the more you work with these associations, the more sensitive you will get. And when you share this information, it's a great conversational opener and a great way to know the people you already know even better."

Learning from the Dog Associations

Then, the conversation turned to how people might learn from their associations to guide their interactions with others, such as knowing when to avoid certain people or situations, as Ellen and Paul reported:

Ellen: "I was just being carefree (during the visualization) and I saw a retriever. It was a nice friendly dog that I liked to be around and felt perfectly safe with. Then, I thought about how if a dog seemed like it was going to be vicious, I would steer away from it. How would I know? By looking at its body language, such as raising its hackles to show it was getting ready for attack.

"Then, that got me thinking about what to look for in people to know if I wanted to be with them or not. For example, I saw some people I knew I would stay away from because their expression showed they didn't want to be bothered. So I bypassed them to keep them from interfering with my happy mood.

Paul: "I thought about getting cues on who or what to avoid, too. The visualization was like a reminder to pay more attention to this and be careful. For instance, I saw people when walking around with my dog, where I could tell by reading their body language that I didn't want to be around them, because they might be dangerous. Then, my dog signaled me by tugging on its leash, saying: "Let's go this way." Likewise, when my own dog sees a dog he knows is a problem, he'll avoid it. He'll shy away indicating that 'I'm scared of that dog. Let's go this way.'"

As Paul and Ellen's experience suggested, it's important to pay attention to the dog images and associations to better get to know others and decide what to do as a result. As I explained:

"Say you are walking down the street, see some people ahead of you and get an image of your dog tugging on its leash. That's a message from your unconscious to avoid the situation, perhaps by walking on the other side of the block or finding another route. You get such messages from your unconscious in the form of sudden feelings of tension or anxiety. Then, the images and associates you get by working with these techniques magnify those messages, so they are clearer and you pay more attention to them."

What about the problem of getting mixed messages? How do you interpret the signals then, David wondered. As he noted: "Sometimes the body language of dogs is contradictory. Usually, you can tell when a dog's hackles are up that he's ready to attack. But sometimes dogs have their hackles up, but their tail wagging, so they appear friendly. Then, you get close, and boom, they really love to attack. So they're just drawing you in and putting you off your guard."

David's image of real-life experiences during the visualization suggested the need for extra caution, not only with dogs showing these contradictory signs with these same characteristics.

"I've had an experience in offices with backstabbers, and I can imagine a number of dogs that might be like that, such as a Pit Bull who's friendly as long as you keep him fed and happy. But once you slip up on a meal, watch out. You could be the next victim. Backstabbers are like that, too. They just wait for the right opportunity. Then, boom, they plunge in the knife."

"That's right," I said, wrapping up the discussion with a last comment. "By being sensitive to these different kinds of dogs, you become sensitive to the type of people who might be like that – people who are tail wagging, yet ready to attack you. So if you sense these mixed signals, such as while you're talking to this person and the image of a tail-wagging dog ready to pounce comes to mind, you know it's time to put up your defenses. Or maybe you might even try a pre-emptive offensive, since you're dealing with someone you can't trust."

Making Changes in a Relationship

The workshop concluded with two exercises on changing a situation. One was to create a warmer, personal relationship or reduce tension in a conflict by sending warm feelings to another person. The other was to increase one's feelings of power and confidence in a relationship.

As I explained the process:

"In this first visualization, you will imagine you are sending feelings of love, affection, or warmth to a person you want to feel closer to or overcome a conflict with using the help of your Power Dog or Guide Dog. Then, in the visualization on increasing your power in a relationship, you will imagine your Power Dog coming with you to help."

After each visualization, there was a brief discussion about what each person experienced and how to apply that experience in everyday life.

For example, after the "Sending Love" visualization, Sharon described turning to a St. Bernard for help, because, "They're so big and lovable." Though Sharon didn't have any particular person in mind, she felt she could use the technique to meet someone in a more receptive frame of mind. As she commented:

"This might be a good approach to create a warmer, more comfortable setting for a date or romantic encounter. But I want to do this in a restrained, controlled way, since you could overwhelm someone if you send out your feelings too intensely. You don't want to come on too strong."

Finally, I set the stage for the last visualization about increasing one's power in a relationship.

"Now, to increase your power, you'll see yourself as being very powerful. You'll also call on your Power Dog, a dog you associate with being powerful, to make you feel even more powerful. Then, you'll see yourself in the relationship or situation where you want this additional power. You'll imagine a scene that is likely to happen, you'll express this newly found sense of power there. Later, when you are with that person or in that situation for real, you'll carry those increased feelings of power with you, and you'll be better able to act to express that power."

After the visualization, there was a final discussion about everyone's experience and how to apply this feeling of greater power in their situations. This time everyone chose work situations, since that was the setting in which one is most concerned with power in relationships. "It's where alpha and beta are most relevant – at work, Paul observed, "Either you're on top or somebody else is, and you want to know."

How did everyone feel they could apply their experience of power in the workplace? Here are some highlights from the discussion.

Paul: "After the experience of being more powerful, I imagined being at work dealing with my boss. At first, I saw my boss as being very snappy as before, and then I saw myself saying things to her before she could say them to me, because I knew she would say them. I wanted to say them first, because if she did, she would take control, and if she did, that would be unsettling. But if I could say them first, I could take control. So it was a little like my boss and I were playing a power game, like "Who goes first?" But this was my way of pulling out the rug from under her by saying what she expected to say first. For instance, I'd tell her: 'Okay, I know how well I did, which wasn't enough, and I know I have to do better.'

"Afterwards, I worked on adding power to my response, so in the future I would feel even stronger and better able to stand up to her."

Then, Paul had even more ideas about ways of working with his boss in the future.

Paul: "Besides standing up to her, I could find a more creative way of working with her and take on more responsibility. For example, one image that came to mind is of my sled dog pulling the sled up to the problem, identifying it, and thinking of the quickest and easiest way around it. So increasing power doesn't always mean having a confrontation with someone. It's more about working smarter and independently and being able to do more myself. So I think that would be a better strategy to use – the way of the sled dog, rather than playing the pit bull and getting knocked out of the ring."

As I commented: "One way this process can work is when you haven't expressed this power before in a relationship. Visualizing this gives you a charge of power so you feel ready to go do it. It's also a way to identify different possibilities in advance so you can try them out mentally. The process helps you feel like you can do almost anything, since you're safe to imagine it now. Then, in reality, you can do it or not. But since you have gone through that scenario before, you are prepared if that's a good way to act. It's like a pre-exercise. Plus the process adds an extra charge of power, since you are associating your Power Dog with it."

Andrea had exactly that experience, explaining that: "My Power Dog was a Doberman. They know how to sit quietly in the corner, just watching and feeling out what different people are like, like they are preparing their strategy on how to respond and how much power to use if they are called on to attack. So they are not too overpowering or use too little power. So they have a power they can control, and I would like that kind of power myself. That's why I chose a Doberman as my Power Dog. It's a dog that can be controlled, but has a lot of power and is watchful."

GSS: "And then you take that image and experience with you to remind yourself how to exercise your own power and control, and that reinforces how you want to act."

By contrast, David chose a Power Dog he associated with using more subterfuge to exercise power. As he described his experience, "My Power Dog was a sled dog, and I thought about how the Alpha Beta dynamic is very strong in work relationships, like in a dog pack, where the top dog wants all the other dogs to know who's the most powerful. So if you're not the Alpha dog but you want to get what you want, you have to do this in a more roundabout way. I do field work doing interviews in the neighborhoods, so I don't have to be around the boss. So I imagined this sled dog in the snow getting the ball to the goal while avoiding the boss. The other dogs were still hooked up to the sled, so they were going along with pack leader, but my dog was out on his own, so he had the power to be free.

I explained, "A sled dog is the perfect example of this more surreptitious use of power and that many sled dogs may be part of the pack and learn to follow the lead dog, but they can be very independent and stubborn, like Siberian Huskies. So if they don't respect the dog or person exercising authority or you open the door, out they go. And it sounds like your boss is very much like this."

David: "Yes, she is. She may still own the sled, but I can find ways to get where I am without being hooked up to it. That approach works well for me, so that's what I'll keep doing."

On that note, the workshop ended, with everyone eager to apply their experiences with their Guide Dogs and Power Dogs in their real life work situation, though Paul had one last question as he flipped through the profiles of different types of dogs.

"What if you don't see an association you have with a particular dog listed as a personality trait, and you're trying to imagine a better way to relate to that person?"

"That doesn't matter," I explained. "The associations listed are the ones most commonly thought to characterize that dog. But what's important is not the images that others have, but your own associations with each dogs. Think of the ones that are listed as a way to get you started thinking about the common characteristics of these different dogs. Then, add your own trait – whether for your Power Dog or the person you are working or interacting with. Then, use these associations – the common ones and your own – to help you both increase your feelings of power and decide the best approach to use in drawing on your power in that situation to better get what you want in that relationship."

Setting Up Your Own Workshop

Here are some tips for setting up your own workshop.
- Start off with an introduction on using the Guide Dogs for getting advice.
- After participants choose their Guide Dogs, ask everyone to describe the dog they chose, why, and how their Guide Dog helped them.
- Ask people to think about the people in their life and the dogs they associate with them.
- Discuss how people can apply these associations to make changes in relationships.
- Invite people to share about their experiences or their reactions to others' experiences or ask questions.
- Have fun.

PART V: APPLYING THE DOG TYPE SYSTEM IN EVERYDAY LIFE

CHAPTER 12: GETTING SOME EXTRA HELP FOR MORE ENERGY AND POWER

Once you know the basics of using the Dog Type system to understand yourself and others, you can apply it in multiple ways in your everyday life. Essentially, you call on your Guide Dogs and Top Dog for advice and guidance in daily life and on your Power Dogs for additional power and support in different situations. The process of visualization, mental imagery, self-talk, and other techniques allow you to tap into your intuitive, creative powers; and the relationship you develop with different types of dogs helps to increase that power. In short, wherever you call on your inner powers for advice, strength, and support – from making decisions and solving problems to practicing skills and becoming more creative – you can call on your dogs for help.

Getting Some Extra Help from a Rescue Dog

A Rescue Dog is one you call that has additional qualities you feel will be helpful in a particular situation. Later, you can continue to call on that Rescue Dog for help when that situation arises again.

For example, say you feel you need to relax more, and the dogs you have already selected as your Guide Dogs, Top Dog, or Power Dogs, are hard driving, aggressive, strong dogs, usually fast and on the go – not the kind of dogs you associate with relaxing and chilling out. So now it's time to bring in a different type of dog with the needed qualities as your "Rescue Dog" to come to your "rescue".

In some cases, this helpful Rescue Dog may even be your Underdog, because you don't normally have these qualities, but could develop them. But that's fine. You can get help from all sorts of unexpected places.

You find a Rescue Dog using the same techniques for connecting with your Guide Dogs, Top Dog, and Power Dog. The difference is that you are calling on your Rescue Dog for additional help in a particular situation.

First think of what help you need or of what goal you want to accomplish. Then think of what type of dog you associate with that kind of activity. An image or the name of this dog may come to mind immediately, if you are familiar with this system. Or take a few minutes to relax, think of the situation in which you need help, and ask for your Rescue Dog to appear to help you, and soon your dog will.

For instance, say you want to increase your energy. You might visualize a Greyhound or Whippet, which are very fast dogs; then call on that dog to appear in your mind's eye or sit beside you to give you an infusion of energy. Or suppose you want to relax and calm down. You might call on an English Sheepdog or Puli, which is a very calm, relaxed dog. The Puli even looks like a huge pillow of fur you can sink into to get really relaxed. Or say you are going to a meeting where you have to be very assertive to stand up for what you want to persuade others to go along with you. The image of a Mastiff or Pit Bull might help.

In some cases, you may already have a Power Dog, Top Dog, or Watch Dog, that is ideal for helping in a particular situation. Then, simply call on your Power Dog, Top Dog, or Watch Dog to help. But if you don't already have the type of dog best suited to help in that situation, that's when you need to call on a Rescue Dog – or a team of them – to appear on the scene with the qualities and assistance you need.

Following are a variety of ways to apply these methods with your Guide Dogs, Top Dog, Power Dogs, or Rescue Dogs. As you continue working with these techniques and get to know the different dogs even better, you'll find still other ways to use these dogs and these techniques – the subject of future books in this series.

This chapter focuses on techniques for overcoming stress and tension, increasing your energy, feeling more confidence and self-esteem, and achieving your goals. The next deals with ways to increase your skills and creativity, solve problems, and make better decisions.

To Overcome Stress and Tension

With many people complaining about too much stress, given today's fast paced, competitive life, calling on your dogs can help you relax and get rid of unwanted tension. You need the appropriate balance so you aren't over-tense or overstressed, and are sufficiently relaxed to feel confident, composed, and carry out any task smoothly and efficiently.

Here are some ways to do this.

Create a Mental Trigger with Your Dog for Yourself

You can use a mental trigger to help you relax. First, use a visualization or self-talk to think of a dog that suggests relaxation to you. Then whenever you feel tense or feel sensations of stress coming on, you can use the trigger to remain calm and relaxed or quickly calm down.

To create this trigger, take a few minutes to get very relaxed, and as you do, think of a dog you associate with being relaxed (such as a Beagle, English Shepherd, or Puli).Then, repeat this process a few times a day over the next few days, and each time you relax, think of this kind of dog. Eventually, just thinking of this type of dog will relax you, since you have created a conditioned response by making an association between relaxation and this dog. Once you have created this association, think of this dog any time you want to relax, and you can use this same process to create an association between any other activity and a selected dog.

Use a Relaxing Visualization with Your Dog to Help You Calm Down.

Another approach to calming down is to take a few minutes in a quiet place to visualize yourself in a relaxed setting with your Top Dog, Guide Dogs, or Rescue Dog you associate with getting relaxed.

Then, see yourself engaging in an enjoyable and relaxing activity with this dog, such as going to the beach and walking by the water or taking a leisurely walk in a sunny meadow. As you participate in this activity, feel yourself getting more and more relaxed, and if you want, have your Top Dog, Guide Dog, or Rescue Dog repeat the words to you: "Relax…Relax…You are getting more and more relaxed, more and more relaxed."

Keep doing this exercise for a few minutes, and you'll experience your body feeling more and more relaxed, too. So after a few minutes, you should feel much calmer, as well as more refreshed and reenergized.

Chase Away Your Anxieties with Your Dog to Help You Calm Down

You can chase away the anxiety you feel about something you have to do by building up your confidence that you can do it.

One way to build up your confidence for a task is to call on your Guide Dog from time to time during the day to remind you that you can and will do it. To do so, take a few quiet minutes now and then to get calm and centered. Then, imagine that your Guide Dog is telling you again and again: "You do can do it (fill in the image of whatever you want to do). You can do it."

Next, turn this into an "I" statement and by saying to yourself: "I can do it. I am doing it (fill in the image of yourself doing it)." At the same time, feel the support and confidence of your Guide Dog.

Then, see yourself doing what you want now, so your inner mind gets used to your doing it. Also, feel a sense of assurance and confidence that you are participating in this activity correctly and effectively.

You might additionally visualize others being pleased and complimenting you on whatever you have done (such as writing a good report, giving a good presentation, leading a successful meeting).

After this exercise, you'll feel better immediately. You'll be calmer, more relaxed, less worried about whatever you have to do. In addition, when it comes time to perform the activity, you'll do it better, because you feel more confident and have practiced doing it in your mind.

To Increase Your Energy and Feel Less Tired

Calling on your dogs can help you get a quick charge or recharge of energy, such as if you feel sleepy or drowsy, have to start a big project that seems overwhelming, or need a rush to get you going in the morning and keep you going at night. These techniques work because you are using an image of a high-energy dog to give you the energy you need – whether one of your Power Dogs, your Top Dog, or a Rescue Dog you call on for the occasion. This kind of energy charge can often substitute for using anything artificial, like a pep pill, since you are drawing the needed energy from inside you, with the help of your dogs. The process works much like other types of energy techniques, using visualizations, except here you are using the visualization with some help from your dogs, as in the following two techniques.

Creating Your Own Energy and Enthusiasm

This is a technique to create a quick burst of energy and enthusiasm at any time, with a little dogged help. First, visualize or think of a fast, high energy dog.

Then, with this dog's image in mind, stand with your feet slightly apart and make a fist with one hand. Then, see this dog running rapidly either in a race or chasing a very fast animal, such as a rabbit. You see it going faster and faster, with mounting excitement in your mind's eye.

Now, as you see this dog running, quickly raise your hand to your head and lower it several times. Each time you bring it down, shout out something like: "I am awake," "I feel energetic," "I am enthusiastic and excited," or "I am raring to get up and go."

Repeat this five to ten times, and each time feel a rush of energy and enthusiasm surge through you. Soon you'll be awake and alert and ready to tackle any project. In fact, after you have repeatedly practiced this exercise, you can simply imagine this dog racing or chasing something and your energy and enthusiasm will increase, because of the power of repeated association.

Ideally, do this exercise initially in reality, since it's more stimulating to use your whole body. But if other people are around, so you can't actively participate without seeming strange or disruptive, imagine yourself doing this exercise in your mind's eye. Then, your mental imagery or self-talk can help to wake you up or motivate you to act. Eventually, the whole process will become a habit so just thinking of a dog racing or chasing will be enough to energize you.

Drawing on the Energies of the Universe

In this technique, which Gini adapted from a technique she first described in *Mind Power,* you get a little help from your dogs to make the experience even more vivid. You imagine that you have columns of energy flowing into and through you, with one stream of energy coming up from the earth and the other from the air. Meanwhile, one of your Power Dogs, Top Dog, or an especially strong Rescue Dog is seated beside you, helping to gather this energy. For example, visualize the dog digging in the ground to unleash the earth energy that pours into you, and then see him facing the wind to draw the energy of the air toward you. As you feel these two streams of energy pour into you, you feel energized – and this process has real biological effects, since it stimulates the molecules of energy in your body to move more quickly, so you both feel and become more energetic.

As these two types of energy pour into your body, notice they are slightly different. Notice that the earth energy that pours into your feet and surges up through your body feels very strong, giving you increased energy and power. Meanwhile, the air energy that streams in through the top of your head and down into your body feels light, airy, and expansive, giving you a sense of buoyancy.

Next, focus on the two energies meeting at the base of your spine, and see them join and spiral around together. Then they move up and down your spine and fill you with energy. You can balance the two energies, if you wish, by drawing on extra energy from the earth (heavy) or from the universe (light) as you wish. Meanwhile, your dog is outside, helping to direct more and more energy to you.

Keep running this energy up and down your spine until you feel filled with energy. Then, if you have a project or task you want to do, direct this energy toward doing this project. Even if you haven't felt especially motivated and enthused to do this task, you will feel this increased energy and enthusiasm to work on this project now, and you will feel increased confidence knowing you can do it with all this extra energy.

Whatever the project is, as you go to tackle it, feel this energy pouring from you into the project, while your dog sends you even more energy. It's like the dog you called on to help is acting like a pump, drawing the energy from the earth and the air and directing it to you, so you experience it energizing and can direct that energy into whatever task you want to do.

For example, if you want to write or type something, visualize the energy surging out through your hands. If you plan to lift some heavy objects, visualize the energy coming out through your feet, body, and arms. If you are going to teach a class or sell something, see the energy pouring into your voice as you speak. Or just see this energy pour into you as you start the day.

Both these and the previous techniques are great energy builders. But they're not designed to replace the sleep you need. Think of them more like quick energy-fixers to be used on a short-term basis. Should you keep drifting off while doing something or find yourself continually tired, after using these exercises, get more sleep.

To Increase Your Feelings of Confidence and Self-Esteem

You can build up your feelings of confidence and self-esteem with the help of your Power Dogs, Top Dog, and Rescue Dogs, too, to better get what you want in life. Even if you haven't done something before, being confident, can help you do it; it can help you get better at something more quickly, because you are more focused and sure of yourself as you practice. And, when you feel more confident, you don't let any negative criticisms get you down; you don't take them personally, because you feel certain you can deal with the problem and overcome it. You are confident you can do better, and so you will.

This approach works because *if you believe you are great, you are great!* Then, that belief helps to create the experiences you have that support this belief. For example, if you are convinced you should have a certain job or promotion, you'll exude an aura of confidence and act like you belong in that job, so people will think of you in that role. Plus, with that belief, you'll know you can do whatever is required and will be able to do it. And you will have that ability because you believe you can and confidently do what is necessary to turn your belief into a reality.

Where do your dogs come in? In several ways. Your Guide Dogs can help you as you think about your good qualities that help build your esteem. Your Power Dogs can give you support and increase your feelings of confidence about your abilities, skills, and likelihood of success as you engage in activities. And, as needed, a Rescue Dog can provide you with even more confidence to build you up. Here are some key techniques to use to build confidence.

Acknowledge your Good Qualities, Talents, and Accomplishments

You gain confidence in yourself and what you can do by acknowledging your good qualities, talents, and accomplishments. Here's where your Guide Dogs can be especially helpful in identifying what these attributes are and helping you concentrate on them to remind yourself how great you are.

One way to do this exercise is to find a place where you can quietly think about what you like about yourself and what you have done well. Before you start, imagine that one or more of your Guide Dogs are with you. Though you can think about your qualities, talents, and accomplishments on your own, your Guide Dog adds additional support as you think about these qualities. Also, sometimes people are hesitant to praise themselves, thinking this seems too prideful or boastful. But if you have someone else, such as a friend or in this case your Guide Dog praising you to the skies, that's okay.

So now get started thinking about all your good qualities. To do so, get a sheet of paper and a pencil, divide the paper into three columns, and head each one: "My Good Qualities", "What I Can Do Well", and "What I Have Accomplished". It should look something like this:

	What Are My Good Qualities?	What I Can Do Well?	What Are My Biggest Accomplishments?
1			
2			
3			
4			
Etc.			

With this paper in front of you, get very relaxed, and imagine your Guide Dog is sitting beside you giving you answers. Ask your Guide Dog the question at the head of each column and listen to the answers. Then, as quickly as you can, write down whatever your Guide Dog says. When you start to slow down, repeat the question again, listen and write some more. Conclude by asking: "Anything else?" write down these last items, and go on to the next heading.

After you are finished, review your list. As you read each item, see yourself with that quality, talent, or accomplishment, and feel your Guide Dog praising you, telling you how "Great" and "Wonderful" you are. Experience how good it feels to get this praise. Finally, see your Guide Dog giving you a large blue "Best of Show" ribbon – just like a judge might give a show dog a ribbon. Then, pat yourself on the back to congratulate yourself and hear your Guide Dog barking out his or her excited approval, too.

Affirm Yourself and All Your Talents and Abilities

Affirmations are another great way to build confidence and self-esteem by asserting that you already have the qualities you want to develop. You keep making these affirmations as you work on developing these qualities with even more confidence.

This approach works because you are what you think. So if you think positively you'll feel positively. And if you think you have certain qualities and talents, that's how you'll be. Even if you don't have these characteristics now, by thinking you have them, you'll develop them and your self-esteem will soar.

In this case, your Power Dogs can contribute to the process by being there as your cheerleaders, making these affirmations that much stronger. So imagine one or more of your Power Dogs by your side as you do this exercise, and experience them cheering for you as you say each affirmation. Should you want help in deciding what your affirmations should be, call on one of your Guide Dogs to help you create your affirmations.

Take a sheet of paper, write down an appropriate header (i.e.: "Who I Am Now"), and begin writing down your affirmations about who you are, want to be, or what you have or want. Choose whatever is most important to you, and affirm it in the present tense, even if you don't have that thing or quality now. Use the present tense, because we become the way we see ourselves now. You can ask your Guide Dog for help with what to write or for additional ideas.

For example, you might affirm that:
I have an exciting, interesting job I really enjoy.
I have gotten that new job I want and I enjoy my new office.
I am a dynamic speaker and can keep an audience excited about what I say.
I have met the partner I want and we are getting married in a gala celebration.
Etc.

After you finish writing, select your most important affirmation and focus on it for about a minute. Close your eyes if you prefer. Repeat your affirmation over and over to yourself aloud or mentally, and as you do, see yourself in this imagined situation. Don't just say the words, but see yourself there. At the same time, as you engage in this activity, see your Power Dog eagerly jumping up and down or barking, giving you its strength and support.

Do this technique daily for about a week, and you'll notice that you feel more confident and that the things you want will start coming into your life. These affirmations work, because this mental and visual reinforcement helps to change your attitude about yourself, so you not only see yourself in a different way, but you feel better and therefore more confident about yourself, too. Then, your changed self-image will lead others to perceive and respond to you differently, because they can sense this air of increased confidence – much like you can stare down a dog that might be ready to attack. When you look like you are confident and sure of yourself, typically, the dog will sense that strength coming from you and back off, not wanting to challenge you.

Visualize Yourself as a Successful Person Achieving a Goal or Having Everything You Want

Seeing yourself as a success in achieving a goal, having what you want, or being recognized for your accomplishments can increase your confidence, too, since success builds self-esteem. So does visualizing yourself as successful. You see that desired vision as a reality, which helps you feel more self-assured. You feel more powerful, dynamic, and recognized, and these positive feelings contribute to your being more confident.

Here your Guide Dog can help you decide what you most want, and your Power Dog can give you more strength, as you imagine you now have what you want in the here and now. Once you decide to do this technique, repeat it regularly for several days to reinforce this success image and strengthen your feelings of self-esteem. Later, turn these feelings into reality by initiating new actions for success or responding confidently to new opportunities, knowing you have the ability to achieve them.

To start the process, decide what type of goal is most important to you in your work or personal life. To help with this process, you can imagine your Guide Dog is beside you. Then, ask the question: "What goal do I most want to achieve now?" and listen for the answer. Should several goals come to mind, pick the one that feels the most important to work on now.

Next, get relaxed, close your eyes, and see yourself realizing this goal. Make your image of this achievement as vivid as possible, and see your success happening in the here and now. Meanwhile, as you see this image appear in your mind's eye, imagine that your Power Dog is seated beside you, happily watching and cheering you on. It may be jumping up and down, barking happily, wagging its tail excitedly, or otherwise showing enthusiasm and support.

As you visualize your success, experience the feeling of satisfaction and power this brings. Feel elated, excited, strong, powerful, fully self-confident, and in charge. See others come over to you or call to congratulate you. You feel warm and glowing as you receive their praise. They tell you how successful you are. And you feel wonderful, able to do anything you want.

To Set and Achieve Goals

You can also call on your dogs to help with setting and achieving your goals. Their primary role is to help you make choices when you use various goal-setting techniques. Essentially, you ask your questions, and your Guide Dogs help you answer them, sometimes more honestly, since calling on them helps you tap into your unconscious desires and needs. Your dogs can also help you establish more specific and realistic goals and set priorities, which are critical for reaching your goals. If you are too vague, don't feel an intense conviction that you really want something, and don't prioritize, you diffuse your energy by going after too many things simultaneously, rather than focusing on what you want the most.

In short, to get what you want, do the following:
1. Have a clear specific picture of what you want
2. Prioritize your most important goals.

3. Focus on your more important goals first — at most, two or three at a time.
4. Make sure each goal is realistically achievable.
5. Infuse your goal with a determined conviction that you really want it and are willing to do what it takes to get it.

These are fairly basic goal-setting principles. The following techniques can help you better set and achieve these goals by calling on your Power Dogs or Top Dog for help.

Getting a Clear Specific Picture of What You Want and Prioritizing What to Do

This technique will help you focus on what you really want and set your priorities by using visualization or self-talk, combined with automatic writing, to record your answers. The process helps you get at what you really think and feel by letting go of your conscious mind, so your thoughts flow more spontaneously.

Get prepared by taking a sheet of paper and writing down the questions you want answered, such as, "What Do I Want to Gain or Achieve?", "Why is This Goal Important to Me Now?", "What is My Most Important Goal or Goals?", "How Realistic is This Goal?"

Your sheet of paper will look something like the following table:

What Do I Want to Gain or Achieve?	Why is This Goal Important to Me Now?	What is My Most Important Goal or Goals?	How Realistic Is This Goal?

Then, get very relaxed and imagine one of your Guide Dogs (or your Top Dog) sitting across from you. Your dog is there, eager to listen and help you first determine your goals and prioritize your most important goal or goals. Later, you can ask your dog what you need to do to get there.

Now start asking your questions. Don't try to guide the answer yourself. Instead, let your Guide Dog (or Top Dog) answer. And write down whatever comes to you.

First ask, "What do I want to gain or achieve?" and list whatever answers you get. Then, for each goal, asking "Why is this goal important to me now?" and record your answers. As you look at these different goals, ask your Guide (or Top) Dog: "What goal or goals are most important to me now?" or "Which goal or goal should I concentrate on achieving first?" Then, note the first of the three goals that come to mind.

For those goals you have listed, ask: "How realistic is achieving this goal?" and ask your Guide (or Top) Dog to give you one of three answers: "Realistic", "Maybe", or "Pipedream". Then, write that down. If you get any pipedreams, eliminate that goal, and concentrate on the others. Should you get all pipedreams, you have a problem setting realistic goals and should look at the other goals you have listed to determine which are most important to do now. Or if you have no more goals listed, start the exercise again, and this time ask your Guide or Top Dog to only suggest goals you can really accomplish.

Once you have selected one to three goals, these are the goals to concentrate on achieving first.

Developing the Conviction and Confidence to Achieve Your Goals

Once you are clear what you want, know your goals are realistic, and are certain this is your most important goal or goals, put your energy and determination into achieving each goal and regularly re-affirm this conviction. This way, you continue to re-energize that goal and remind yourself that you will achieve it and will do what is necessary to do so.

Your Power Dog can help, as a supporter and cheerleader adding its power to increase your conviction and confidence. Here's how.

Get relaxed and close your eyes. Find a few minutes during the day, or do this exercise as you drift off to sleep or right after you wake up.

Imagine your Power Dog is sitting beside you and concentrate all your attention on realizing your goal. See your goal already achieved, whether it's a material possession, job, desired relationship, or new home. And see your Power Dog in the scene with you. Make the images of your goal as clear as possible and be aware of everything you see — colors, objects, people, rooms, furnishings, and so on. Listen to what you hear around you — sounds, voices, conversations. Touch objects around you. Notice anything you smell, taste, or sense moving. And see your Power Dog walking around, looking, listening, and lending you its power and support. In short, experience achieving your goal as fully as possible.

As you see this goal achieved, very vividly, say to yourself: "I will achieve this goal. I will do what is necessary to get it. This goal is completely possible. I just need to act to get it, and it will happen now!"

Finally, end the visualization and return to normal consciousness feeling fully convinced and certain you will get what you want. This feeling will stay with you during the day and will help you take the necessary steps to achieve your goal.

Determining the Steps to Achieve Your Goal

Once you set your goal and have the conviction and determination to achieve it, the next step is breaking it down into specific objectives or steps to accomplish including noting what resources you might need along the way. You also need to work out the sequence of what you will do when. Essentially, this is basic "Goal-setting and Achieving 101", which is much like setting out the steps for designing a project. After you determine these steps, the final stage is implementation – where you put your plan into action and work toward your goal. Whole books are written about this process.

Again, you can call on your Guide or Top Dog to help you decide what you need to do, the resources you require, and how to order and prioritize these activities, so you can carry out your action plan most efficiently. The role of your Guide Dog or Top Dog is to help you get into a frame of mind to see things in a holistic, intuitive way and thereby streamline the goal planning process.

To prepare, get a sheet of paper and a pencil and write the goal you want to accomplish on top. Next make four columns entitled: What I Need to Do, Resources I Need, Order of Execution, and Importance of Activity. Your paper will look something like this:

What I Need to Do	Resources I Need	Order of Execution	Importance of Activity

Then, with this paper before you, get relaxed and imagine your Guide Dog or Top Dog is seated in front of you, eager to help by answering your questions. Once you feel completely relaxed and in a meditative frame of mind, ask your Guide Dog or Top Dog: "What are all the things I need to do to reach my goal?" Don't try to guide the process or judge how important these activities are now. Just write down everything that comes to you in the first column. Keep asking this question and writing down your ideas until you feel finished. The process is like brainstorming, using your Guide Dog or Top Dog to help limber up the process, so you are even more receptive and creative than usual.

Next go to the second column and ask your Guide Dog or Top Dog the following question for each item you have listed in the first column: "What resources do I need to do these activities?" Write down whatever answers you receive. Again, don't try to guide the process or judge or evaluate your thoughts. Just write down whatever resources your Guide Dog or Top Dog tells you. Keep going until you feel finished for each item — and if you don't need anything special for a particular activity, go on to the next.

Now go to the third column and ask your Guide Dog or Top Dog this question to help you order the activities listed in Column 1: "What should I do first? What should I do next? And so on." Number these items accordingly. If you are not sure of the order or feel you will do some activities around the same time, give them the same number.

Finally, go to the last column and ask your Guide Dog or Top Dog to help you prioritize these activities, so if you don't have time to do everything, you can drop the less important activities. Ask: "What is the importance of this activity?" and for each one, ask your Guide Dog or Top Dog to rate these with an "A" for most important, "B" for next most important, and "C" for least important to only do if possible. Again, don't try to guide this process. Just listen as your Guide Dog or Top Dog tells you the ranking.

When you are done, return to your everyday state of consciousness. Now take the information you have acquired to make up an activities list for yourself. List the goal you are going to achieve at the top of the page, and using the numbers listed in column 3, write down the activities you plan to do and the resources you need to do them. Next to each one, write the letter indicating the importance of this activity.

Your sheet of paper will look something like this:

Goal #	Goal	Resources Needed	Priority

Putting Your Goal into Action

Once you know your goal, are committed to achieving it, and know what to do to get it, the final step is to START NOW! Here your Power Dog can help by giving you additional energy, power, and support – or a Rescue Dog might join in as well. The more the merrier, as they say.

This final phase is where you might also use the energy raising techniques in this chapter to infuse you with more energy to get started with enthusiasm. Then, too, you can use some of the confidence and esteem-building techniques to increase your self-assurance that you will attain your goal.

With this conviction, commitment and focused energy, begin the process of going after and getting what you want. As you do, imagine your Power Dogs (and maybe a Rescue Dog if needed) are right beside or just behind you, giving you their energy and support.

As you see yourself moving toward your goal, know you'll get it. Believe you can do it. Do what is necessary to accomplish your goal. And you will! Just thinking, imagining, and knowing what you want and directing your energy and enthusiasm toward your goal will mobilize you to take the appropriate actions to get it.

So send in the dogs and go for it! Use the power of your imagination to call on your dogs to give you even more power. Perhaps a way to think of this process is like driving a dog sled, with a team of very powerful dogs pouring their energy into pulling that sled ever faster and faster until you achieve your goal. You draw on their power and you get there.

So go to it with enthusiasm and confidence. Get going! Do it now! Mush!!!

An Example of How to Use the System

How does the system work in practice? Here's an example.

Take Robert who wants to move into a management job with more responsibility, but he feels cowed by a fellow co-worker, Jim, who is an outgoing go-getter. Jim often gets others to cover for him at the home office, while he is out schmoozing with people and bringing in clients, so he's a natural charismatic fundraiser and it looks like he will get the management nod.

But Robert is much better in managing details in his own quiet way, if only the top executives knew this. Yet Robert feels uncertain about what to do, afraid he won't be able to show off his strengths, and worse, he believes if he says anything to compare himself to Jim, the attempt will backfire, and he could even be out of a job. Thus, he feels highly anxious, lacks confidence, and is unclear about any next steps to take.

Here's how he might use the Dog Type system.

First, since he needs to calm down, he starts with a relaxing visualization. However because the office is usually very busy and noisy, he waits until he gets home, leans back on the recliner in the living room, and turns down the lights. Then, with some soft music playing in the background, he calls on a Rescue Dog to help him relax and feel less anxious. At once the image of a Golden Retriever pops into his mind. So he invites the Retriever to join him as he thinks of a fun, enjoyable activity.

In moments, he recalls how he loves to go to the beach and walk along the sand dunes, and he sees himself walking with this Golden Retriever, he names Sam. As they walk, he concentrates on being fully in the moment, and experiences the waves lapping softly on the beach, as the tide washes in and out. He enjoys the warm sun, while smelling the salty air, and seeing the gently rolling dunes. Meanwhile, he hears Sam saying: "Relax. Relax," as they walk. When he opens his eyes, he feels much calmer, and ready to move on to going after what he really wants.

His next step is to do a little confidence building, since he feels he has the skills and ability, but has trouble showing this to others. So he takes some time to reflect on his good qualities and remind himself of what he does well. Again he sits down on his recliner, this time with a pad and paper, and he begins imagine that his very sensitive, intelligent Poodle, Cheri, is with him as a Guide Dog to answer his questions.

Then, focusing on his desired management job, he uses self-talk to mentally ask Cheri his questions. "What good qualities do I have for this job?" "What tasks can I do well?" "What are my strongest accomplishments at work?" After he asks each question, he holds his pencil poised, ready to write as Cheri responds, telling him about his major strengths. "You have a great sense of loyalty…You're always on time…People can really count on you…People trust you…You are well organized…You are thoughtful…You did a great job leading your team to complete a project…"And so the questions continue until Cheri runs out of answers for him.

Later, as he reviews his lists, seeing himself with each quality or recalling how he completed these tasks, he sees Cheri by his side listening intently. From time to time, she barks her approval or tells him: "You really did a great job" or "You really are good at that." He concludes by seeing Cheri lift up her paw, with a big blue ribbon hanging from it. He grabs the ribbon, holds it, and feels really good, that he really deserves this reward.

Then, as he imagines himself holding the ribbon, he repeats some affirmations to himself: "I have very good management skills," "People in the office really like me," "I'm a great organizer," and he will repeat those affirmations to himself during the week, as a further reinforcement of his abilities.

Finally, after a brief break for dinner, he returns to do some goal setting and planning. This time, after he gets relaxed in his lounge chair and again visualizes Cheri beside him, he asks the question: "What goal do I most want to achieve now?" and he gets the reassurance that yes, he does want to go after the management goal. So he focuses on seeing himself in this new position. He imagines himself in his new office talking to employees, and giving them help and guidance when they have questions about what to do. He visualizes telling his supervisor how much he and his team have accomplished. He also sees Jim, the go-getter, reporting to him and doing an even better job at racking up sales and bringing in new clients, because he's really good at that. Then, he sees himself praising Jim, telling him what a great job he has done, so Jim will keep doing what he has been doing best and get even better.

After that, he asks Cheri to help him decide what to do next to achieve that goal. The answer comes back loud and clear – you need to show your boss you are up to the job, ready to do it, and have a plan about what to do. So, later that night, Robert writes his thoughts into a management plan, suggesting ways to make the office even more productive and how to reward Jim as the office's top producer. As Robert writes, he imagines Bull, his Bullmastiff Power Dog nearby cheering him on, and when he finishes, he takes a few minutes to imagine how he will present himself and his ideas to his boss.

This time he imagines a scenario where he confidently calls up his boss, tells him he's got some ideas for increasing office productivity, and would like to meet with him to share his ideas. As he calls, he imagines Bull right beside him, giving him more power and self-assurance.

Then, in reality, when Robert actually does call up his boss, he feels the strength and confidence he has built up as he asks for the meeting. He even imagines that Cheri and Bull are hovering nearby, lending their strength and support. Finally, when he goes into the meeting, he has that new confidence and assurance as a result of processes he has used to get rid of his anxiety, increase his confidence, be clear about his goal, and know what to do to get it.

The result? Robert shows his boss he really does have the ability and vision to do the job, as well as the confidence to show he is the best person to do it. And so he gets the promotion and new job.

Similarly, other people might use and adapt these techniques for their own purposes – from the workplace to their personal life – to relax, increase energy, build confidence, and set and achieve goals.

You'll see some examples of other ways to use these techniques in the next chapter.

CHAPTER 13: OTHER WAYS OF USING THE DOG TYPE SYSTEM

As you become familiar with using the Dog Type system, you will find more and more ways to use it in everyday life. You may even get a dog if you don't already have one – and your choice of Top Dog, Watch Dog, Guide Dog, Power Dogs, and Rescue Dogs may help you decide what kind of dog to get.

Besides the methods described in previous chapters, other ways of applying the system include: increasing your skills and creativity, solving problems and making decisions, simply having fun, and techniques featured in this chapter. Plus you can use these techniques for virtually any other type of self-help and relationship assistance. Simply call on your different types of dogs to assist.

Increasing Your Skills

As researchers have discovered, using mental imagery can help improve your performance, whether you're rehearsing a speech or performing athletic gymnastics in your mind. Over the past few decades, millions of people have used this widely accepted practice to develop and perfect their skills. The process works by enabling you to practice or rehearse a skill in your mind to supplement your real practice, so you get better at it. You see yourself hitting that tennis serve perfectly; you see yourself in front of an audience of thousands giving a great speech; you imagine yourself typing a letter at your computer and get faster and faster.

Through this mental practice and rehearsal, you reinforce what you have learned through physical practice, since the mind doesn't clearly distinguish between what you do mentally and in reality. The result is that you lay down these neural pathways which are like macros on the computer. You launch them to play for you when you engage in this skill, so you cut down on actual practice time and speed up the time you need to improve.

Furthermore, when you work with the skill you want to acquire in your mind, you can see yourself performing it perfectly, thereby providing an ideal model to achieve when you perform the activity in reality. But you need to do it correctly in your mind for this to work. Otherwise, your mental mistakes will translate into real world ones. Thus, be sure to know in advance the ideal way to perform this skill (such as watching an expert play a good game of tennis; listening to an expert speaker give a speech), so you have a role model in mind when you practice mentally. Or initially visualize yourself using a method you have learned to do physically.

However you learn this ideal method for performing this skill, see yourself doing it correctly and effectively, as your mental image will eventually translate into reality. Also, imagine yourself practicing the skills you desire as vividly as possible. Visualize the setting; see yourself or others dressed appropriately to practice that skill; notice others in the environment. The more real you can make your mental experience, the more powerful it will be in translating into a real life event.

Just as you get better at a skill in reality through repeated practice, so you should repeat this visualization again and again, to give it more power. As you practice, feel yourself becoming more skilled, confident, and assured, and this feeling will carry over into real time and will help you perform better.

The way the Dog Type system works with this process in that you call on your dogs to help you get even better at perfecting a skill. They do so by acting as advisers, supporters, and cheerleaders to give you even more power and confidence as you engage in these skill visualizations. They also make these visualizations more vivid and intense, and therefore, more powerful.

Use the following visualization to practice with the help of your chosen dog or dogs.

Close your eyes and get very relaxed. Imagine that your Top Dog, Power Dog, Guide Dog, or any other dog you feel can help is there with you to give you advice and support.

Then, see yourself participating in whatever skill you want to practice. You can practice by yourself, or you can see people in the audience watching you if this is a skill you perform in front of a group or crowd.

Now, whether you are practicing alone or in front of a group, you see your chosen dog helping you by your side or in the stands cheering you on. If you are practicing this skill for the first time, ask your Guide Dog for advice on exactly how to do it. As you get ready to perform, listen to his suggestions about what to do, such as how and where to stand, how to move, or whatever you need to do.

Then, as you perform the skill, your Top Dog, Power Dog, or any other dog you want there, are enthusiastically cheering you on. Each time you complete an activity, they call out their praise with cheers or barks, and show their excitement for how well you are doing. They may jump up and down, clap their paws together, wag their tail energetically. And you feel that enthusiasm, giving you even more assurance and confidence as you continue to perform that skill perfectly well.

Finally, after you have repeated this practice for several minutes, stop practicing, and take a bow to your Top Dog, Power Dog, or any other audience that has been watching. Then, come back into present reality.

You'll find that this mental practice, particularly when you repeat it for several days, will soon translate into an improved performance. Continue doing this visualization until you have acquired the facility you want with that skill. Once you attain this level, if you continue to perform this skill regularly, your everyday habit reflexes will take over. As a result, soon you'll be able to perform this skill automatically and effectively, whether you practice mentally or not, and you won't need to practice mentally on a regular basis.

However, from time to time, to polish your abilities, go over your skill in your mind, and as before, imagine that your Top Dog, Power Dog, or other dogs you want to invite are watching you and enthusiastically praising your performance. If you expect to use these skills for a particularly critical occasion, such as a sports competition or speech to an important group, mentally review, so you feel completely prepared and psyched up to put on your best possible performance.

Increasing Your Creativity

You can call on your dogs to up your creativity, too. Just using this system is an exercise in being creative, because you are developing your powers to visualize and tap into your intuition, which are at the heart of creativity. Through your creative visuals, you're envisioning all sorts of things – from goals to achieve to new ways to organize an organization or your life.

The essence of creativity is coming up with new ideas, doing things differently, thinking of alternative approaches, and seeing things in new ways. In today's world of continual change and transformation, creativity is especially important, because you have to continually adapt and even remake yourself to take on new roles in new situations with new people. By increasing your creativity, you increase your ability to change and adapt.

There are all sorts of ways to increase your creativity, which Gini has written about in *Mind Power, The Empowered Mind,* and *The Intuitive Edge.* The Dog Type system is still another way to increase your ability to come up with new ideas and direct your creative processes so they are more effective and productive. Calling on your dogs is a way to build on other systems for developing creativity by using them for advice, support, and intensifying the experience, so you become even more creative.

The following techniques will to help you increase your creativity by further developing the qualities and attitudes that make up creativity, such as:
- seeing new ways of doing things,
- perceiving and thinking in innovative ways,
- being open to alternative ways of doing things.

As you develop these qualities and attitudes, you can apply this outlook to any area you choose to express your creativity. These possibilities are endless, ranging from being innovative in how you dress or design your room to coming up with ideas for new products, programs, and organizational systems at work.

The following techniques illustrate three ways to be creative and call on your dogs to further increase your creativity in the workplace and in your personal life. As you work with these techniques, you'll limber up your brain to think and perceive in new ways, which enables you to apply your creativity in multiple areas of your life, since your creative abilities can easily be adapted from one sphere of activity to another.

Seeing New Uses for Things

The advantage of coming up with new uses for things is you can maximize what something does. On a practical note, this is a good way to increase the value of something or reduce expenses, because you have more uses for the same thing. For example, besides reading a book, you can use it to make measurements when you don't have a ruler, or use it for a weight to press flowers.

This technique will get you thinking about new uses for things – with a little help from your Guide Dog. You begin by imagining new uses for familiar items as a warm up to attune your brain for quickly sliding from one idea to another. Then, you apply the process to a specific situation, say at work, where you want to discover new uses for things. So get ready, get relaxed, and go, using the following exercise.

First, see how many new and unusual uses you can come up with for a series of familiar objects. Begin by getting some paper and a pencil. As you hold the paper, imagine that your Guide Dog is beside you, ready to give you ideas.

Divide each page into three or four columns, and write down the name of one familiar object in each column. To come up with objects, look around your office or house and write down the names of objects your see. Or turn to your Guide Dog and ask: "What are some familiar objects I can use?" Then, listen to the answers and write them down, one per column.

Now, look at the name of each object in turn, and as you do, mentally ask this question to your Guide Dog: "What are all the uses you can think of for this object?" Then, listen and write as quickly as you can. As soon as the suggestions for uses stop flowing, ask your Guide Dog again: "What other uses can you think of?" Again, listen and write as quickly as possible. When the process slows again, go to the next object.

Seek to make these uses as novel as possible, and feel free to change the size, shape, or color of the object to do so. You can also combine this object with other objects. Invite your Guide Dog to come up with ideas reflecting these changes and combinations.

When you feel warmed up, think about any situations in your life in which you might want to apply this technique. If you aren't sure which situation to use, ask your Guide Dog: "What situation in my life would I like to change?" Then, listen to what your Guide Dog says, without trying to guide the process.

For example, if your company is marketing a new product, think of all the possible uses for it, or think of all the ways the company might advertise it. Or, say you are planning a party. Think of all the things you might do to make this a unique experience for everyone.

Finding New Methods or Materials to Achieve a Goal

Another way to increase your creativity is coming up with alternate methods or discover different resources that enable you to reach a goal – whether it's a goal at work (like completing a task or launching a product) or in your personal life (like all the ways you can amuse the relatives when they come to visit).

The process of finding new methods or materials can apply to anything. Just think "I can do it," and think of all the ways you can accomplish that task and what you need to accomplish it. You may be able to use what you already have although in new ways. Or maybe you need to get other resources and come up with creative ways to get them.

For instance, suppose you have to get across town and you discover the road you usually take is blocked. Maybe there is another route across unfamiliar roads you can take in your car. Or maybe it would be better not to go by car at all. Maybe you would do better taking a bike. Or maybe you don't need to take the trip now and can go another day. Or maybe…maybe… In other words, you may come up with all sorts of alternate ways to achieve that goal or even change the goal to something else.

Again, your Guide Dog can assist by helping you come up with all sorts of creative suggestions – more than you might think of yourself – helping you to tap more deeply into your intuitive and unconscious thinking.

Use the following guidelines to help loosen up your thinking processes to better come up with new approaches to achieve your goals. As before, first work with the technique to limber up your mind; then apply it to a particular goal you want to achieve.

First, get a sheet of paper and pencil, get relaxed, and imagine your Guide Dog is seated in front of you, eager to come up with ideas for you.

Now think of how many ways you can come up with to fill a need or achieve a goal. Start with some simple needs or goals to practice the process. For example, use a goal such as: "to plan a great party...to take a unique trip...to get across town faster...to keep burglars away." Should you need help thinking of what goals to use, ask your Guide Dog, and listen for the answers and write them down.

Next, look at each activity individually, imagine you have unlimited resources to create solutions, and start brainstorming. To do so, ask your Guide Dog: "How many new approaches can you think of to reach this goal?" Then, let the answers come as quickly as possible. Don't try to critique them or explain them. Just write them down. If your Guide Dog slows down, ask the question: "What other new approaches can you think of to reach this goal?" Then, listen uncritically and write down whatever your Guide Dog tells you.

Later, you can evaluate these ideas and think about which ones you might choose if you were going to do so.

Once you are comfortable using this process, apply it to a real situation where you want to come up with ideas. Afterward, you can assess these ideas, rate them based on how much you would like to use them, and finally choose any ideas you can use to implement in the future.

Changing What Already Exists – or Finding New Combinations

A third key creativity method is changing what already exists in different ways or finding new ways to combine and recombine what already exists. Such a change can contribute to keeping people stimulated and enthusiastic at work or in a relationship. It prevents boredom and keeps motivation high. Those in the entertainment business know the power of creative change, so they are always looking for something new to keep people entertained. They don't just follow "the show must go on!"

motto, but the adage, "The NEW show must be developed to keep going." And, those in the high-tech industry are continually looking for the next new thing.

Likewise, you can use this creative change approach to improve your life at work and in your personal life. For example, change the décor or your fashion to add more excitement to your life. Reorganize the way you do things in the office to promote efficiency and improve motivation. Or if you're on a tight budget, find ways to create some inexpensive furniture, such as by turning a pile of colorful cushions into a comfortable couch.

Use the following exercises to help you think change, and as before, invite your Guide Dog to sit in front of you and help you brainstorm ideas. After you practice limbering up your brain power in this way, you can apply this process to specific situations where real change would be useful.

To start each exercise, get a sheet of paper, get relaxed, imagine your Guide Dog eagerly seated in front of you, and ask the question: "What are all the ways I can change…"You fill in the blanks. Just listen and write as your Guide Dog makes suggestions to you.

- Changing Things *(especially useful for developing new inventions, creating new products, devising new systems, etc.) See how many changes you can make in familiar objects. Imagine the different uses these objects might have when changed. Think of all the ways you can change each object — in size, color, style, construction. Don't expect every idea to be useful and practical. Rather, come up with as many ideas as you can as quickly as possible. Later you can go through these ideas and pick out those that might work.*

- Changing Places *(especially useful for changing landscaping and the look of your home or work environment). Discover how many changes you can make in what you see. Use a picture or look around you. To alter what you see, mentally add something, modify or rearrange things, change size relationships, or take something away. For example, add in flowers or pictures to a room; see different plants in a garden; imagine that a building on the street is no longer there. Don't feel your ideas have to be practical ones. Just let your mental processes flow and generate as many ideas as you can. Later, you can select out what's practical and make changes accordingly.*

- Changing People *(especially useful for changing your own look to better project the image you want or changing the way you interact with others.) Think of the many ways you can change people or yourself. While you can do this exercise wherever you are – say at a cocktail party or while waiting for a plane as people rush by, you can also visualize making these changes in your head. For example, ask your Guide Dog: "What would this person look like if..." Then, see the picture of this person change before you. For instance, suppose a man has a mustache or a beard. Ask your Guide Dog: "How would he look without it?" Or suppose a woman has long hair? Ask what she would look like if she had very short hair. Or take an elderly man? What might he look like if young? Keep going with other questions and be receptive to whatever comes to you. Later, you can apply this process to a real situation where you want to make changes, such as if you are thinking of changing your style to be more up-to-date or with it by wearing different clothes or adopting a new hair style.*

- Changing Your Interaction Style. *(especially useful for improving your relationships with others). Look at the different ways you can act and react in social situations. Imagine yourself in different situations, starting with a not very important setting so you get familiar with this technique, and see yourself acting and reacting in different ways, while your Guide Dog accompanies you, giving you tips on what to say or do and cheering you on. For example, see yourself going into a store and starting the conversation with a different opening remark. See yourself going up to someone you never met at a party and trying out different greetings. Imagine you are at a talk asking different questions. Once you get comfortable using this technique, try applying it to a real life situation that is important to you. When you do, note which approach gets a better response from others, and use that in real life to improve your interaction with that person.*

- Making New Combinations *(especially useful for inventing new products, creating new designs for your home or office, or reorganizing a group of people). Now you want to combine familiar objects or people to create unique arrangements. First practice the process by thinking of two or three familiar objects or people, and later apply this approach to practical situations. To begin, write down the names of the objects or people. Then, ask your Guide Dog to help you come up with suggestions, and in your mind's eye, see the objects or people on a stage in front of you. Make the setting as wild and fantastic as you want to inspire your creativity. You can make the objects or people larger or smaller than normal, too. The idea is to be as innovative and creative as you can. Later, you can apply your ideas to practical matters, because your ideas will come more quickly and freely.*

Solving Problems and Making Decisions

The Dog Type system can help you solve problems and make decisions, too, through brainstorming or using your intuition to know what to do.

The brainstorming process has become widely known, usually when done in a group. You can also do this very effectively as an individual, and for many people who are not comfortable sharing in a group setting, individual brainstorming is generally the most productive, creative way to come up with ideas. In either case, the goal of the brainstorming process is to first come up with as many alternative ideas or problem solutions as quickly as possible. Then, in the second phase of the process, the goal is to select the most appropriate ideas from this list and seek to implement them.

The brainstorming process is extremely effective at producing a variety of ideas, because you quickly generating whatever you think of without any restrictive attempts to evaluate them. That's why you need a two stage process, whether you do this individually or as a group — the first to generate ideas; the second to review them critically to eliminate unworkable ideas and prioritize those that are left.

Thus, the technique has become very popular not only for generating creative ideas, but for solving problems by coming up with a variety of alternative solutions. Such problems can be literally anything – from personal problems to problems at work.

Probably you are already familiar with some types of brainstorming. However, now you can call on your dogs, especially your Guide Dog, to help you brainstorm even more effectively. Generally, this process works best when you are brainstorming individually, since you can combine it with getting relaxed and visualizing. Besides, if other people aren't familiar with the Dog Type system, it may seem a little nutty to call on your dogs to help you brainstorm. (But as more and more people learn about the system and use it, sure, do this as a group...though, ummm, keep the barking down).

Here are two techniques using individual brainstorming, where you first generate as many ideas as possible, write them down, and then go over these ideas critically to select the best ones with the help of your Guide Dog. Here's how your Guide Dog can help at each phase of the two-step brainstorming process:

1) To further stimulate your imagination and intuition to think of as many ideas as possible, imagine your Guide Dog seated before you and ask him the question you are brainstorming. As in a usual brainstorming process, make the question clear, precise, and open-ended, such as: "What should I do about…?" or "What are some alternate solutions to…?" You fill in the blanks with the problem. Then, without trying to direct your Guide Dog, let him answer however he wants, listen to the answer, and, write it down.

2) To help you review these ideas to decide which are best for further development, ask your Guide Dog to sit beside you and help you rate these ideas to give you a quick assessment as you review each one. For example, ask for an "A" for the best ideas; "B" for the next best, and "C" for the next best after that. If any are clearly unsuitable, ask for an "X" to mark the spot. As an alternative, invite your Guide Dog to bark out his assessments – a loud enthusiastic bark or three barks for "great"; a regular bark or two barks for "good", a soft bark or one bark for "maybe", and a growl or no bark for "a definite no".

You can use this process to come up with alternative possibilities for just about anything from the smallest problem to complex long-term undertakings. The following technique will help you limber up your mental processes to start generating alternatives. Ideally, start with a less important or hypothetical problem to gain skill at using this process; then apply this technique to resolving an issue you are really concerned about.

Coming Up With Alternatives to Find Solutions

Start by writing down the problem you want to solve or objective you want to achieve on a sheet of paper. The problem or objective can be anything – a physical one such as building a house; an organizational one, such as resolving a personality clash between two people; or a personal matter, such as figuring out how to better get along with your mother-in-law. Next, divide your sheet of paper into three columns, headed approaches, persons, and objects. It will look something like this:

Problem I Want to Solve:		
Approaches	**Persons**	**Objects**

Now get very relaxed and imagine your Guide Dog is seated in front of you, eager to help, as in previous exercises.

For each column, ask your Guide Dog the following questions and listen to the answer. Don't try to guide the process. Just listen to what your Guide Dog says and write down whatever comes. Don't try to evaluate the comments either. Just listen and record.

The questions to ask for each of the columns are these:
- What are all the ways I can solve this problem?
- Who are the people or groups I need help from to make this happen?
- What are the objects I need to solve this problem?

Keep listening for answers as long as your Guide Dog has something to say. When the answers slow down or stop, ask this question: "Is there anything else you would suggest?" Again listen and write down whatever your Guide Dog says.

After you finish the three columns, review your list critically to determine which approaches are the best and which persons or items you really need. Ask your Guide Dog to give each one a "Yea" or "Nay" as good possibilities or not good at all using whatever method of communication you prefer (for example, he can tell you "Yea", bark, or wag his tail for a yes, or he can tell you "Nay," growl, or hold his tail down for "No".

After you've eliminated all the clearly bad ideas, rank the circled ideas in order of priority from "A" (highest priority) to "C" (lowest priority). You can ask your Guide Dog to help by telling you the rating as you go through each item on the list.

For practice, use this technique for simple or test problems. Then, apply it to more complex or real life problems in your work or personal life.

Using Your Intuition to Make Better Decisions

Besides coming up with alternatives and selecting the best one, another approach is using a more intuitive, holistic "ah-ha" method. Again you can get help from your Guide Dog to achieve this knowing ah-ha. This intuitive approach to making decisions is helpful when you have difficulty choosing among alternatives, or you don't have many alternatives, since your choice is basically "yes", "no", or deferring the decision to a later time when you are ready to decide. For instance, a limited alternative situation might be: Should you take the job offer or turn it down? Do you want to marry this person or not?

Sometimes it's hard to decide based on your reason alone, such as by weighing all the pros and cons to make your decision worse, using your logic can sometimes lead you to make a decision that makes rational sense, but you don't feel right about the result. By contrast, if you can tap directly into your unconscious or intuition, you can make that gut-level decision that expresses what you really want.

What if you have trouble hearing that inner intuitive voice? That's where your Guide Dog can help you tap into that inner response and pay attention to what it says to do.

The following techniques will help you do just that – connect with your inner self with a assistance from your Guide Dog. These techniques reflect different ways of making that connection: through automatic writing, visual symbols or thoughts or signals from your body. You call on your Guide Dog to help you experience and interpret these different forms of inner communication. Since different people get information in different ways and vary how they prefer to get it, these techniques provide alternate ways of getting this information. Try out these different methods; then choose the technique or techniques that work best for you in different situations.

Getting a Quick Yes or No

Here's a way to get a quick "Yes" or "No" to help you make a decision, when an extended visualization to find an answer will take too long, since you need an immediate decision. In this quickie approach, you see the words on a screen in your mind saying "Yes" or "No," or you hear a little voice telling you that. And to make the "Yes" or "No" even more clear and intense, call up a quick picture in your mind of your Guide Dog giving you the "Yes" sign (i.e.: smiling, wagging his tail) or the "No" sign (i.e.: lowering his head or tail) or you can hear your dog bark happily for "Yes" and growl or whine for "No". For a "Not sure", you can see your Guide Dog simply shake his head.

To program yourself to use the process, go through a list of questions where you already have a clear "Yes" or "No" answer, such as "Was I born in _____?" (your birth year); is my mother's name_____? And so on. As you answer, notice how you get the get the answer. You may see a "Yes" or "No" on the screen in your mind, or you may hear your inner voice say the answer. At the same time, use or hear your Guide Dog respond. However this response comes, concentrate on getting your future answers the same way, so you reinforce and validate that method of getting answers. Then, if both answers are the same, you can feel even more sure this is the correct answer for you. If not, take some time to assess your answers. The lack of consistency may suggest you aren't really sure. So it is better to wait before you make a decision and perhaps you might later do this exercise again, until your answers from two sources are the same and reassure you that your decision is now correct.

In first using this method, continue to ask yourself questions to which you know the answers and work on getting your response to come more quickly, until you hear or see it come like a flash, where you see or hear the "Yes" or "No" and your Guide Dog responding right away.

Initially, you will have to consciously call up this visualization, but gradually it will become a matter of habit, programmed into your mind. To make this happen, keep doing the process of answering "Yes" and "No" for several minutes, as you see and/or hear your Guide Dog respond appropriately.

Continue to practice this technique regularly for about a week and start using it to get answers for things where you really do want to know the answers as you go about your everyday life. You'll find that the process gradually becomes automatic. You'll find the "Yes", "No", or "Not sure" answers start popping up automatically on your mental screen along with your Guide Dog responding too, or you'll hear the answers spoken by your Guide Dog as your inner voice.

Keep using this technique every day, whenever you want to make a quick yes or no decision, and if you don't use it for a while, do a refresher to practice the technique, so it becomes automatic again.

Deciding the "Write" Way

The write way technique involves using automatic writing along with some input from your Guide Dog to help you decide. Start by having paper and pencil available or sit in front of your computer, so you can immediately begin to write. It also helps to set up a comfortable writing environment to help tap into your intuition, say by using candles or dim lighting. Then, get very relaxed and imagine your Guide Dog beside you, ready to give you suggestions.

Now ask your Guide Dog questions about your decision, such as "What should I do about_____?" "What is in my best interest to do about_____?" "What would I really like to do about _____?" You can also ask about options, such as asking: "What are my alternatives?" and "Which alternatives would I prefer?"

Then wait for your Guide Dog to answer. Don't try to guide the answers. Just be receptive, listen, and start writing as the answers come to you. Don't think or analyze. Just write. Keep asking questions and recording the answers until the questions and responses stop coming.

Finally, review what you have written. The course you want to take should be clear.

<u>Asking Your Guide Dog for Advice</u>

In this technique, use a visualization of a computer and monitor or a movie screen to contact an expert counselor who knows all the answers. You can choose any kind of person or being as your counselor though your Guide Dog is ideal. Plus feel free to invite in other experts and consultants for their input – even real people as well as dogs! So now, let's go. You can use the following as a general guide, or read it into a recorder and play it back as a guided fantasy.

> *To start the process, get relaxed. Then imagine that you have an office or other place in your house where you can go to find out whatever you want to know. It may be in the attic, basement, garage; any place you can be alone.*
>
> *Wherever it is, take a walk there with your Guide Dog. Imagine him walking beside you, ready to help. As you walk there, notice what is around you. When you get to that room, open the door and go inside. As you look around, you see all kinds of books and papers. You see large stacks of computer printouts. Then, at the far wall,*

you notice a long desk and above it a computer console, with numerous gadgets and buttons. Above this you see a large monitor that looks like a movie screen. Just press a button, and you can see a movie of your own experiences on this screen.

Now, to work on resolving a problem or getting advice, press the button and you'll see the situation you want to resolve unfold on the screen. Or you may see the question you want to ask. Once the problem or question is clear, you can seek a solution or answer.

To obtain this answer, turn to your Guide Dog and ask for help. Tell him or her what is wrong and ask for advice on what to do or say to resolve matters.

Now listen as your Guide Dog tells you what to do. If the answer is simple, he or she will reply briefly. Or your counselor may ask you to press a button on your console, to see the solution. Then, some action you can take will appear on the screen.

If you have more questions, continue to ask them and your Guide Dog will reply. Again, wait for your answer in whatever form it comes. When you have no more questions, tell your Guide Dog you are done, and thank your Guide Dog for his or her help.

Then, turn off your computer console and leave your workshop. Return to the regular part of your house. As you do, return to normal consciousness and open your eyes.

Usually, you will have clear answers as a result of this process. However, if your Guide Dog didn't have any answers or asks you to wait, this means you don't have enough information or the situation is unclear. If so, wait a day or two and ask your questions again; or use another technique to obtain more information or increase your confidence, so you are in a better position to take action.

Taking a Journey to Find Your Answer

In this journey technique, you travel to the top of a mountain to learn your answers with the help of your Guide Dog and others you meet along the way. In some versions of this technique, the journey is to meet a wise man or woman who lives in the mountains. But, since this is the 21st century, not many wise men or women live in the mountains anymore. Besides, you've been learning to get help from your Guide Dog, so that's who'll help now. I've adapted this journey from one in *Mind Power*.

To take this journey, first get very relaxed and comfortable. Use this description as a general guide for your experience or record the journey and play it back while you listen.

> *This journey begins in the midst of a beautiful meadow. See yourself there surrounded by lush green foliage. Your Guide Dog is beside you. The air is clear and warmed by the sun. Nearby, you hear the soft buzz of bees and the chatter of birds. Off in the distance, you see a large mountain and walk toward it with your Guide Dog. As you walk, notice the tiny flowers. Little mushrooms pop up in the shade of trees. You can feel the carpet of moss beneath your feet. Cows grazing on the hillside low softly.*
>
> *As you walk toward the mountain, the trees begin to thin out and you pass patches of grassland. The wind feels stronger and cooler. Now you pass a small stream. Sit down for a moment with your Guide Dog to relax. Let your feet dangle in the stream. Feel the water move past them. It's so relaxing, and you feel very peaceful. You sit very still and listen.*
>
> *Now go on. As you walk uphill, note that the trees give way to bushes. You come to a clearing and look down on the meadow and valley below. Notice how far away it seems.*

Now as you climb higher and higher, notice how the air begins to cool. Yet the sun shines on you directly and warms you. As you climb further, experience a sense of clarity and self-understanding, as you get farther and farther away from the things that usually concern you. It is as if you are leaving the world and all its cares behind. Realizing this, you feel an intense sense of peace.

Now you come near the top of the mountain, where you see a tall rock and tree. Go there with your Guide Dog and sit down by the tree. This rock and tree are the source of great wisdom.

Now, with your question clearly in mind, ask your Guide Dog, who will turn to the rock and tree, and listen for the answer. As your Guide Dog hears the answer, he will tell you, or you will hear the answer at the same time. Just listen to the answer.

If you have additional questions, go ahead and ask them. Again, your Guide Dog will turn to the rock and tree to obtain the answers.

Afterward, thank your Guide Dog for his help, and go back down the mountain as you came, and return to the meadow where you began your journey.

Asking Your Body – and Your Guide Dog – For Answers

Another way to get yes, no, and maybe answers is by asking your body, since your body holds the key to your subconscious, when you learn to read your body's cues and train your body to give them. A little nudge by your Guide Dog will help your body respond with those cues.

As with the technique of seeing the answer on your mental screen or hearing it from your inner voice, you need to do some initial practice to train your responses until they become automatic. In this case, you must physically move your body to get answers. But after some practice, you can visualize these bodily movements in your mind or can develop a voice inside you to answer for your body. Alternatively, you can learn to feel very subtle motions within your body, such as the speed of your pulse or your heartbeat.

One way to start asking your body for information is to train it to act like a pendulum, which will move forward and back to give you "yes" answers; to the side to give you "nos", and in a circle to give you "maybes" or "not sures." Your Guide Dog is there to give you that little nudge to get your body moving. To condition your body to respond this way, use the following technique.

Stand straight and imagine your body as a pendulum. See your Guide Dog standing close beside you.

As your Guide Dog gives you a gentle push, sway backward and forward. That means 'yes". As your Guide Dog gives you another push, sway to the right and left. That means "no". Now with another push from your Guide Dog, sway in a circular motion.

Go through this process several times, alternating the order in which you go forward and back, left and right, and move in a circular motion, so the signals become automatic.

Then ask yourself some yes-no questions to which you know the answers. Your body, with a push from your Guide Dog, should respond with the appropriate swaying motion. Once it does this consistently, you are ready to begin asking it for answers.

Ask your questions as yes-no questions, such as: "Is it in my best interest to do this?" or "Should I do this?" After you ask, observe how your Guide Dog pushes you and your body responds — with a back and forward yes motion, a side to side no, or a circular maybe. With practice, you should get clear yeses and nos. Once you do, you can decide whether to act accordingly.

If you get a lot of circular motions for maybes or get alternating yeses and no's to the same question, you may not be asking the question clearly or your conscious self may be getting in the way. To find out, ask: "'Is my question unclear?" or "Is my conscious self getting in the way?" If so, clarify or reframe your question, or push your conscious thoughts and feelings aside to let your inner self speak. Or ask your question another time.

At first, you will have to physically assume this pendulum position when you ask a question. But once you are familiar with this technique and consistently get clear answers, you can make it a mental process. Just imagine your body as a pendulum with your Guide Dog beside you and ask your question. Then observe how your body responds in your mind's eye, or listen to what your inner voice tells you about your body.

Later, you won't need to imagine the pendulum. You can merely ask your question and feel your body respond with a yes or a no or maybe.

New Ways to Just Have Fun

Besides these practical applications, you can use the Dog Type system to just have fun. How? Simply call on any of your dogs to join you when you participate in real life fun activities, especially when you're on your own, such as hiking the mountains, walking along a beach, or taking a swim. Or use a visualization to go on a mental journey or participate in a fun activity with one of your dogs. Imagine your dog is beside you as you experience this journey or activity.

Here are a few examples to get you started. Then, come up with other ways to have fun with your dogs.

- As you listen to music, imagine that your Top Dog or Guide Dog is with you. As he or she moves to the music, you feel the music even more intensely and vividly yourself.

- When you go to an art gallery, imagine that your Top Dog or Guide Dog is with you, commenting on the art you see as you move from piece to piece.
- When you participate in any activity by yourself – from going on a hike, swimming, or going for a run, imagine that your Top Dog or Guide is with you. Then, let your imagination go. For instance, as you run faster, imagine you are racing with your dog. As you find sea creatures along the beach, imagine that your dog is commenting on them.
- When you exercise, imagine that your Top Dog or Power Dog is beside you, cheering you on and giving you even more energy.
- Go on a mental journey with your dog. For example, imagine you are blasting off to outer space, and your Top Dog or Guide Dog is beside you. Or journey back in time to another place and age, and your Guide Dog is there to advise you and your Power Dog is there to protect you. Or think of other places you would like to visit, say on vacation.

In short, the possibilities for having fun with your dogs are endless. Just let your imagination go.

Still Other Ways of Working with the Dog Type System

Now that you've learned many methods for working with the Dog Type system, you can think of many other ways to use it. For example, call on your dogs to help you eliminate bad habits, improve your memory, increase your ability to concentrate and pay attention, help with your health, and more.

Plus you can find many ways to share and participate in these techniques with others. You can also use these techniques to help and counsel others, say by using the insights from your Guide

Dogs and Top Dog to provide guidance. Or call on your Power Dog to assist you in helping to energize and motivate others.

So what kind of dog are you? What kind of dogs are the people you interact with? And how can your dogs help you and others? Just call on your dogs and you're off and running. And if anyone tells you that "the world is going to the dogs", well, maybe that's a good thing to happen now, as you think about and work with your dogs in this new way.

CHAPTER 14: SUMMING UP AND EVEN MORE POSSIBILITIES

In the previous chapters, I have illustrated the many ways this system can be applied, from understanding yourself to improving your relationships with others. It can be used in one's personal life or in the workplace for a variety of everyday activities and just to have fun.

In short, this is a new system that can take its place alongside other systems for personal and organizational development – from Myers-Briggs to astrology and Tarot cards. A reason this approach of working with different dogs is so helpful is because for many thousands of years, dogs have been humans' closet companion, and they have been bred in hundreds of cultures for many different purposes – from being a tough hard-working dog to a loyal, affectionate companion.

Here I just want to sum up the major ways you can continue to work with this system to gain insights about yourself and your relationships. I'll conclude with a few suggestions on how to use this system in other ways – including just for fun.

For Self-Understanding and Personal Development

Since the dog you picked as your favorite (your Top Dog) or your next favorite dog (your Watch Dog) reflects the qualities you already have or would like to develop, some exercises to become more aware of these qualities can help you acquire or develop them. While you can do these exercises on your own, sharing with others can contribute to even broader insights, so if you can, set up a group to share your experiences. The major exercises to practice for greater self-understanding and personal development include these:

- Once you select your Top Dog and Watch Dog, take some time to think of the qualities associated with these dogs and

how the choice reflects who you are. Pick any quality you want to work on experiencing and developing. You can do this as a "Top of Mind" exercise, coming up with the first idea you think of by looking through the dog profiles to see which one seems most right for you, or as a relaxed visualization where you see yourself expressing those qualities in various situations. This processing helps you think about the many qualities you have.
- Next think about the qualities you would like to further develop and pick one. Then, quickly think of or visualize a situation in which you would like to use that quality at home or in work, having more strength to do something or being a more outgoing, warm person. See yourself as already having that quality, and feel confident that you can express that quality effectively. Then, watch the scene play out before you. Notice what happens when you express that quality. After the visualization, notice how you felt about expressing that quality and ask yourself these questions: "How did that quality help me gain what I want? What can I do now to further develop that quality in my life?
- Now that you have identified the qualities to develop, put them into practice in everyday life in one of two ways:
  1. Visualize yourself with these qualities before you go into a situation and seek to express those qualities (i.e.: be warmer and more outgoing like a Cocker Spaniel; have more strength and endurance like a Bullmastiff);
  2. Set up a situation where you can express those qualities, possibly with people you don't already know (i.e.: join a group of strangers waiting somewhere, like in a bus terminal, so you can experiment with being warmer and more outgoing).
- Call on your inner Guide Dog(s) for additional advice and/or ask your Power Dog(s) for more support, particularly when seeking new ways to increase or use your power.

For Understanding and Improving Relationships

Since the type of dog you associate with others gives you insight into what they are like and how to better interact with them, some exercises to become more aware of these qualities and how to deal with others can help you do this. Plus you can gain additional help from your Guide Dogs, Power Dogs, and Rescue Dogs by doing these exercises on your own or sharing with others in a group. The major exercises to practice for greater understanding about others and how to have better relationships with them include:

- Imagine that someone you know at work or in your personal life is a dog and consider what dog would that person is. Then, consider what traits that dog would have.
- Think how you might better interact with this person in the future, based on the qualities you associate with this dog.
- Think about the types of dogs you most like to interact with and how this knowledge might guide you in the future, such as in deciding whether to initiate or remain in a close relationship with someone.
- Think about the how knowing a person's preferences for different dogs might help you put groups of people or teams together.
- Call on your Guide Dog(s) for additional advice and/or on your Power Dog(s) for their support, particularly when you are dealing with an already strong, powerful, and unfair person, such as a "Machiavellian" boss, who is interested in showing off what he or she has accomplished and taking all the credit for it.

For a Variety of Everyday Purposes

When it comes to everyday activities, you can use the system for just about anything, since you are calling on your Guide Dogs for advice; your Power dogs for power; and your Rescue Dogs for more assistance. In short, you are calling on whatever dog you associate with the qualities you feel will help in that situation – and if you are drawn to mixed breeds, well the more the merrier. Among the many activities where you can gain help, as previously described, you can call in the dogs to help you:
- Relax and calm down
- Increase your energy and power
- Increase your feelings of confidence and self-esteem
- Set and achieve goals
- Improve your skills
- Increase your creativity
- Resolve problems and make better decisions

In short, whenever you might use any other self-help system, you can apply this system – with a little extra help from your dogs.

Mostly Just for Fun

Finally, besides using these techniques for insight, personal development, and relationships building, you can use various techniques just for fun. You might gain some insight in the process, but otherwise, just enjoy. Some ways to have fun with these techniques include the following – and certainly, you can think of many more ideas. To get you started:
- After choosing your Top Dog and imagining what dog someone else is, imagine you are both interacting as dogs, and notice what happens. Are you playful? Warm? In a power struggle? Imagine the scene.

- Once you pick a dog for a person, imagine that you could change the person into another type of dog. As you interact with that person, notice what happens. For example, you go to talk to your usually tough Bulldog boss, but now he's gentle and playful like an Old English Sheepdog.

Still Other Ways to Use this System for Getting to Know Others and Having Fun

Here are a few last suggestions for having fun with this system and meeting and getting to know others.
- Put together a workshop based on any of these chapters, such as the two illustrated in this book. If the group is large enough, divide people into smaller groups based on the dog they pick as their Top Dog and the number of people in the group. Ideally, end up with groups with 4-6 people, and combine similar types of dogs together (for instance, combine everyone who has selected large, tough dogs into one group; people who have picked small, toy dogs into another. Then, focus the program around what people are interested in; choose appropriate exercises; adapt the techniques to suit the group, such as using visualization if people like this, or using "top of mind" responses if preferred.
- After each technique, invite people to share in their small group and with the group as a whole. You'll find that people enjoy sharing with others with similar choices as well as seeing how those in different groups do it differently. Creating teams is a great approach for a social mixer, too.
- Use the system to put on a fun singles event, where people choose their favorite or Top Dog. Then they move around meeting others who have made similar choices and at times mix and meet with people making a different choice. For

instance, imagine the German Shepherds meeting in one group, the Dobermans in another, the Poodles in a third. If a guy who's a German Shepherd wants to meet a woman who's a Poodle, there will be some time for cross-choice mingling, too.

- Use the system to create interactive social games. For instance, imagine a game where people pair up, spend a brief time talking, then each person puts the name of a dog he or she thinks the other person is on his or her back. Then, the game is for each person to figure out what dog he or she is by moving around from person to person and asking a single "yes" or "no" question of each one. The winner is the first person to discover and announce what kind of dog he or she is.

- Create an ad to meet others for friendship or dating based on the type of dog you each are. For example, a singles ad might go something like this: "I'm a German Shepherd looking for a Poodle."

- Have a "Come as Your Favorite Dog" party, in which everyone comes as their Top Dog. Plan a variety of fun games and skits where people participate as Top Dog. Or as an alternative make it a "Come as Your Underdog" party, and see what happens when everyone turns up as their least favorite dog.

- Use some exercises on understanding others for team-building or as a fun incentive to motivate the sales team.

- Put on a Dog Type program for people with dogs, and invite them to come with their dogs.

- And now…well, you get the picture. Keep going and think of even more fun ways to play with the Dog Type system – and let us know when you do. We'd like to include the ideas in a future book. So keep the ideas coming and have fun. Woof!

Sources

The historical material on the different breeds of dogs is drawn from these five books. The information in each book is organized by breed.

AMERICAN KENNEL CLUB. *The Complete Dog Book, 19th Edition Revised.* New York: Howell Book House, 1998.

COILE, D. Caroline. *Encyclopedia of Dog Breeds.* Hauppauge, New York: Barron's Educational Series, 1998.

DEPRISCO, Andrew and Johnson, James B. *The Mini-Atlas of Dog Breeds.* Neptune City, New Jersey: T.F.H. Publications, 1990.

SCHULER, Elizabeth Meriwether. *Simon & Schuster's Guide to Dogs.* New York: Simon & Schuster, 1980.

WILCOX, Donnie and Walkowicz, Chris. *The Atlas of Dog Breeds of the World, 5th Edition.* Neptune City, New Jersey: T.F.H. Publications, 1995.

ABOUT THE AUTHORS

Jana Collins

JANA COLLINS is the CEO of an internationally-known publicity firm: Jones and O'Malley, based in Los Angeles. During the past 30 years, Jana has worked for numerous A-List celebrities, and has placed her clients and their products in almost every nationally distributed publication, every major television network and every top-rated cable station, including; ABC, NBC, CBS, FOX, Discovery, Nat Geo, "E", HGTV, DIY Network and many others, with shows as diverse as *The Today Show, Nancy Grace, Doctor Phil, Dateline, Good Morning America, This Morning, 60 Minutes, Entertainment Tonight, CSI, Law & Order,* and *20/20,* as well as a number of big-budget motion pictures. She also has conducted extensive social media campaigns for clients in recent years. She works with clients as a strategist in determining the best approach for gaining traction for their brand and message in today's fast-paced marketplace.

She became fascinated by the dog and cat projects developed by Gini Graham Scott, since she owns several dogs and cats, has long been interested in the activities of groups supporting the environment, nature, and animals. Plus, she has a deep interest in psychology.

Gini Graham Scott

GINI GRAHAM SCOTT, Ph.D., J.D., is a nationally known writer, consultant, speaker, and seminar leader, specializing in social trends, popular culture, business and work relationships, and professional and personal development. She has published over 50 books on diverse subjects with major publishers. She has worked with dozens of clients on memoirs, self-help, and popular business books, as well as film scripts. Writing samples are at www.changemakerspublishingandwriting.com and www.ginigrahamscott.com. She is a Huffington Post regular columnist, commenting on social trends, new technology, business, and everyday life at www.huffingtonpost.com/gini-graham-scott.

She is the founder of Changemakers Publishing featuring books on social trends, work, business, psychology, and self-help, which has published over 60 Print, Ebooks, and audiobooks. She has licensed several dozen books for foreign sales, including in the UK, Russia, Korea, Spain, Indonesia, and Japan.

She has written numerous books on creativity and visualization, including *Mind Power: Picture Your Way to Success; The Empowered Mind: How to Harness the Creative Force within You;* and *Want It, See It, Get It!*

She has received national media exposure for her own books, including appearances on *Good Morning America, Oprah, Montel Williams,* and *CNN*. She has been the producer and host of a talk show series, CHANGEMAKERS, featuring interviews on social trends.

Scott is active in a number of community and business groups, including the Lafayette and Danville Chambers of Commerce. She is a graduate of the prestigious Leadership in Contra Costa County program and is a member of a BNI group in Walnut Creek, B2B groups in Danville and Walnut Creek, and Lafayette Savvy Women. She is the organizer of six Meetup groups in the film and publishing industries with over 6000 members in Los Angeles and the San Francisco Bay Area. She also does workshops and seminars on the topics of her books.

She received her Ph.D. from the University of California, Berkeley, and her J.D. from the University of San Francisco Law School. She has received five MAs at Cal State, East Bay, including most recently an MA in Communications in 2017.

www.ingramcontent.com/pod-product-compliance
Lightning Source LLC
Chambersburg PA
CBHW071554080526
44588CB00010B/912